THE KITCHEN

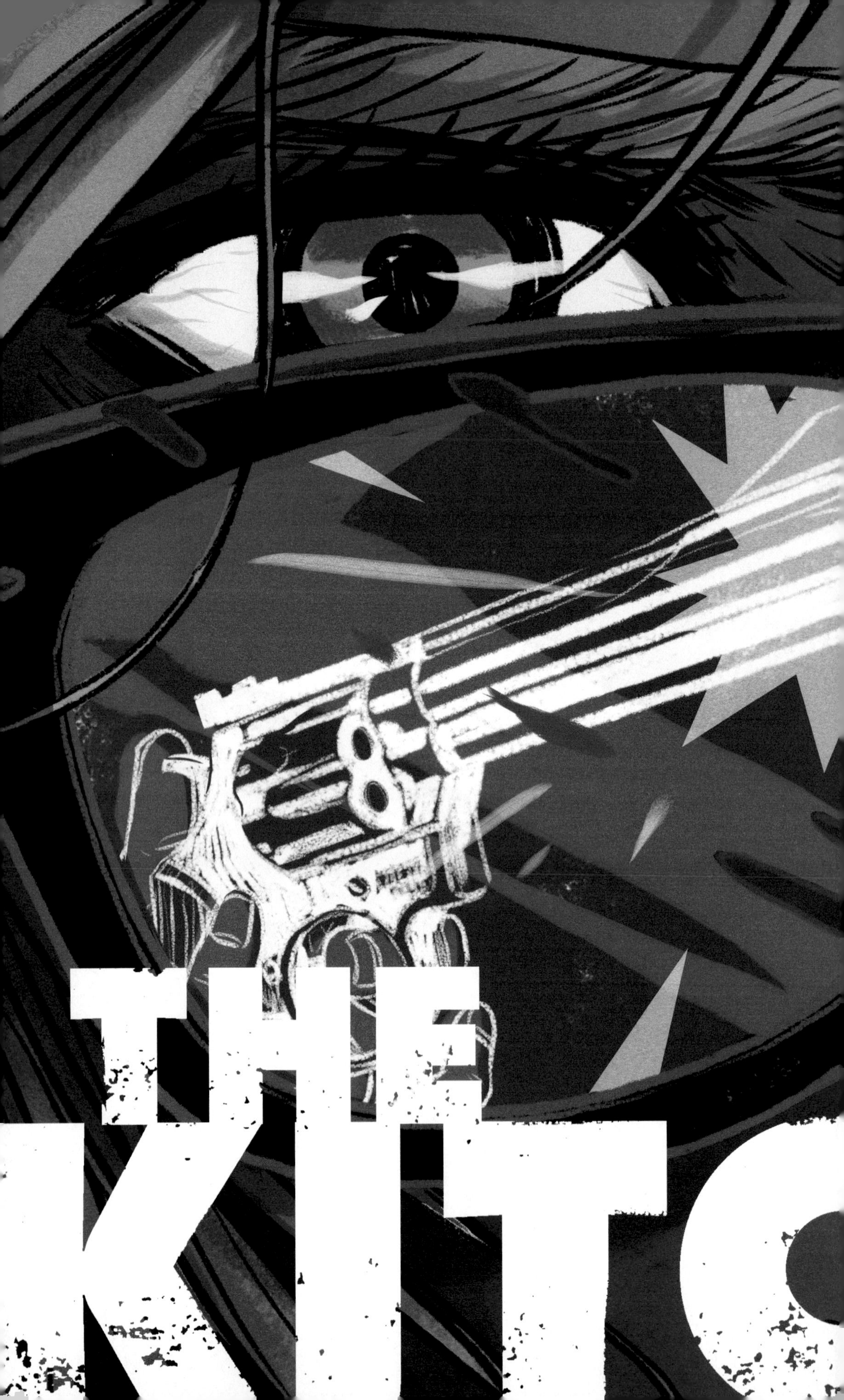
THE
KITC

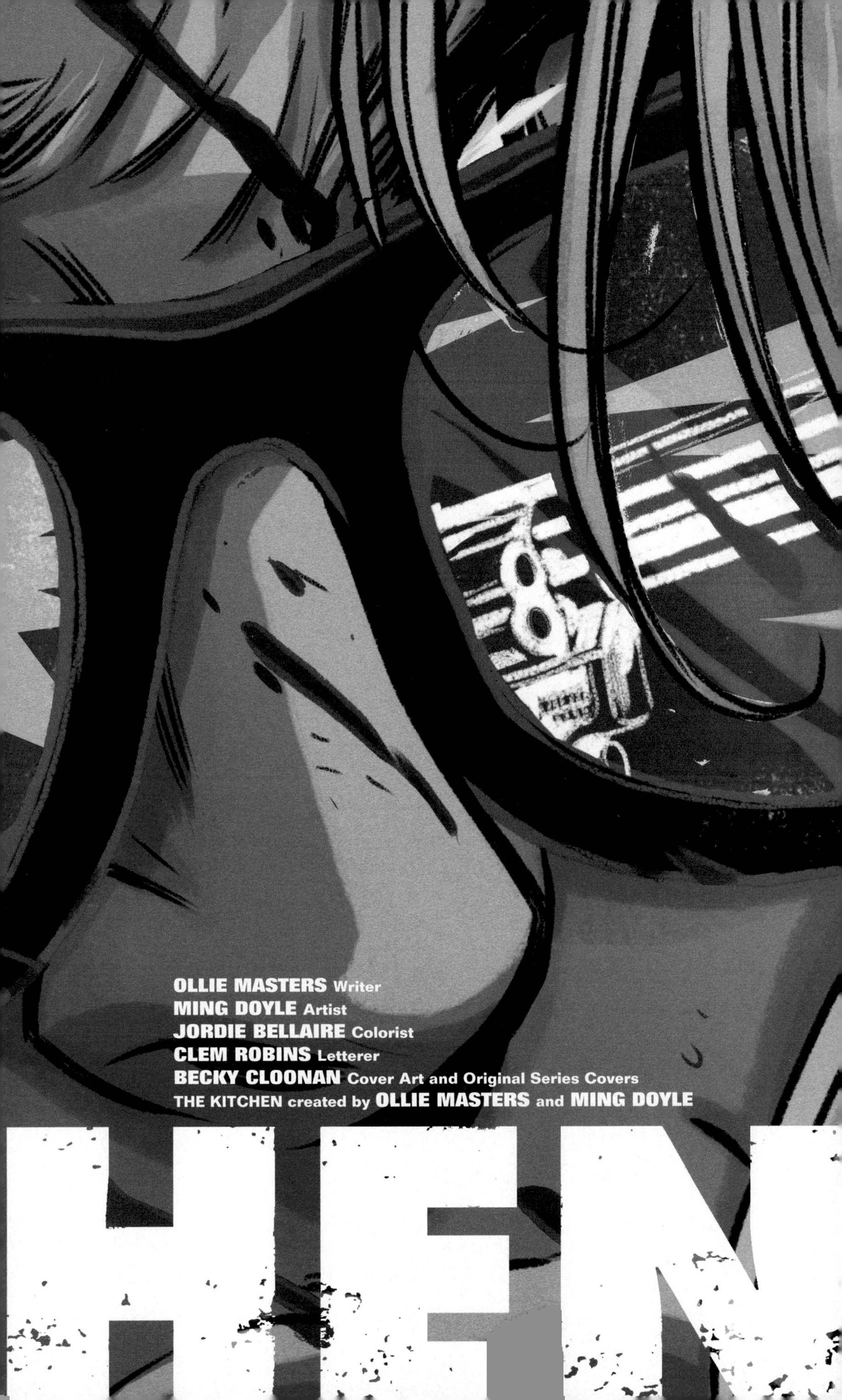
HEN

OLLIE MASTERS Writer
MING DOYLE Artist
JORDIE BELLAIRE Colorist
CLEM ROBINS Letterer
BECKY CLOONAN Cover Art and Original Series Covers
THE KITCHEN created by **OLLIE MASTERS** and **MING DOYLE**

WILL DENNIS Editor – Original Series
GREGORY LOCKARD Associate Editor – Original Series
JEB WOODARD Group Editor – Collected Editions
SCOTT NYBAKKEN Editor – Collected Edition
STEVE COOK Design Director – Books
LOU PRANDI Publication Design

BOB HARRAS Senior VP – Editor-in-Chief, DC Comics
MARK DOYLE Executive Editor, Vertigo & Black Label

DAN DiDIO Publisher
JIM LEE Publisher & Chief Creative Officer
BOBBIE CHASE VP – New Publishing Initiatives & Talent Development
DON FALLETTI VP – Manufacturing Operations & Workflow Management
LAWRENCE GANEM VP – Talent Services
ALISON GILL Senior VP – Manufacturing & Operations
HANK KANALZ Senior VP – Publishing Strategy & Support Services
DAN MIRON VP – Publishing Operations
NICK J. NAPOLITANO VP – Manufacturing Administration & Design
NANCY SPEARS VP – Sales
MICHELE R. WELLS VP & Executive Editor, Young Reader

THE KITCHEN

DC Comics
2900 West Alameda Avenue, Burbank, CA 91505
Printed by LSC Communications, Kendallville, IN, USA. 6/28/19. First Printing.
ISBN: 978-1-77950-049-6

Library of Congress Cataloging-in-Publication Data is available.

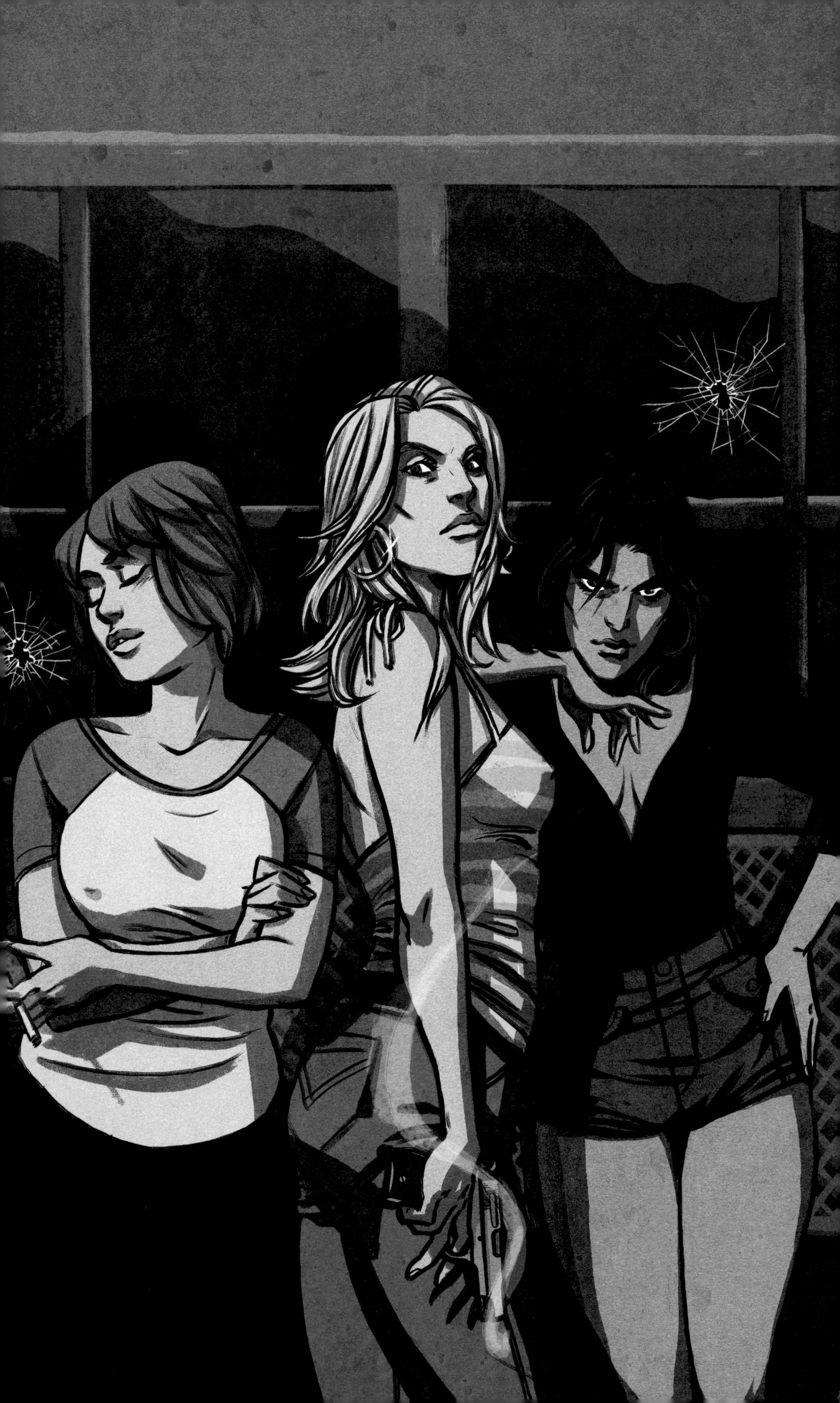

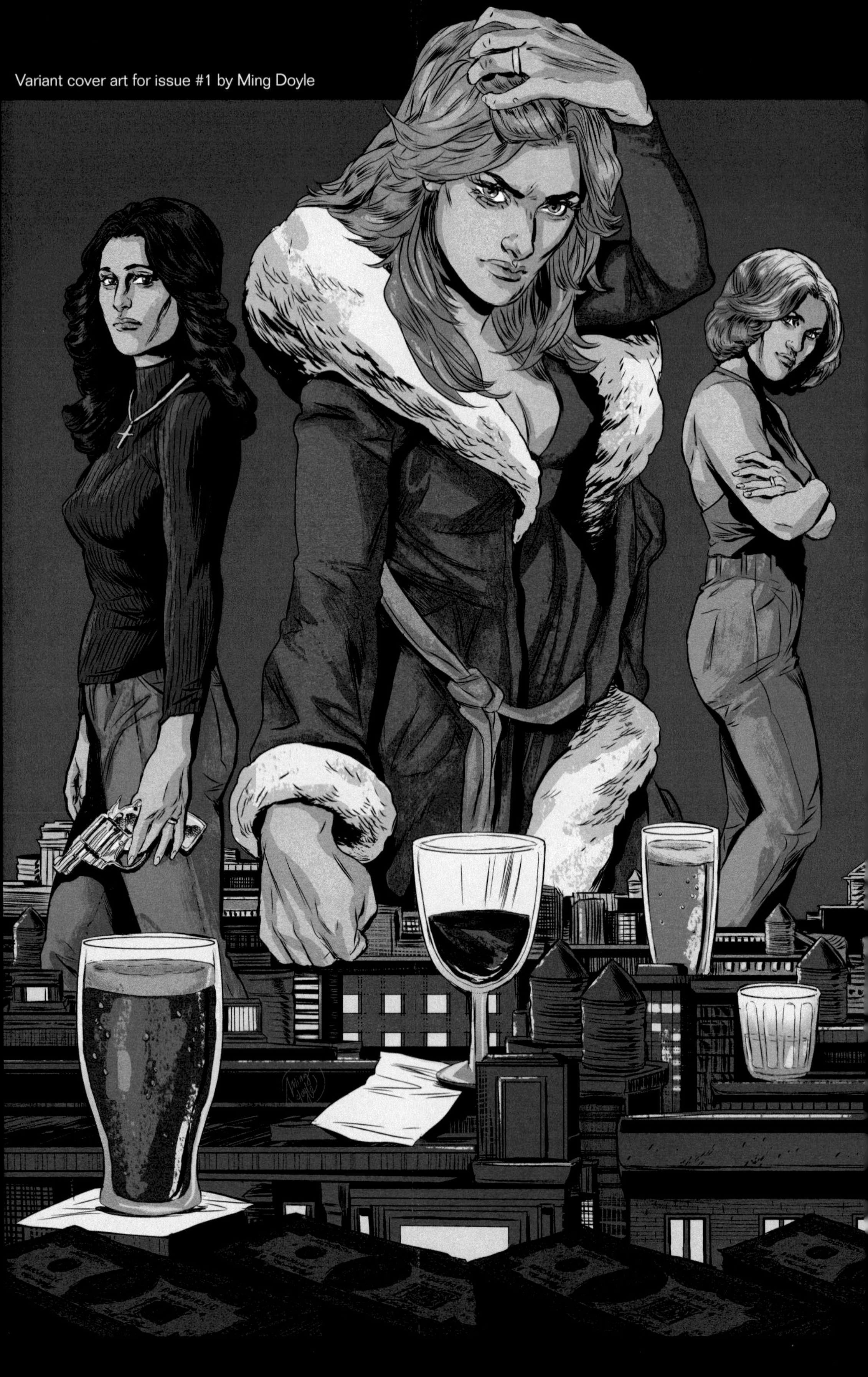

Variant cover art for issue #1 by Ming Doyle

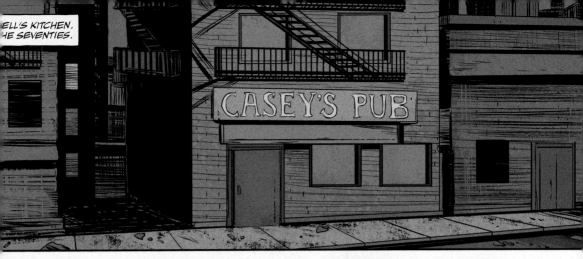

YOU SHOULDA KEPT YOUR FUCKIN' *MOUTH* SHUT, FREDDIE.

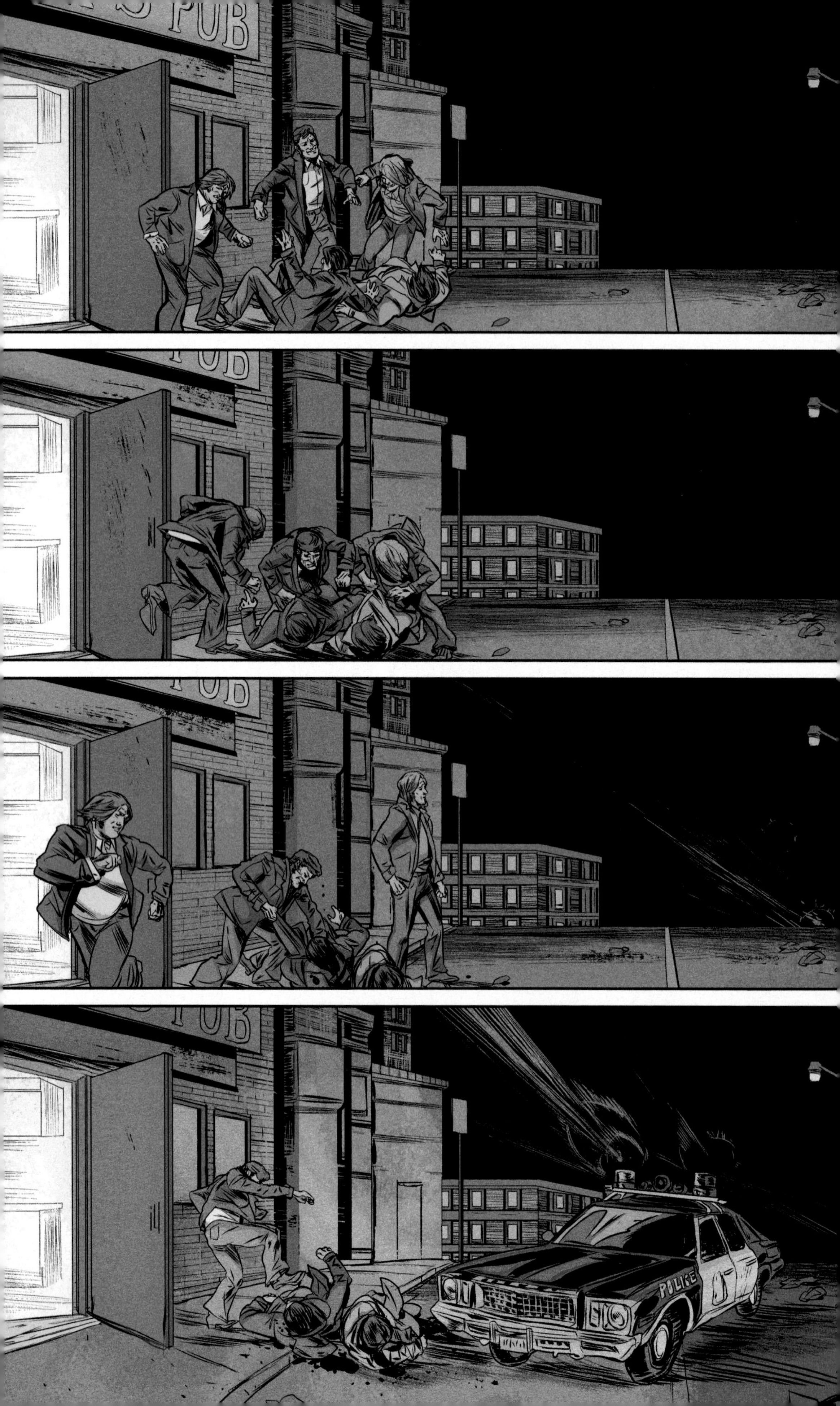
PUB
POLICE

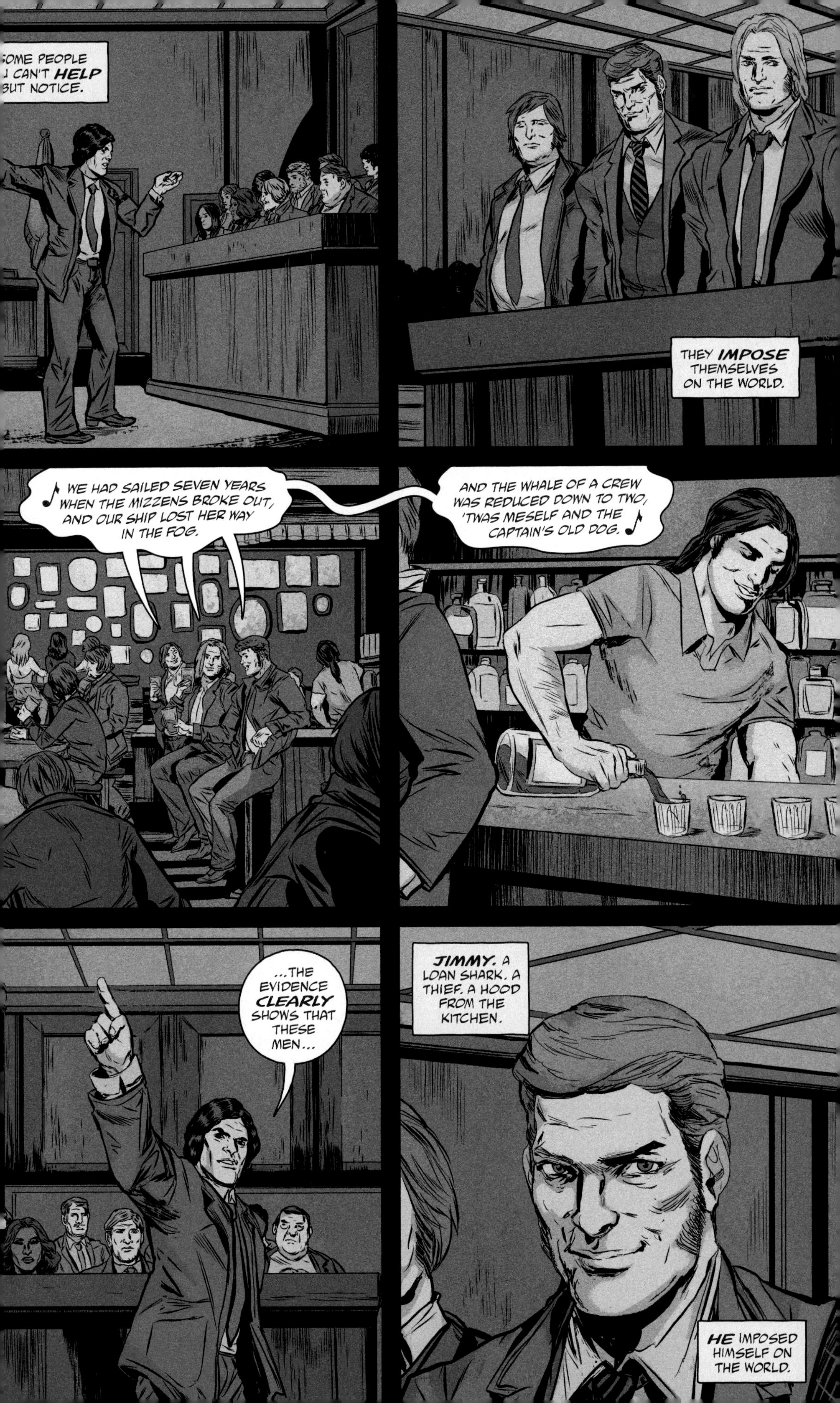
SOME PEOPLE I CAN'T HELP BUT NOTICE.
THEY IMPOSE THEMSELVES ON THE WORLD.
♪ WE HAD SAILED SEVEN YEARS WHEN THE MIZZENS BROKE OUT, AND OUR SHIP LOST HER WAY IN THE FOG.
AND THE WHALE OF A CREW WAS REDUCED DOWN TO TWO, 'TWAS MESELF AND THE CAPTAIN'S OLD DOG. ♪
...THE EVIDENCE CLEARLY SHOWS THAT THESE MEN...
JIMMY. A LOAN SHARK. A THIEF. A HOOD FROM THE KITCHEN.
HE IMPOSED HIMSELF ON THE WORLD.

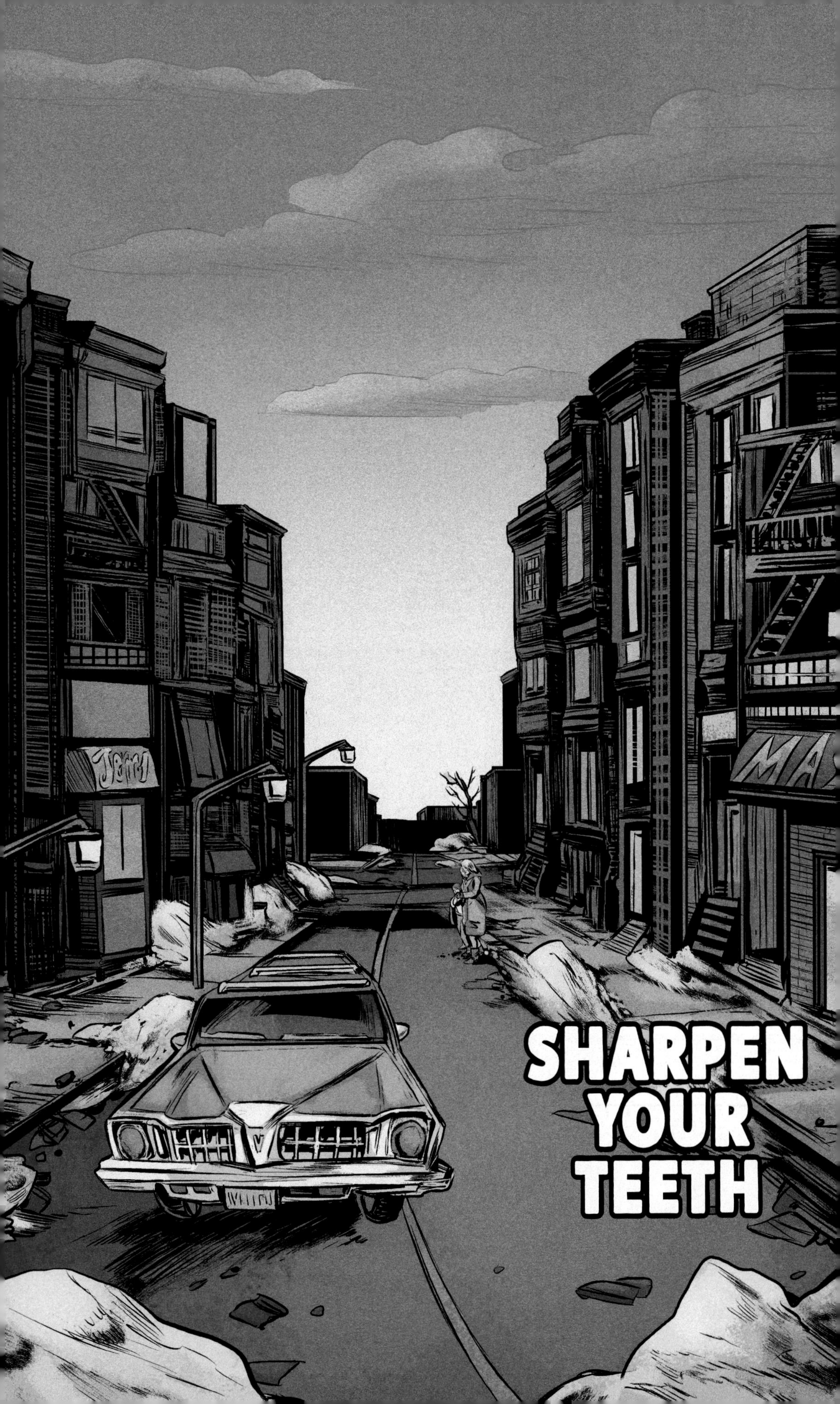
SHARPEN
YOUR
TEETH
MA

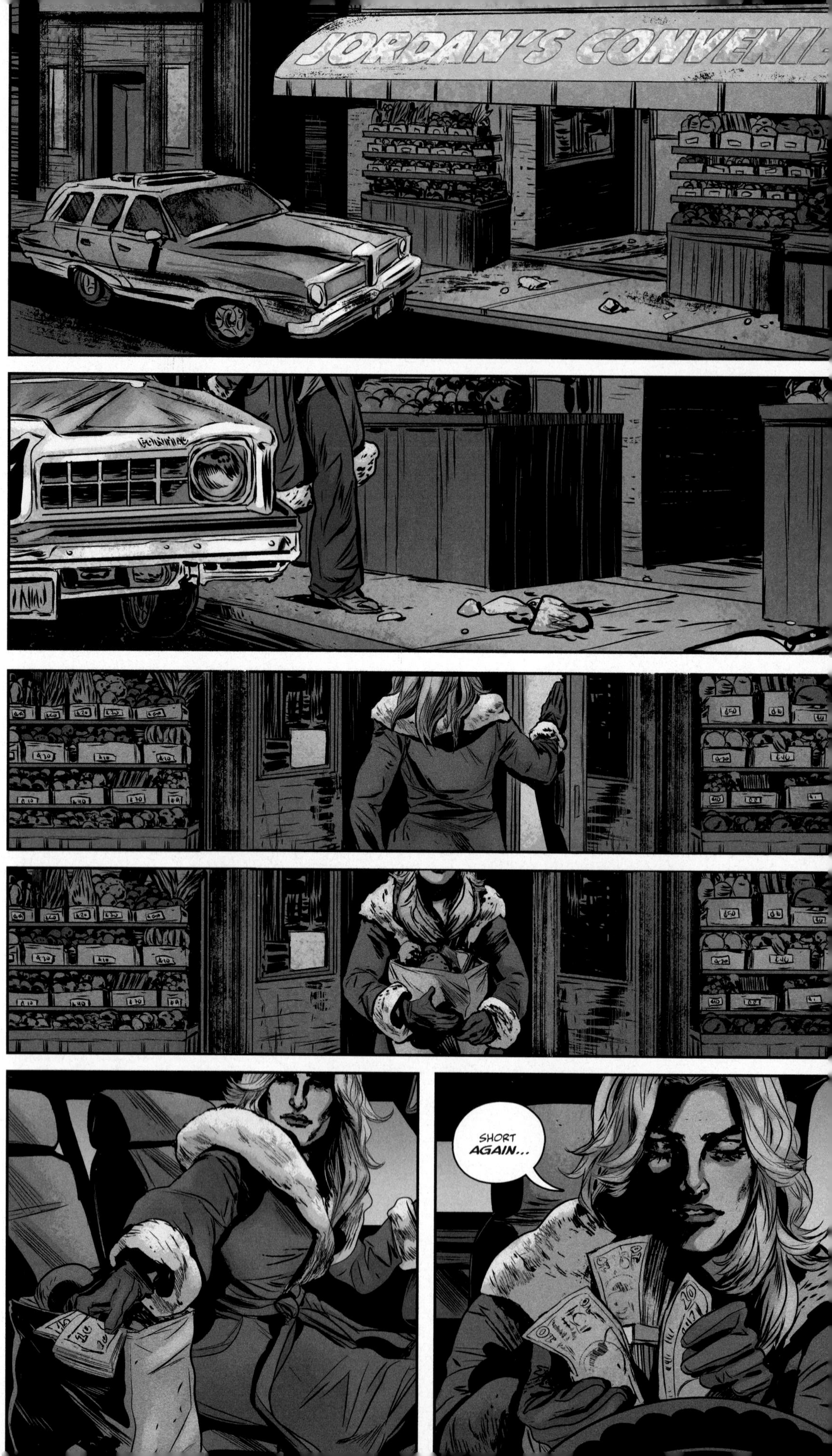
JORDAN'S CONVENI-
SHORT AGAIN...

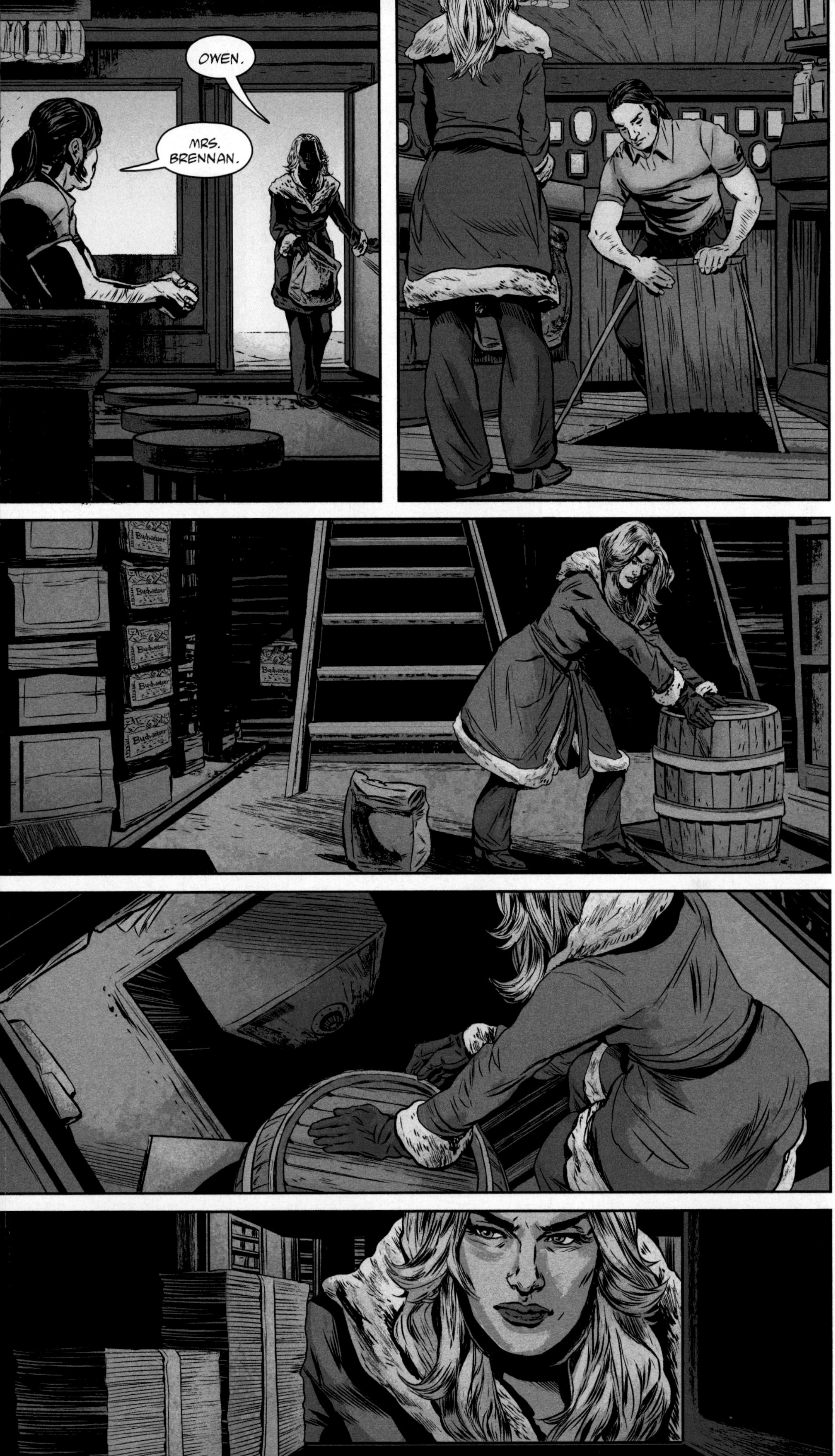
OWEN.
MRS. BRENNAN.
Budweiser

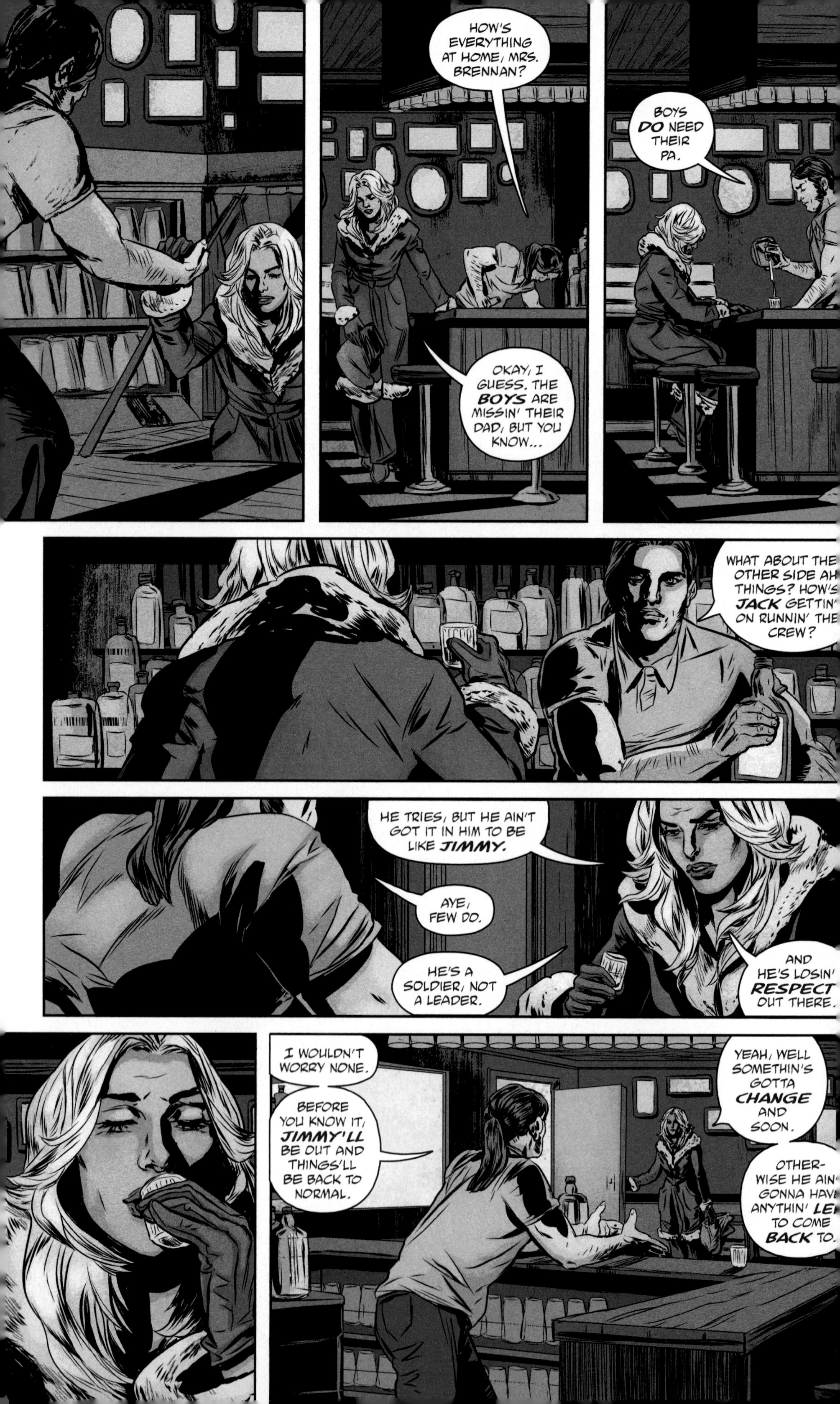
HOW'S EVERYTHING AT HOME, MRS. BRENNAN?
OKAY, I GUESS. THE BOYS ARE MISSIN' THEIR DAD, BUT YOU KNOW...
BOYS DO NEED THEIR PA.
WHAT ABOUT THE OTHER SIDE AH THINGS? HOW'S JACK GETTIN' ON RUNNIN' THE CREW?
HE TRIES, BUT HE AIN'T GOT IT IN HIM TO BE LIKE JIMMY.
AYE, FEW DO.
HE'S A SOLDIER, NOT A LEADER.
AND HE'S LOSIN' RESPECT OUT THERE.
I WOULDN'T WORRY NONE.
BEFORE YOU KNOW IT, JIMMY'LL BE OUT AND THINGS'LL BE BACK TO NORMAL.
YEAH, WELL SOMETHIN'S GOTTA CHANGE AND SOON.
OTHER-WISE HE AIN' GONNA HAV ANYTHIN' LE TO COME BACK TO.

HEY, KATH...

RAVEN.

DRINK? I'VE GOT SOME WINE.

YEAH.

WHAT YOU MAKIN'?

ODA EAD ND TATO UP.

JESUS, THAT SAME IRISH SHIT MOM USED TO MAKE US WHEN WE WERE KIDS?

YEAH, WELL, WE CAN'T ALL AFFORD TO GO OUT TO DINNER EVERY NIGHT.

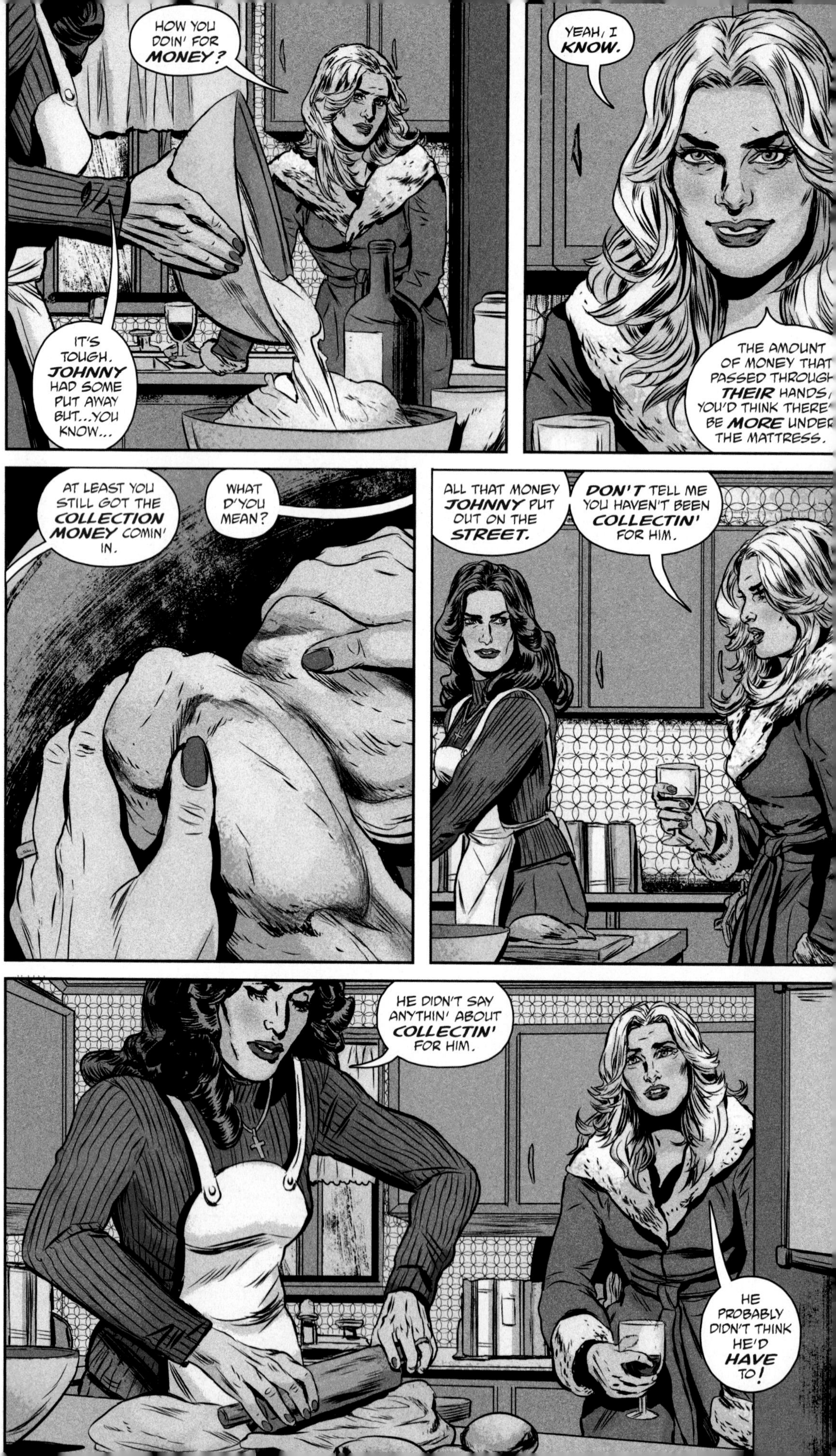
HOW YOU DOIN' FOR MONEY?
IT'S TOUGH. JOHNNY HAD SOME PUT AWAY BUT... YOU KNOW...
YEAH, I KNOW.
THE AMOUNT OF MONEY THAT PASSED THROUGH THEIR HANDS, YOU'D THINK THERE'D BE MORE UNDER THE MATTRESS.
AT LEAST YOU STILL GOT THE COLLECTION MONEY COMIN' IN.
WHAT D'YOU MEAN?
ALL THAT MONEY JOHNNY PUT OUT ON THE STREET.
DON'T TELL ME YOU HAVEN'T BEEN COLLECTIN' FOR HIM.
HE DIDN'T SAY ANYTHIN' ABOUT COLLECTIN' FOR HIM.
HE PROBABLY DIDN'T THINK HE'D HAVE TO!

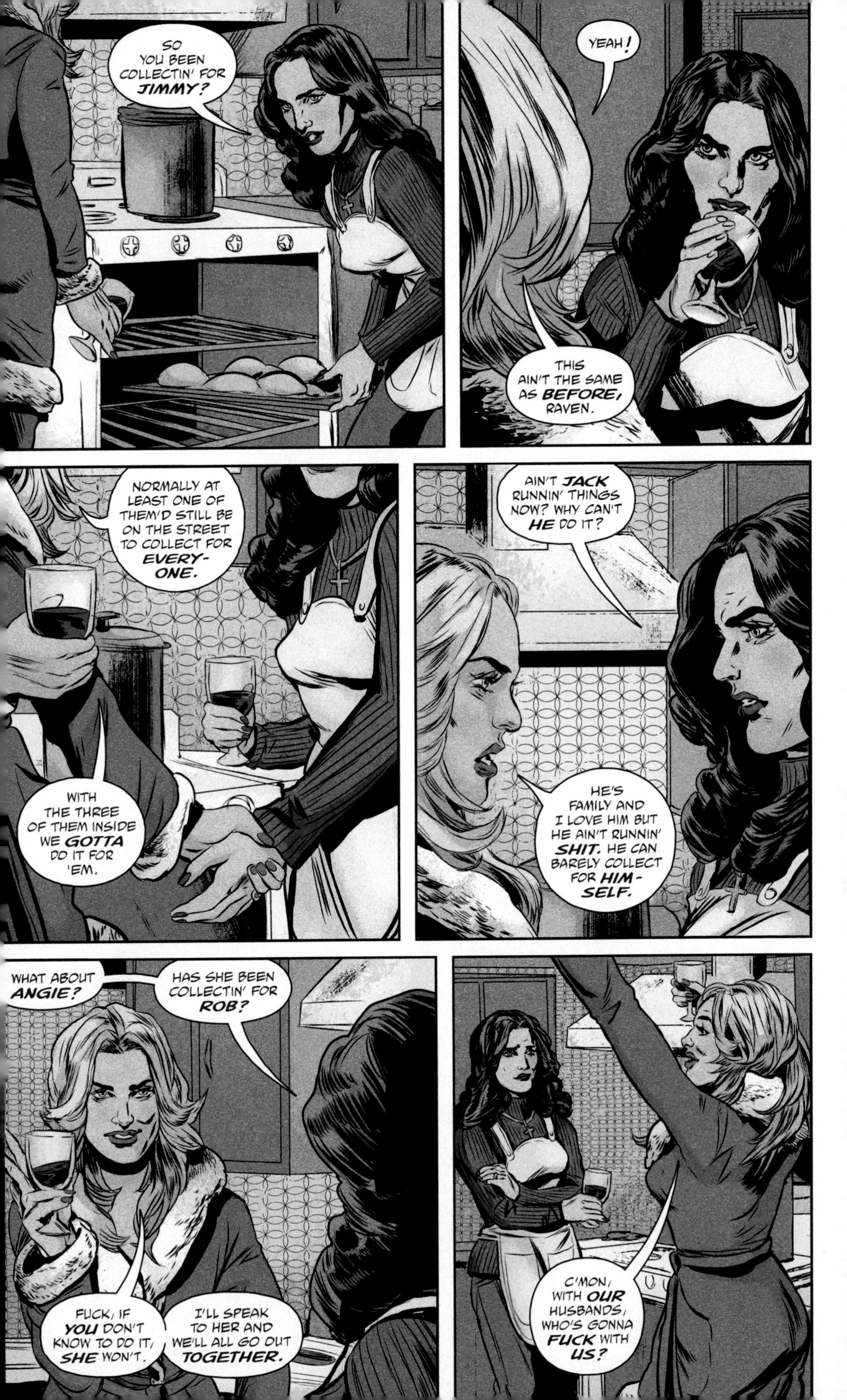
SO YOU BEEN COLLECTIN' FOR JIMMY?
YEAH!
THIS AIN'T THE SAME AS BEFORE, RAVEN.
NORMALLY AT LEAST ONE OF THEM'D STILL BE ON THE STREET TO COLLECT FOR EVERY-ONE.
WITH THE THREE OF THEM INSIDE WE GOTTA DO IT FOR 'EM.
AIN'T JACK RUNNIN' THINGS NOW? WHY CAN'T HE DO IT?
HE'S FAMILY AND I LOVE HIM BUT HE AIN'T RUNNIN' SHIT. HE CAN BARELY COLLECT FOR HIM-SELF.
WHAT ABOUT ANGIE?
HAS SHE BEEN COLLECTIN' FOR ROB?
FUCK, IF YOU DON'T KNOW TO DO IT, SHE WON'T.
I'LL SPEAK TO HER AND WE'LL ALL GO OUT TOGETHER.
C'MON, WITH OUR HUSBANDS, WHO'S GONNA FUCK WITH US?

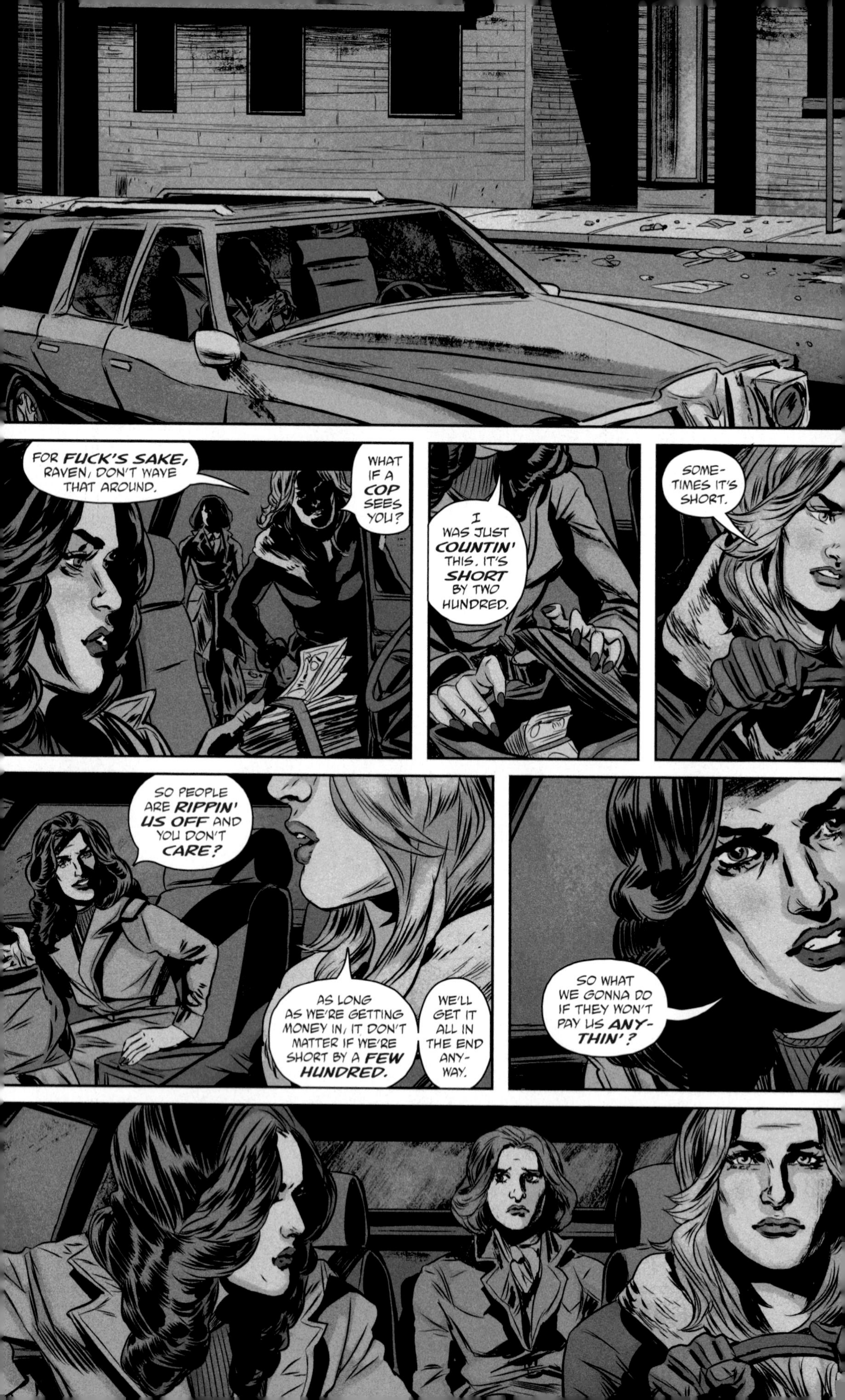
FOR FUCK'S SAKE, RAVEN, DON'T WAVE THAT AROUND.
WHAT IF A COP SEES YOU?
I WAS JUST COUNTIN' THIS. IT'S SHORT BY TWO HUNDRED.
SOME-TIMES IT'S SHORT.
SO PEOPLE ARE RIPPIN' US OFF AND YOU DON'T CARE?
AS LONG AS WE'RE GETTING MONEY IN, IT DON'T MATTER IF WE'RE SHORT BY A FEW HUNDRED.
WE'LL GET IT ALL IN THE END ANY-WAY.
SO WHAT WE GONNA DO IF THEY WON'T PAY US ANY-THIN'?

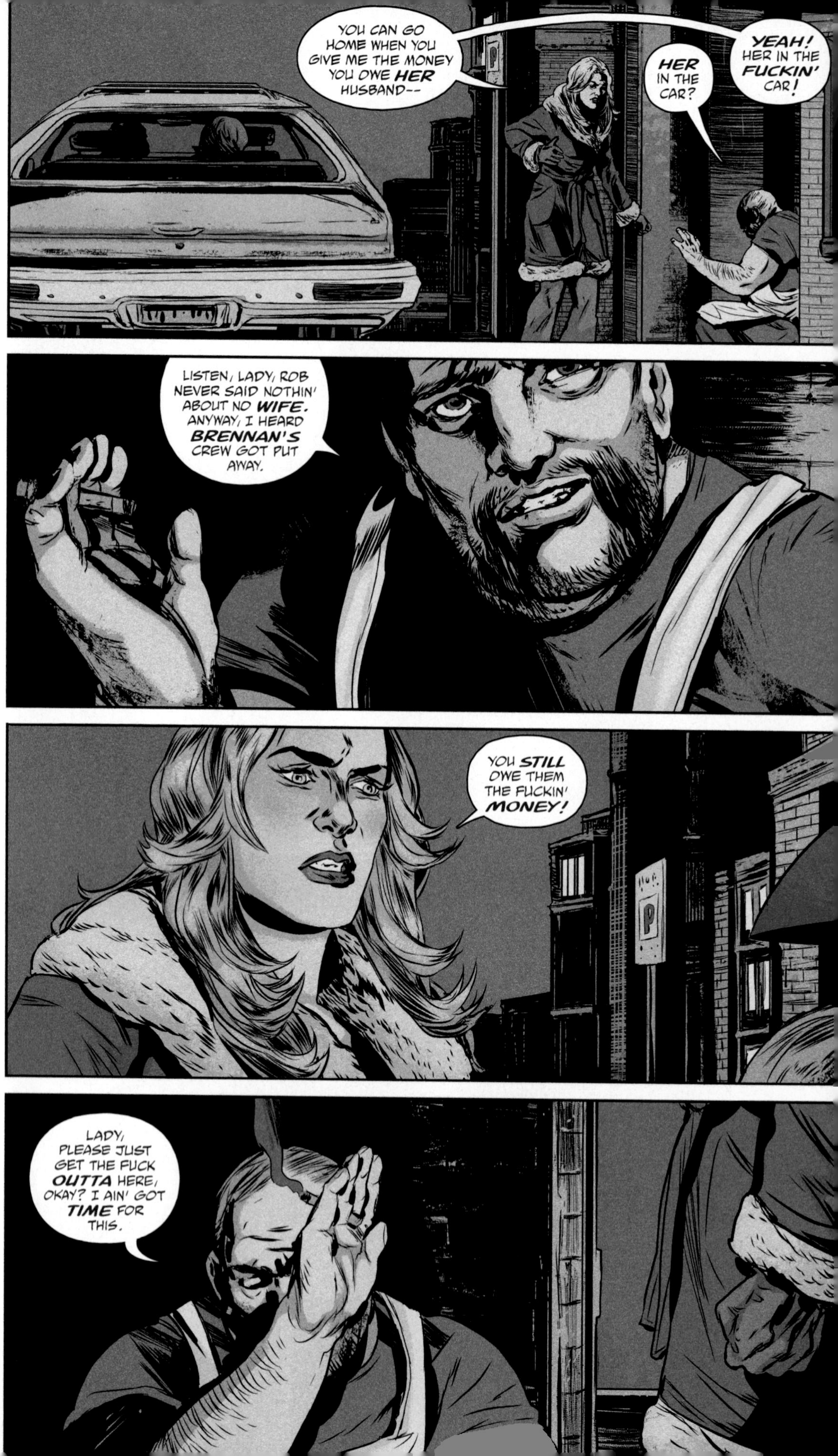
YOU CAN GO HOME WHEN YOU GIVE ME THE MONEY YOU OWE HER HUSBAND--
HER IN THE CAR?
YEAH! HER IN THE FUCKIN' CAR!
LISTEN, LADY, ROB NEVER SAID NOTHIN' ABOUT NO WIFE. ANYWAY, I HEARD BRENNAN'S CREW GOT PUT AWAY.
YOU STILL OWE THEM THE FUCKIN' MONEY!
LADY, PLEASE JUST GET THE FUCK OUTTA HERE, OKAY? I AIN' GOT TIME FOR THIS.

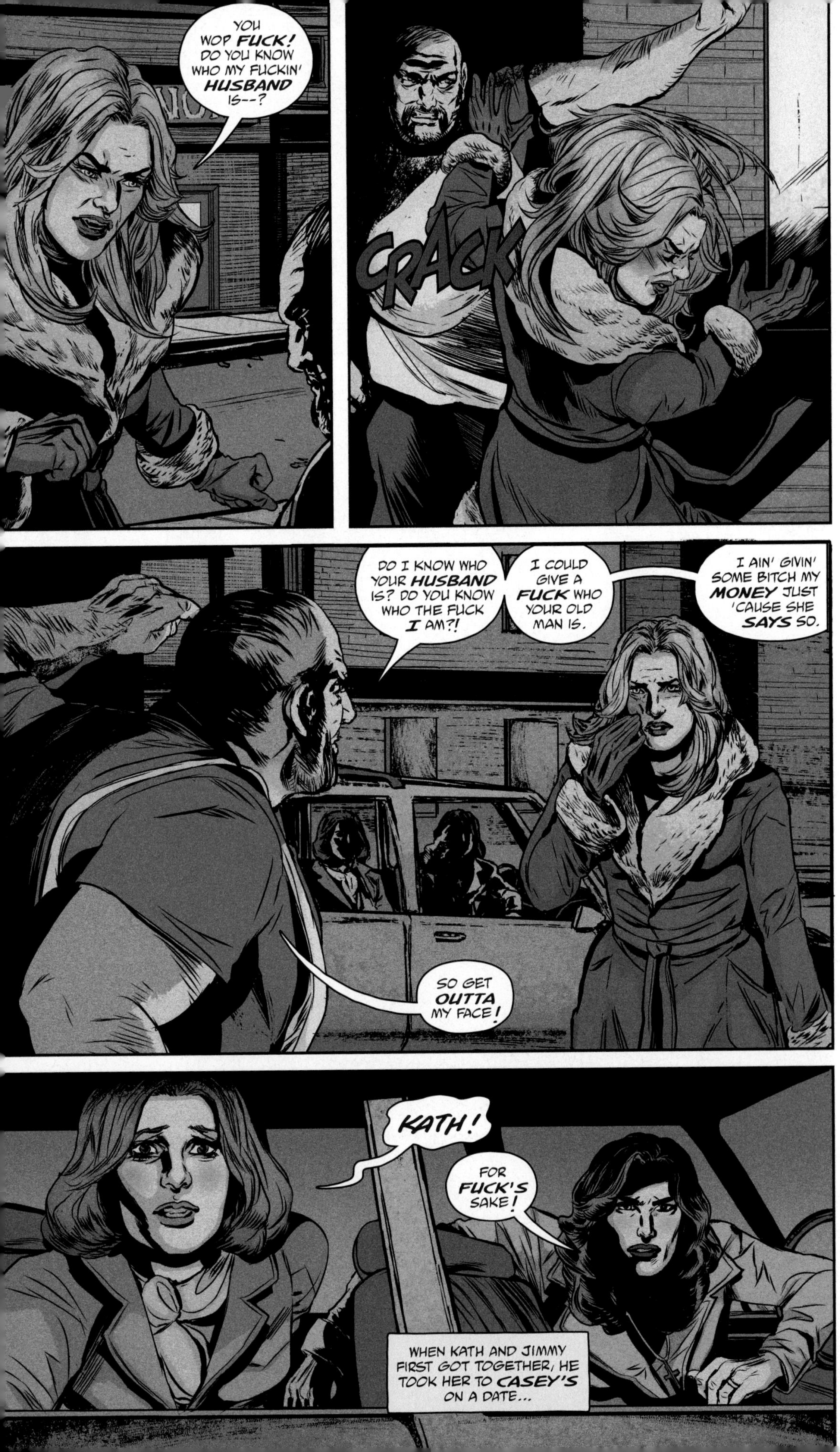
YOU WOP FUCK! DO YOU KNOW WHO MY FUCKIN' HUSBAND IS--?
CRACK
DO I KNOW WHO YOUR HUSBAND IS? DO YOU KNOW WHO THE FUCK I AM?!
I COULD GIVE A FUCK WHO YOUR OLD MAN IS.
I AIN' GIVIN' SOME BITCH MY MONEY JUST 'CAUSE SHE SAYS SO.
SO GET OUTTA MY FACE!
KATH!
FOR FUCK'S SAKE!
WHEN KATH AND JIMMY FIRST GOT TOGETHER, HE TOOK HER TO CASEY'S ON A DATE...

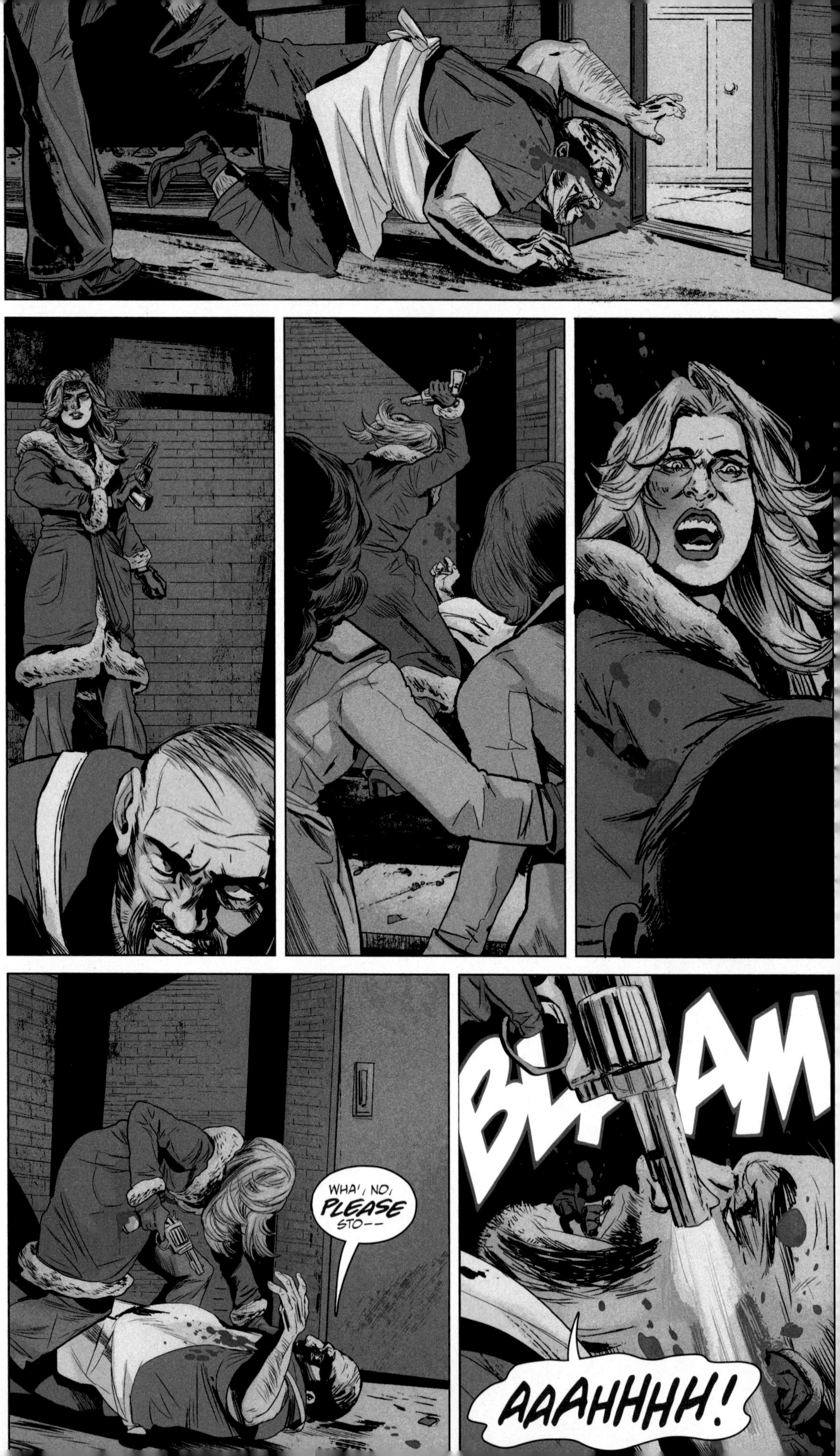
WHA', NO, PLEASE STO--
BLAM
AAAHHHH!

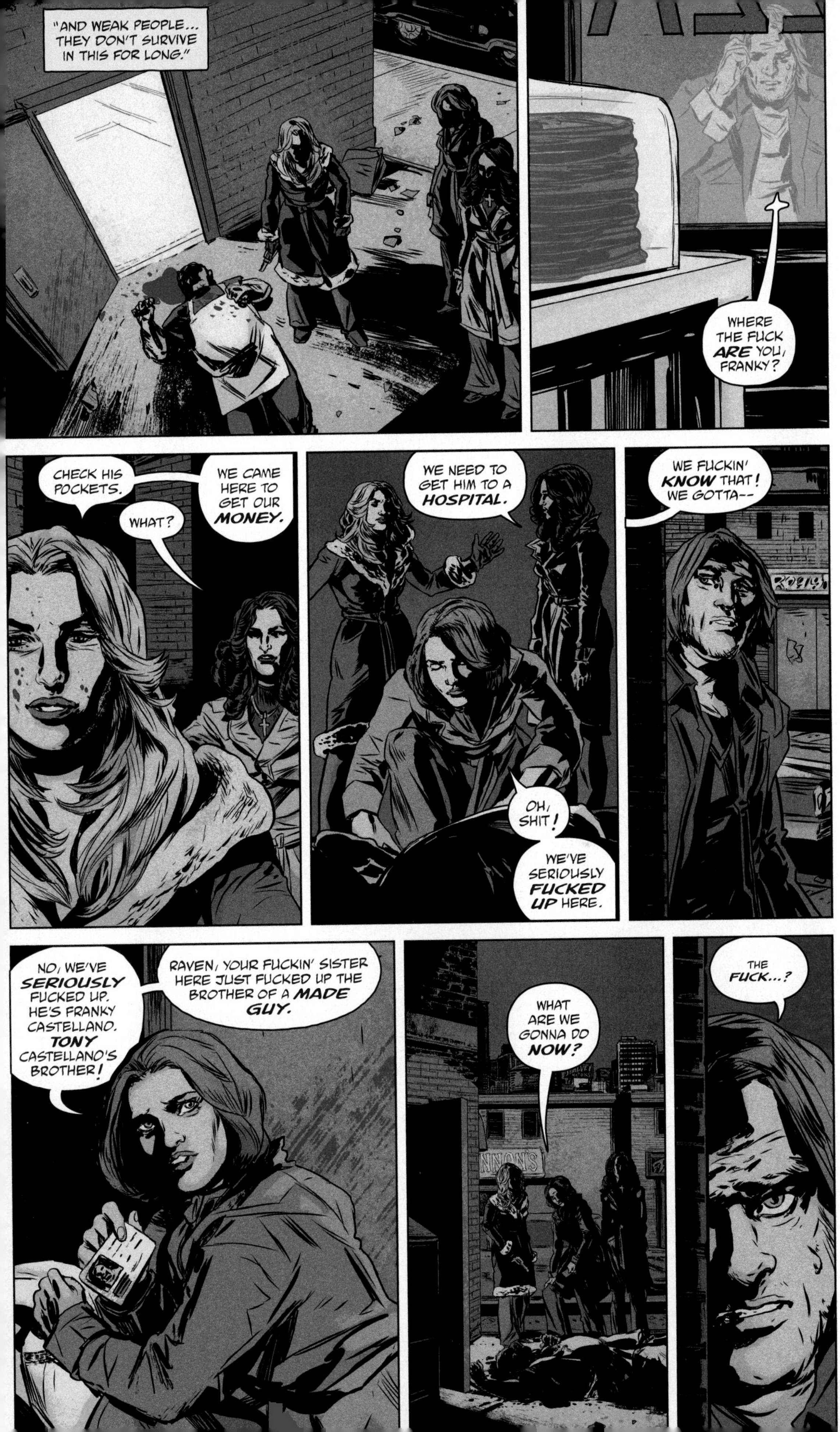
"AND WEAK PEOPLE... THEY DON'T SURVIVE IN THIS FOR LONG."
WHERE THE FUCK ARE YOU, FRANKY?
CHECK HIS POCKETS.
WHAT?
WE CAME HERE TO GET OUR MONEY.
WE NEED TO GET HIM TO A HOSPITAL.
OH, SHIT!
WE'VE SERIOUSLY FUCKED UP HERE.
WE FUCKIN' KNOW THAT! WE GOTTA--
NO, WE'VE SERIOUSLY FUCKED UP. HE'S FRANKY CASTELLANO. TONY CASTELLANO'S BROTHER!
RAVEN, YOUR FUCKIN' SISTER HERE JUST FUCKED UP THE BROTHER OF A MADE GUY.
WHAT ARE WE GONNA DO NOW?
THE FUCK...?

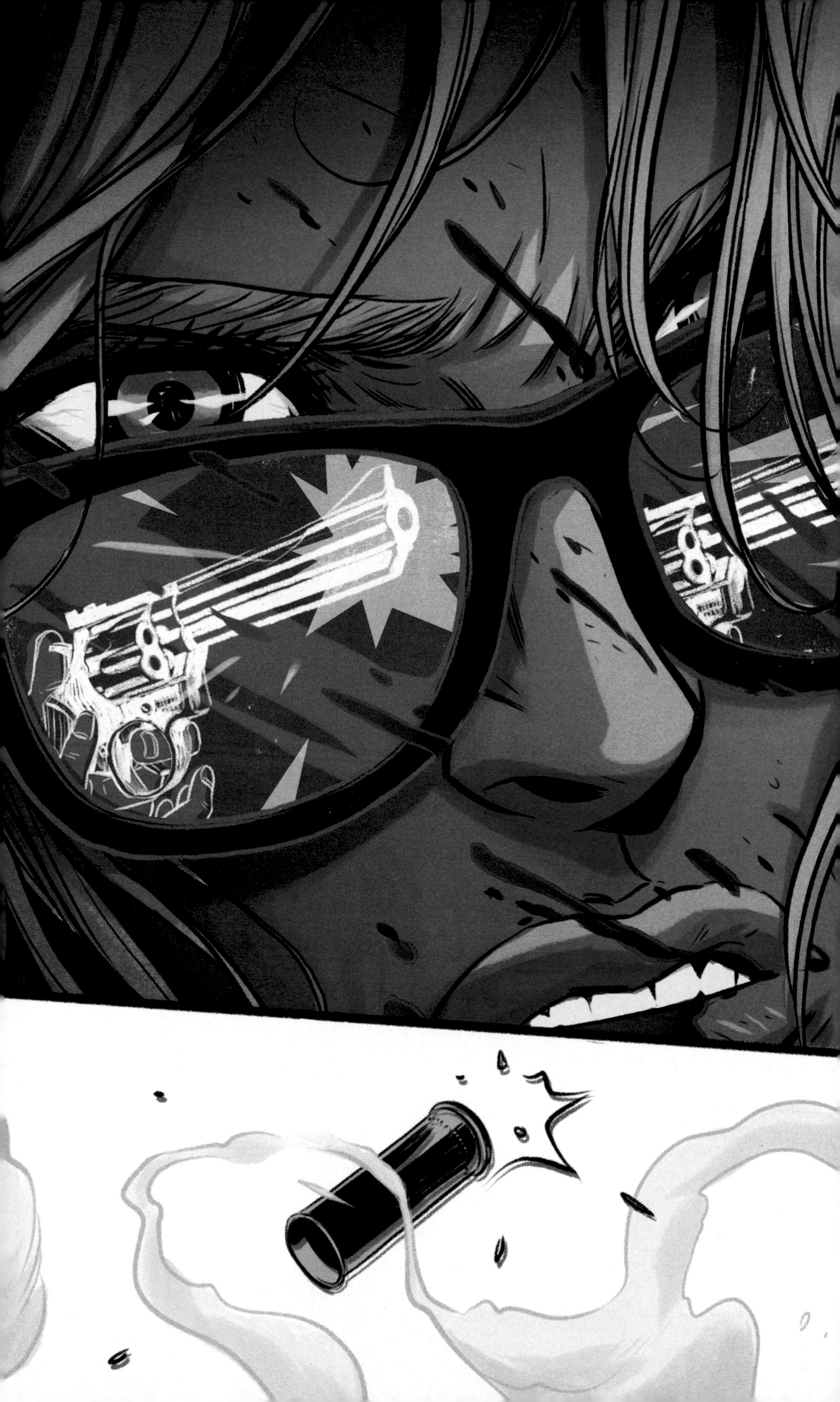

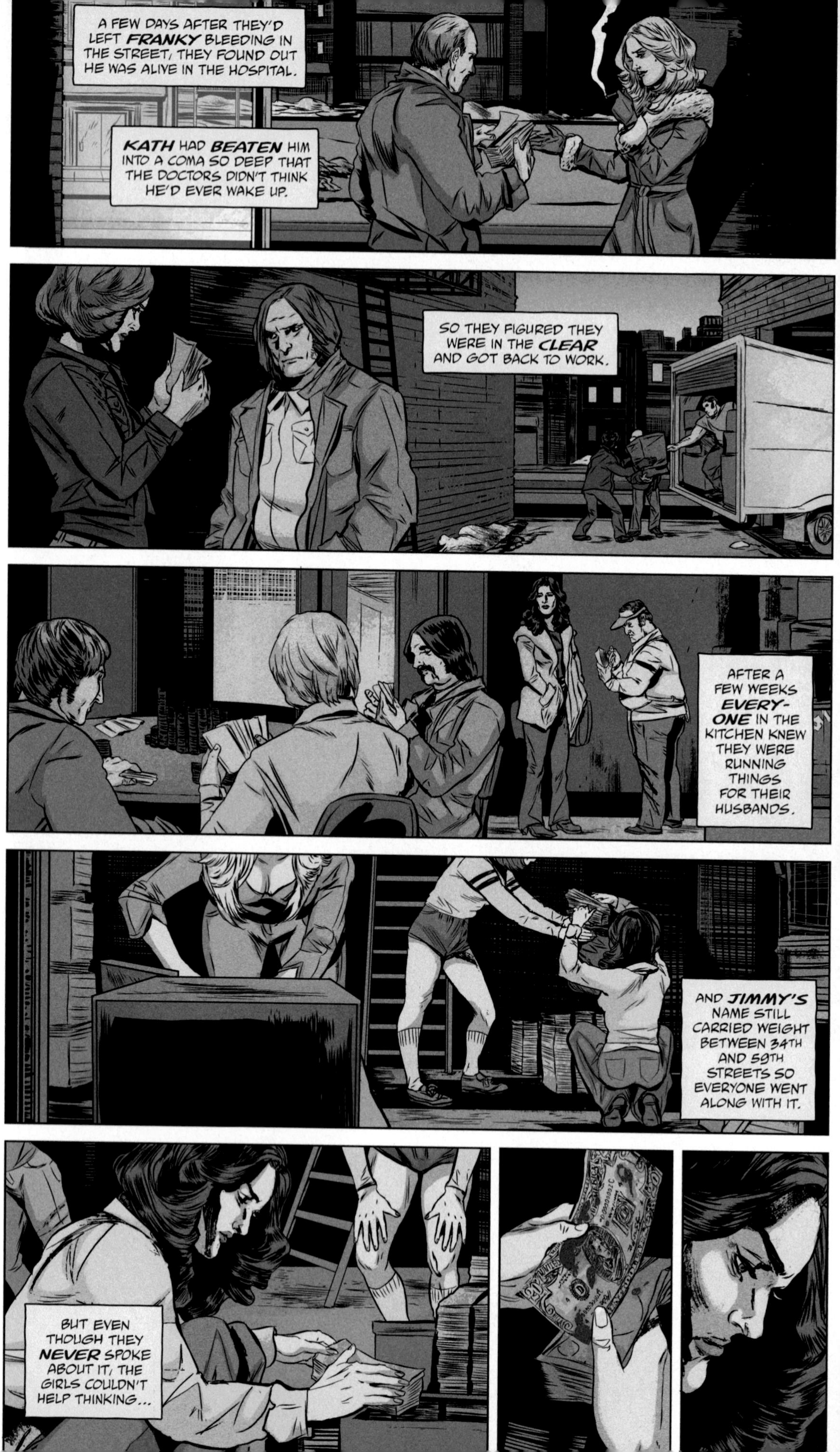
A FEW DAYS AFTER THEY'D LEFT FRANKY BLEEDING IN THE STREET, THEY FOUND OUT HE WAS ALIVE IN THE HOSPITAL.
KATH HAD BEATEN HIM INTO A COMA SO DEEP THAT THE DOCTORS DIDN'T THINK HE'D EVER WAKE UP.
SO THEY FIGURED THEY WERE IN THE CLEAR AND GOT BACK TO WORK.
AFTER A FEW WEEKS EVERY-ONE IN THE KITCHEN KNEW THEY WERE RUNNING THINGS FOR THEIR HUSBANDS.
AND JIMMY'S NAME STILL CARRIED WEIGHT BETWEEN 34TH AND 59TH STREETS SO EVERYONE WENT ALONG WITH IT.
BUT EVEN THOUGH THEY NEVER SPOKE ABOUT IT, THE GIRLS COULDN'T HELP THINKING...

I'M NOT GONNA BE A FUCKIN' *PIMP.*

IT'S JUST AN IDEA, *RAVEN.*

YEAH, WELL *LAST TIME* YOU HAD AN IDEA YOU PUT A GUY INNA' *COMA,* KATH.

ALL *I'M SAYIN'* IS WE'RE MAKIN' MONEY IT WE COULD BE MAKIN' *MORE* AND IT'S A *CLEAN* BUSINESS--

CLEAN? HAVE YOU *SEEN* TIMES SQUARE LATELY?

IT'S *CLEAN* IF YOU DO IT *RIGHT.*

FUCK, EVEN *DAD* USED TO RUN GIRLS OUTTA HIS CLUB.

IF YOU'RE TRYIN' TO WIN ME OVER, YOU SHOULD LEAVE THAT *PRICK* OUT OF IT.

I KNOW YOU'VE FELT LIKE THE FUCKIN' *DON* OF *HELL'S KITCHEN* SINCE YOU FUCKED UP *FRANKY,* BUT YOU AIN'T DAD.

AND IF YOU'VE GOT ANY FUCKIN' *SENSE,* YOU *DON'T* WANT TO BE--

KLINK

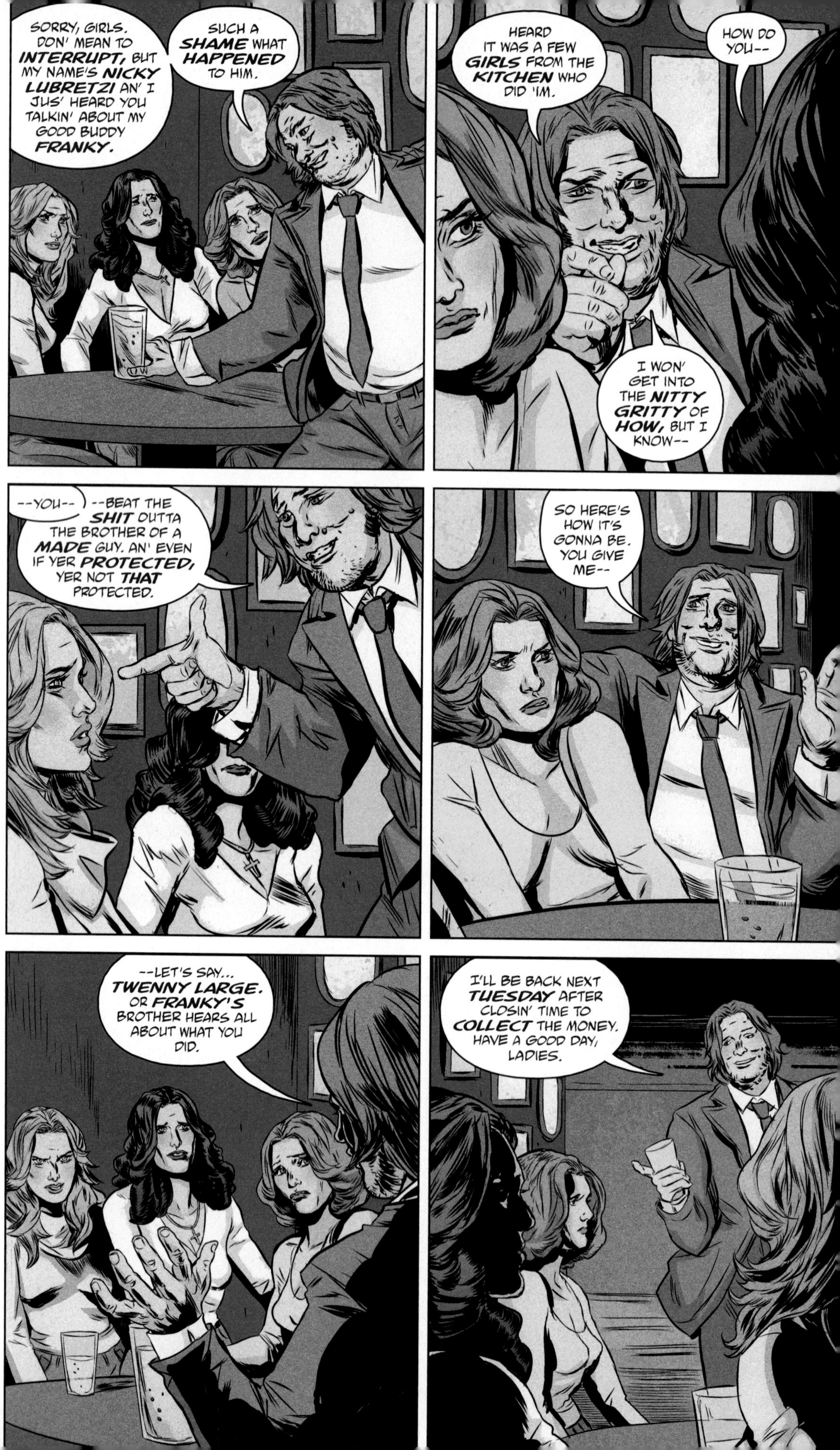
SORRY, GIRLS. DON' MEAN TO INTERRUPT, BUT MY NAME'S NICKY LUBRETZI AN' I JUS' HEARD YOU TALKIN' ABOUT MY GOOD BUDDY FRANKY.
SUCH A SHAME WHAT HAPPENED TO HIM.
HEARD IT WAS A FEW GIRLS FROM THE KITCHEN WHO DID 'IM.
HOW DO YOU--
I WON' GET INTO THE NITTY GRITTY OF HOW, BUT I KNOW--
--YOU--
--BEAT THE SHIT OUTTA THE BROTHER OF A MADE GUY. AN' EVEN IF YER PROTECTED, YER NOT THAT PROTECTED.
SO HERE'S HOW IT'S GONNA BE. YOU GIVE ME--
--LET'S SAY... TWENNY LARGE. OR FRANKY'S BROTHER HEARS ALL ABOUT WHAT YOU DID.
I'LL BE BACK NEXT TUESDAY AFTER CLOSIN' TIME TO COLLECT THE MONEY. HAVE A GOOD DAY, LADIES.

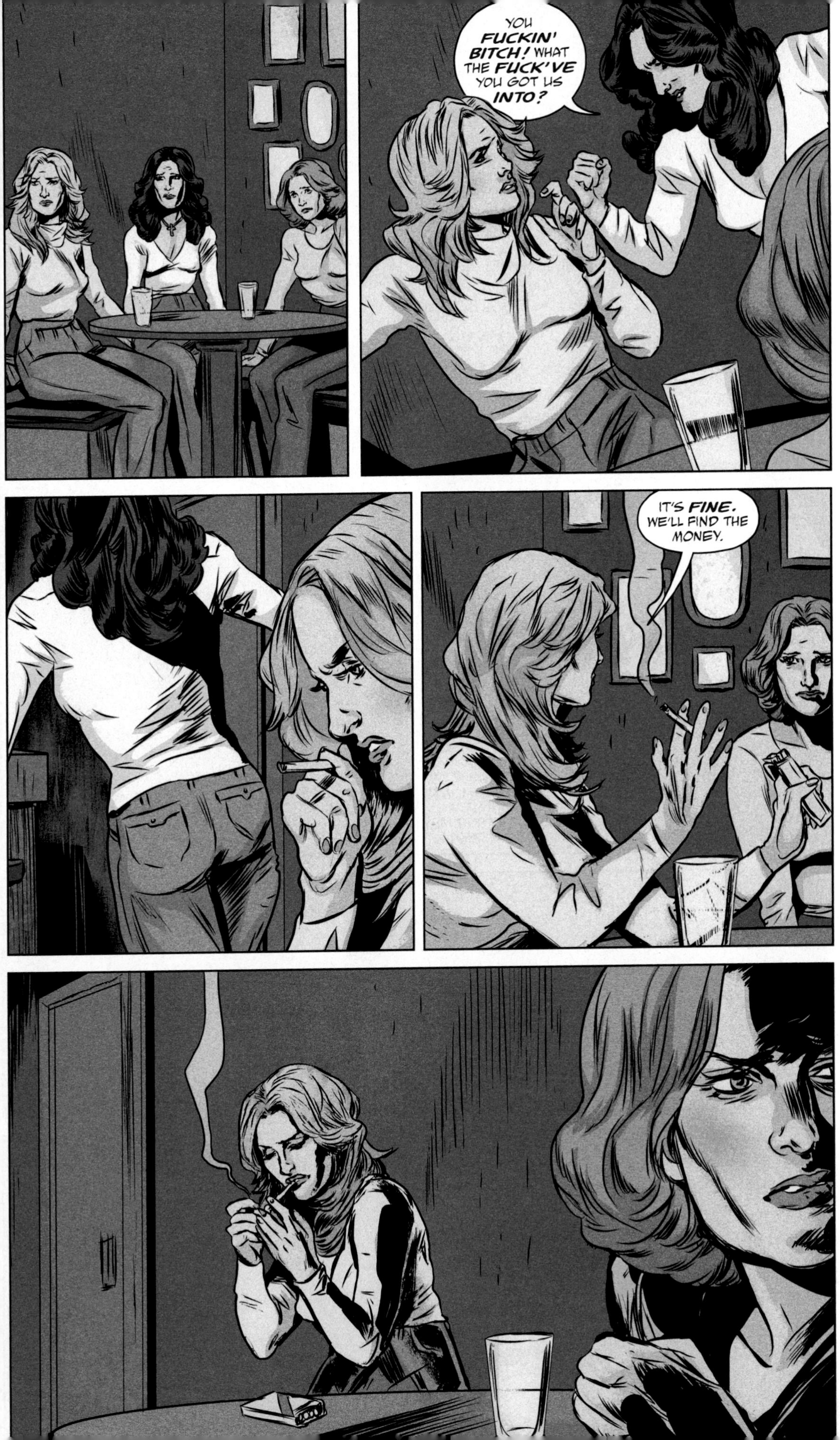
YOU FUCKIN' BITCH! WHAT THE FUCK'VE YOU GOT US INTO?
IT'S FINE. WE'LL FIND THE MONEY.

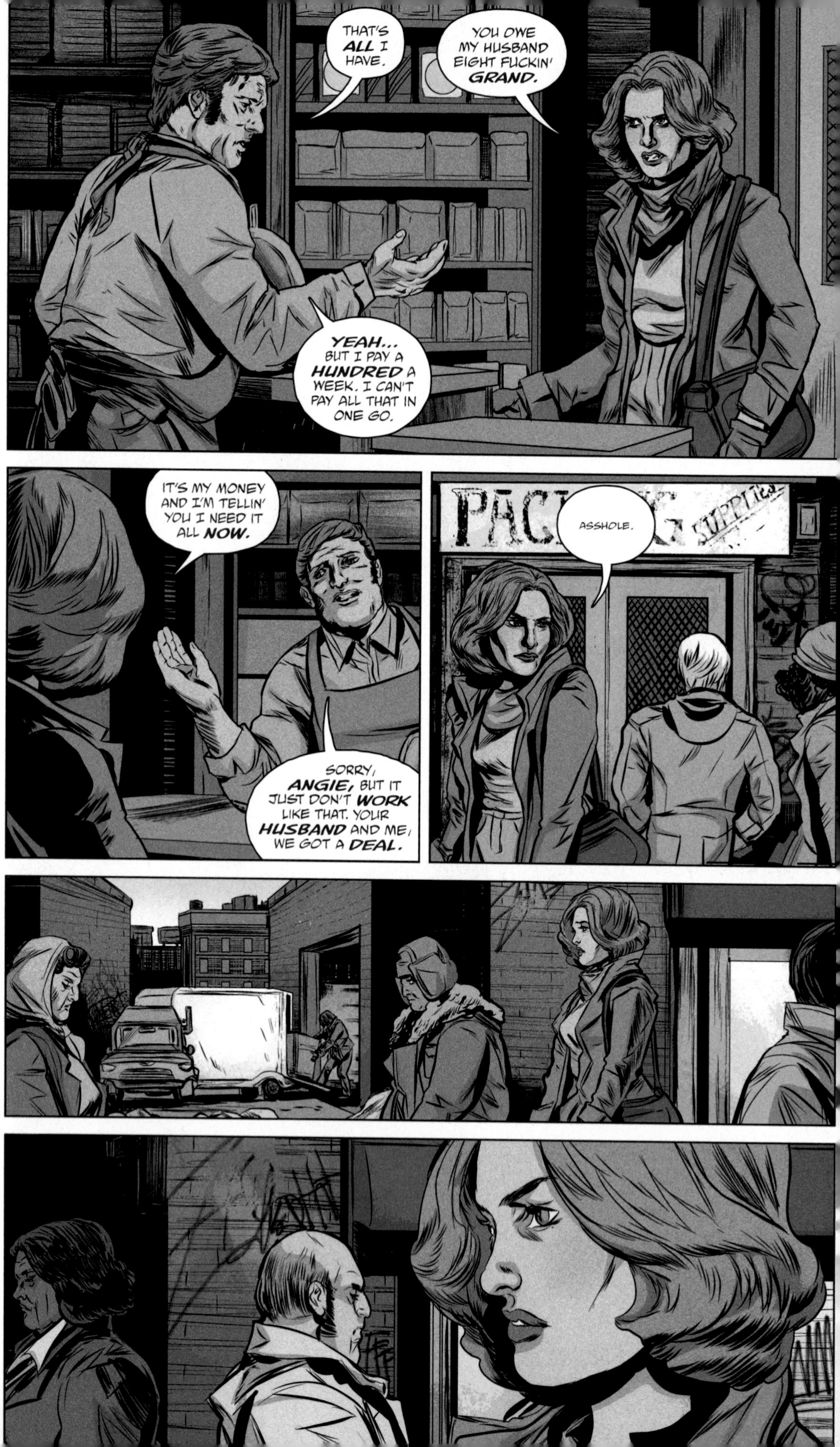
THAT'S ALL I HAVE.
YOU OWE MY HUSBAND EIGHT FUCKIN' GRAND.
YEAH... BUT I PAY A HUNDRED A WEEK. I CAN'T PAY ALL THAT IN ONE GO.
IT'S MY MONEY AND I'M TELLIN' YOU I NEED IT ALL NOW.
SORRY, ANGIE, BUT IT JUST DON'T WORK LIKE THAT. YOUR HUSBAND AND ME, WE GOT A DEAL.
ASSHOLE.

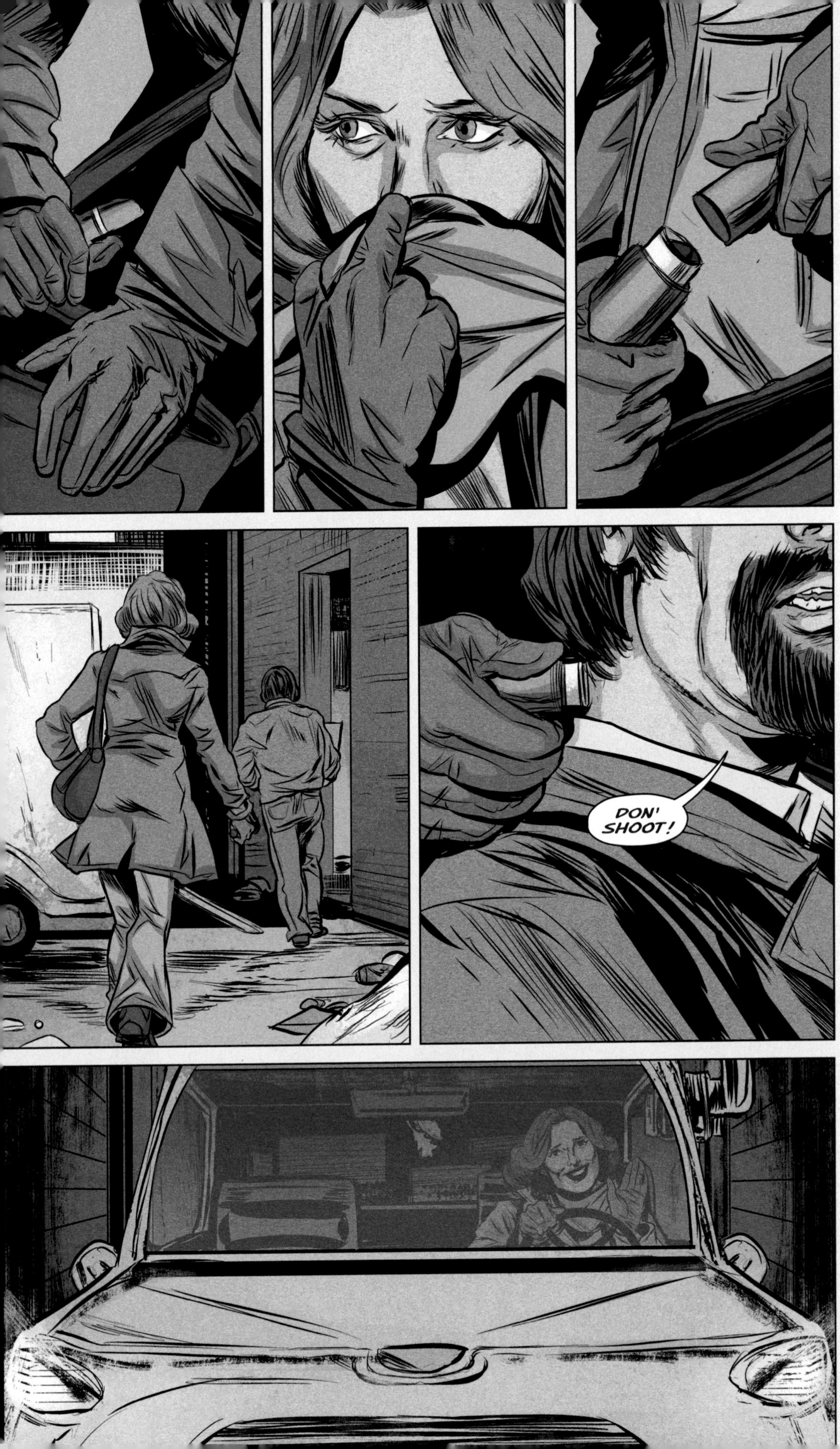
DON'
SHOOT!

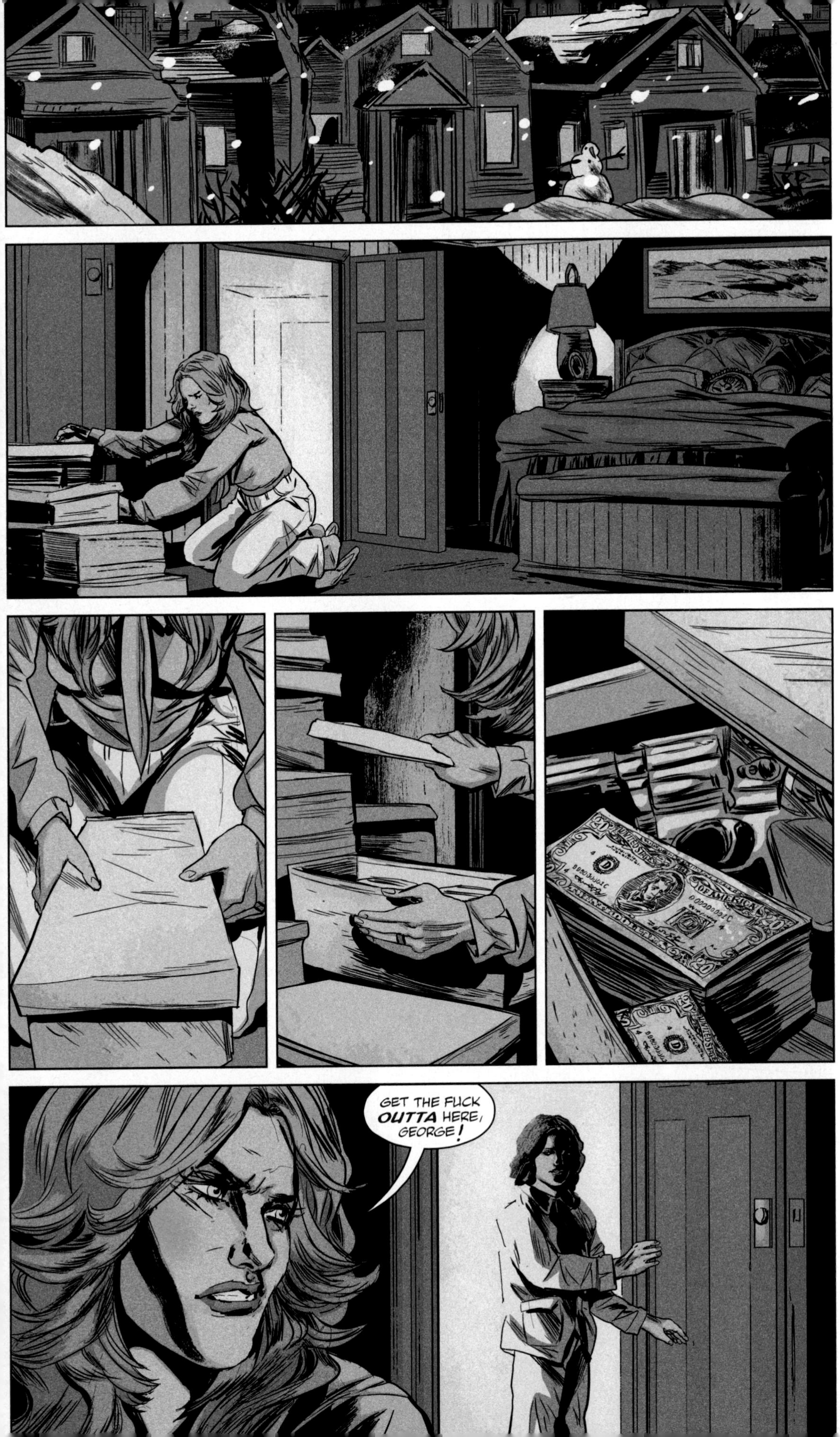
GET THE FUCK OUTTA HERE, GEORGE!

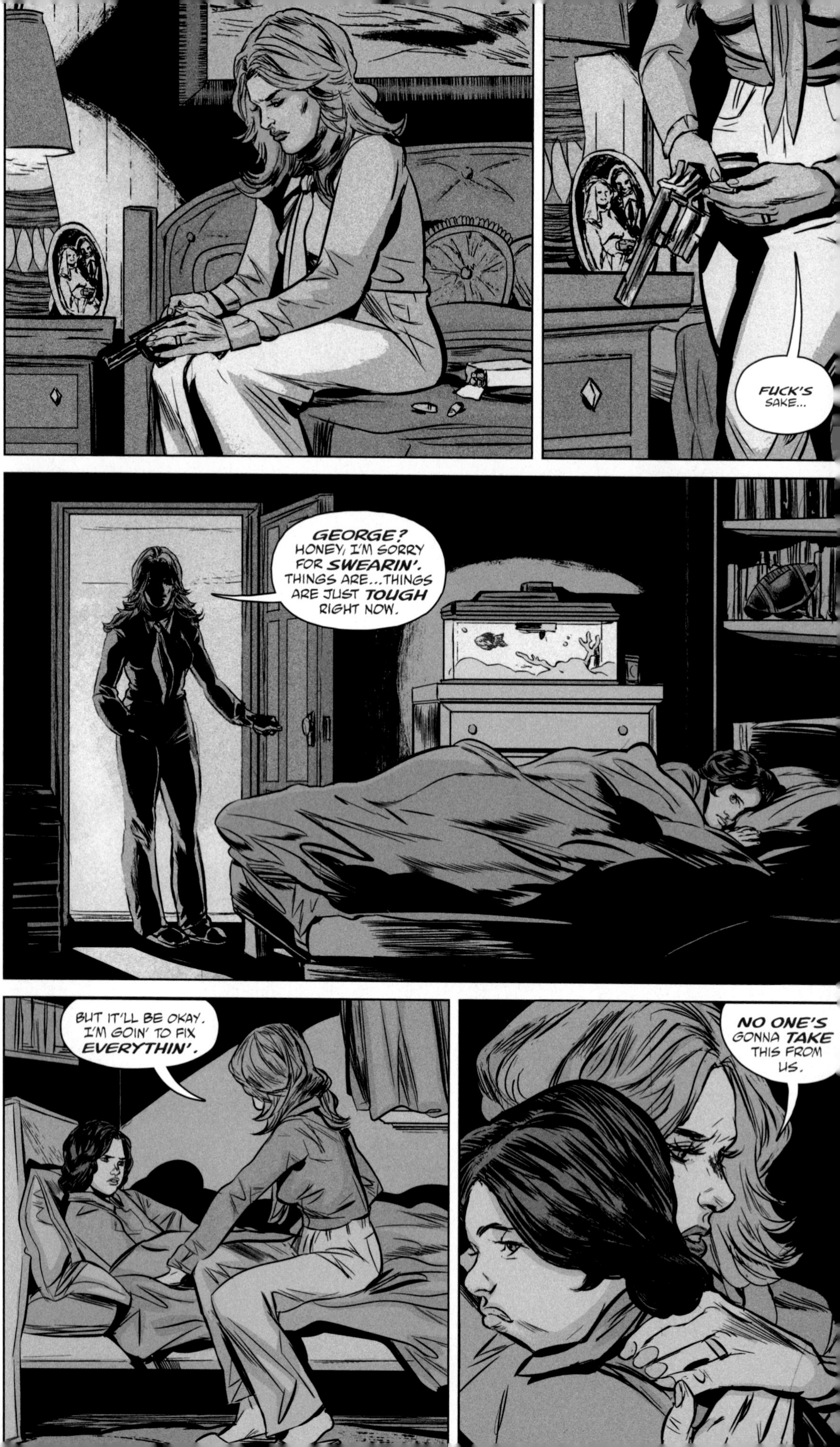
FUCK'S SAKE...
GEORGE? HONEY, I'M SORRY FOR SWEARIN'. THINGS ARE...THINGS ARE JUST TOUGH RIGHT NOW.
BUT IT'LL BE OKAY. I'M GOIN' TO FIX EVERYTHIN'.
NO ONE'S GONNA TAKE THIS FROM US.

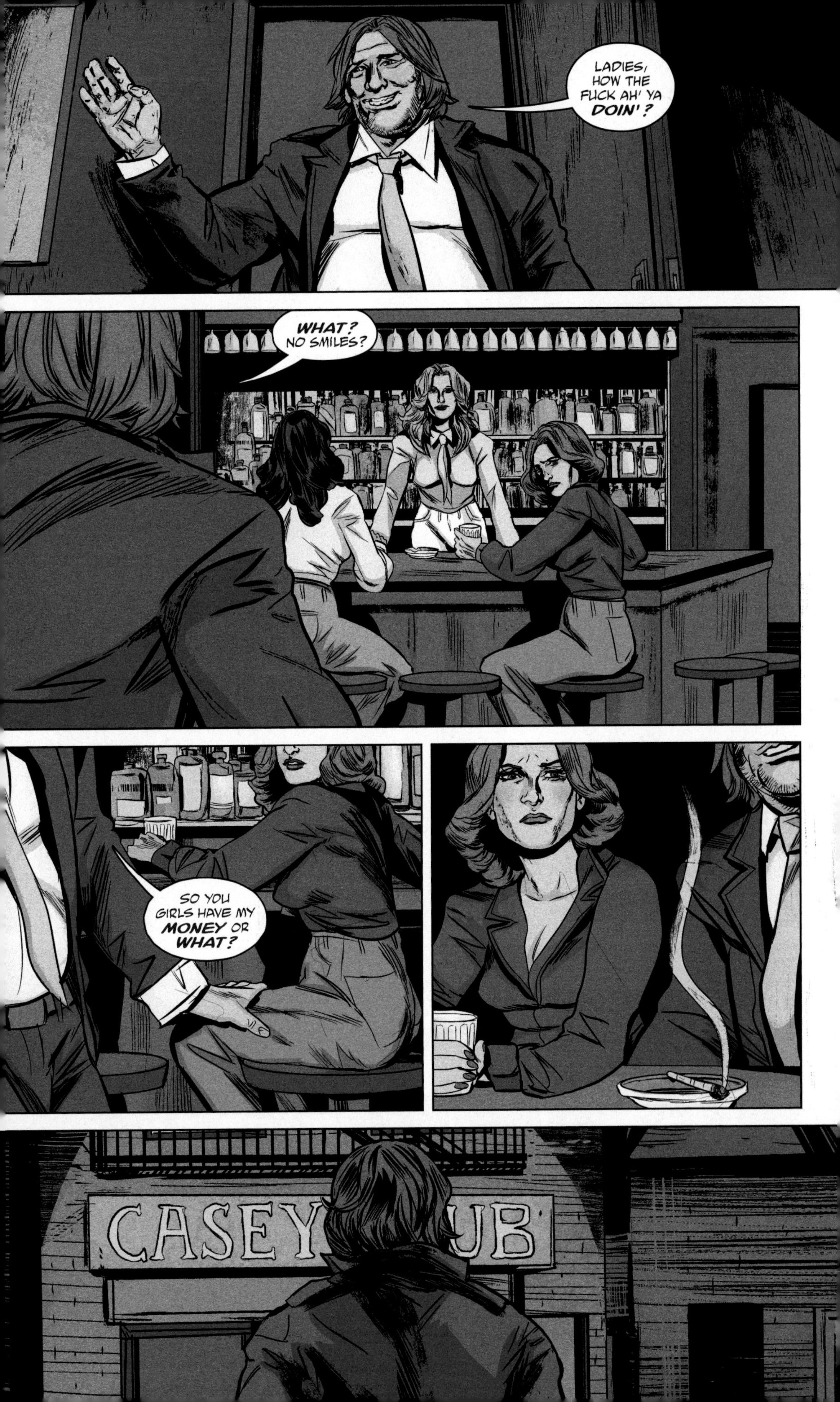

LADIES, HOW THE FUCK AH' YA DOIN'?
WHAT? NO SMILES?
SO YOU GIRLS HAVE MY MONEY OR WHAT?
CASEY UB

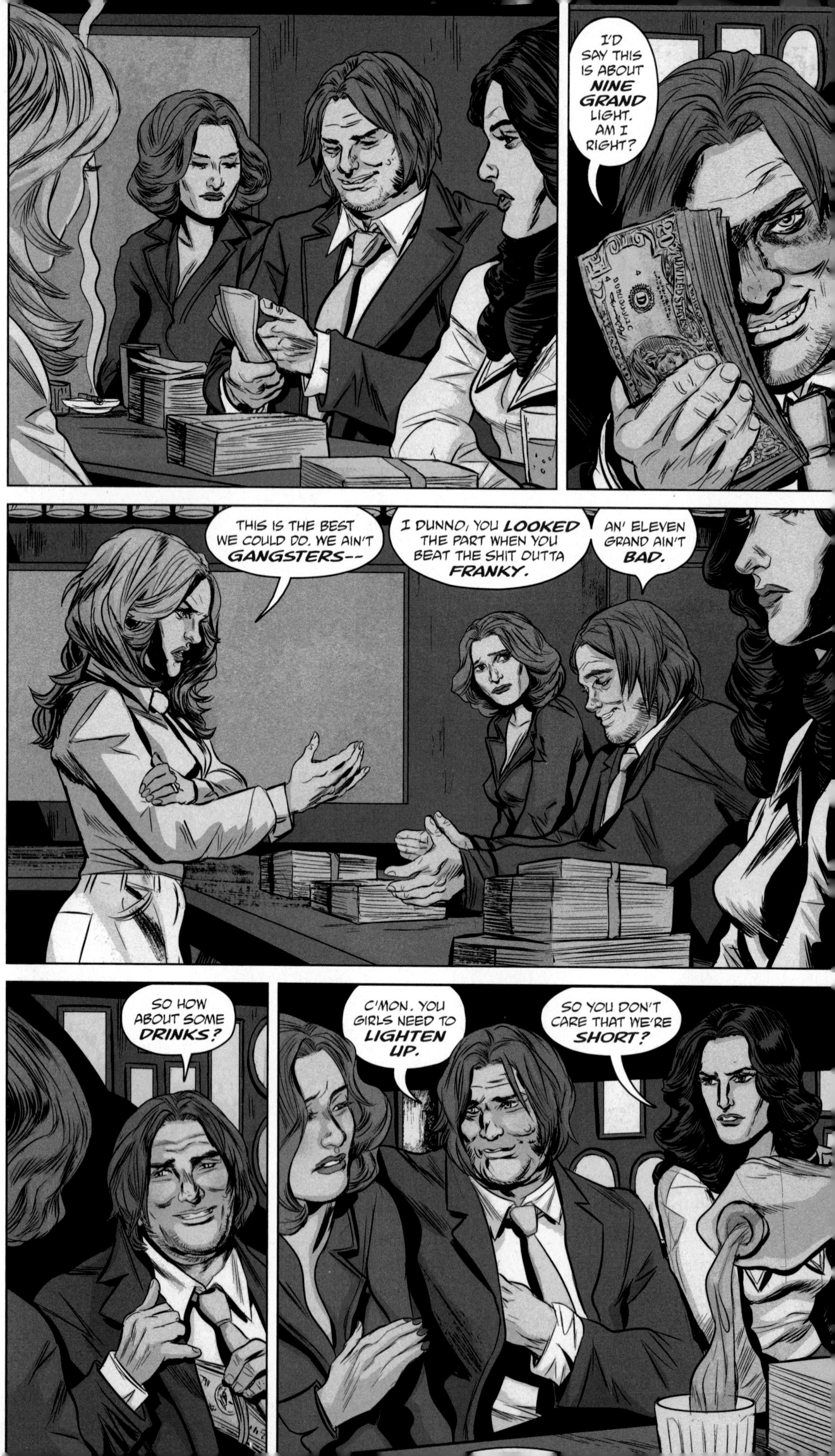
I'D SAY THIS IS ABOUT NINE GRAND LIGHT. AM I RIGHT?
THIS IS THE BEST WE COULD DO. WE AIN'T GANGSTERS--
I DUNNO, YOU LOOKED THE PART WHEN YOU BEAT THE SHIT OUTTA FRANKY.
AN' ELEVEN GRAND AIN'T BAD.
SO HOW ABOUT SOME DRINKS?
C'MON. YOU GIRLS NEED TO LIGHTEN UP.
SO YOU DON'T CARE THAT WE'RE SHORT?

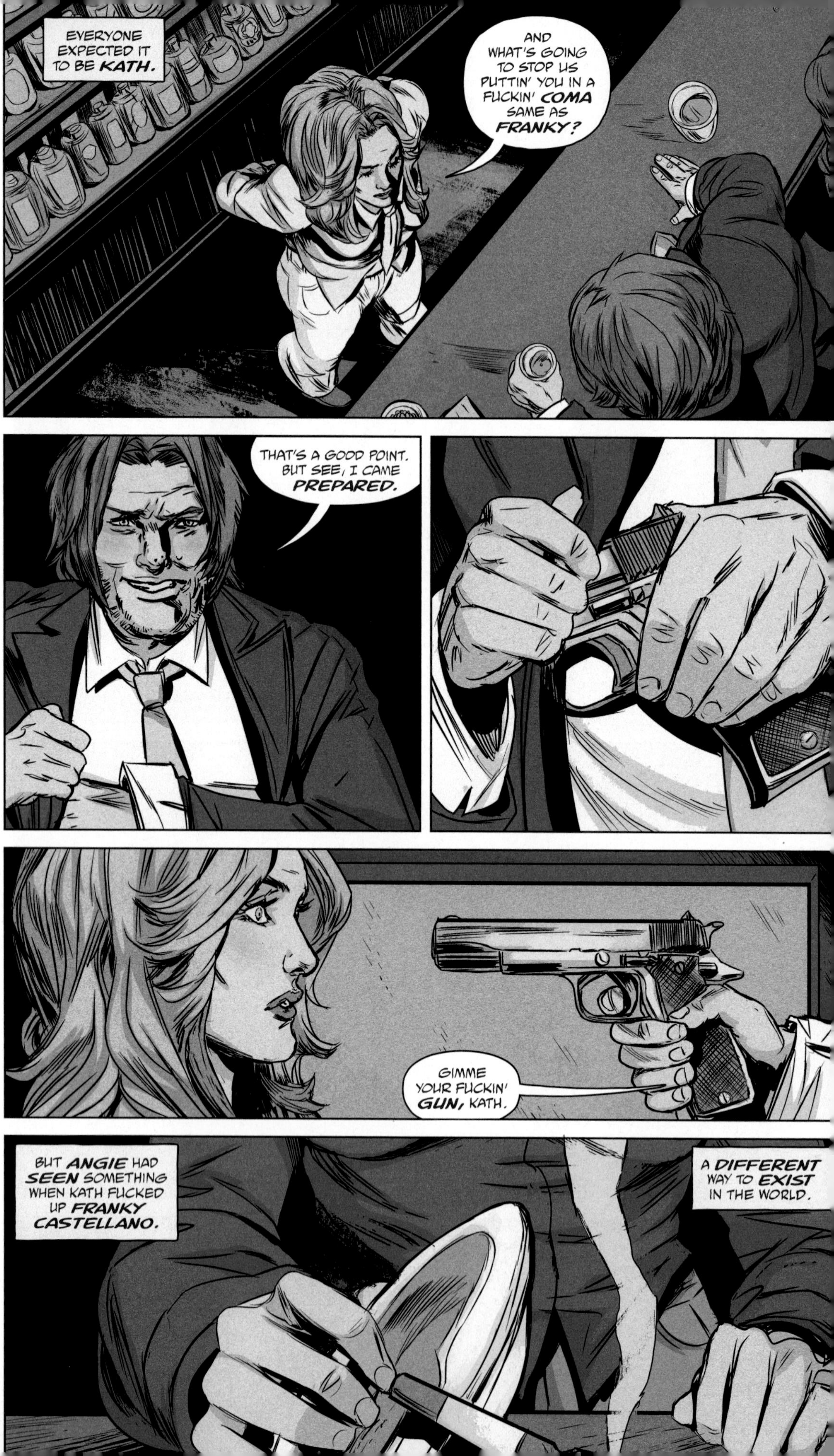

EVERYONE EXPECTED IT TO BE KATH.
AND WHAT'S GOING TO STOP US PUTTIN' YOU IN A FUCKIN' COMA SAME AS FRANKY?
THAT'S A GOOD POINT. BUT SEE, I CAME PREPARED.
GIMME YOUR FUCKIN' GUN, KATH.
BUT ANGIE HAD SEEN SOMETHING WHEN KATH FUCKED UP FRANKY CASTELLANO.
A DIFFERENT WAY TO EXIST IN THE WORLD.

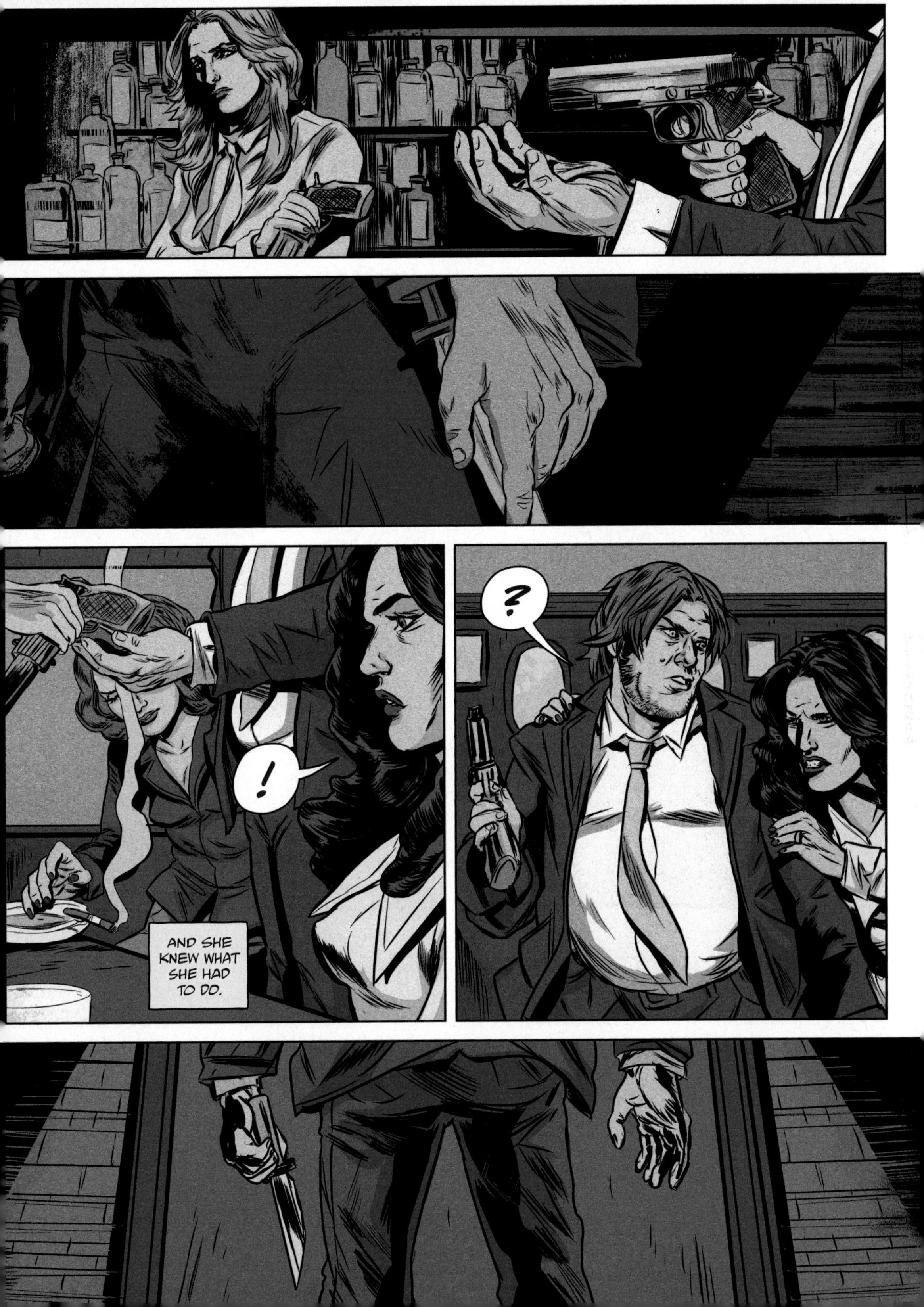
!
AND SHE KNEW WHAT SHE HAD TO DO.
?

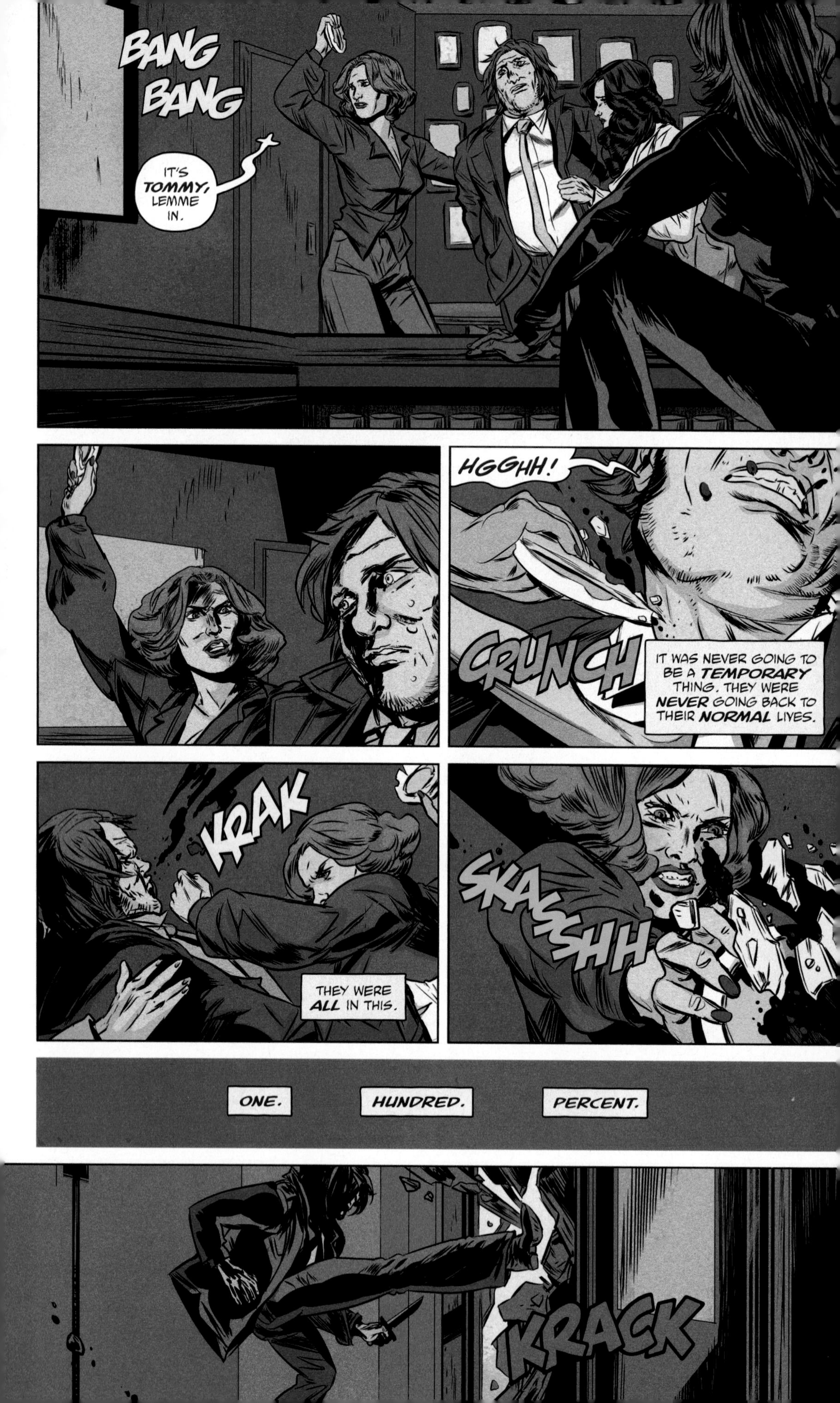
BANG BANG
IT'S TOMMY, LEMME IN.
HGGHH!
CRUNCH
IT WAS NEVER GOING TO BE A TEMPORARY THING. THEY WERE NEVER GOING BACK TO THEIR NORMAL LIVES.
KRAK
THEY WERE ALL IN THIS.
SKASSHH
ONE.
HUNDRED.
PERCENT.
KRACK

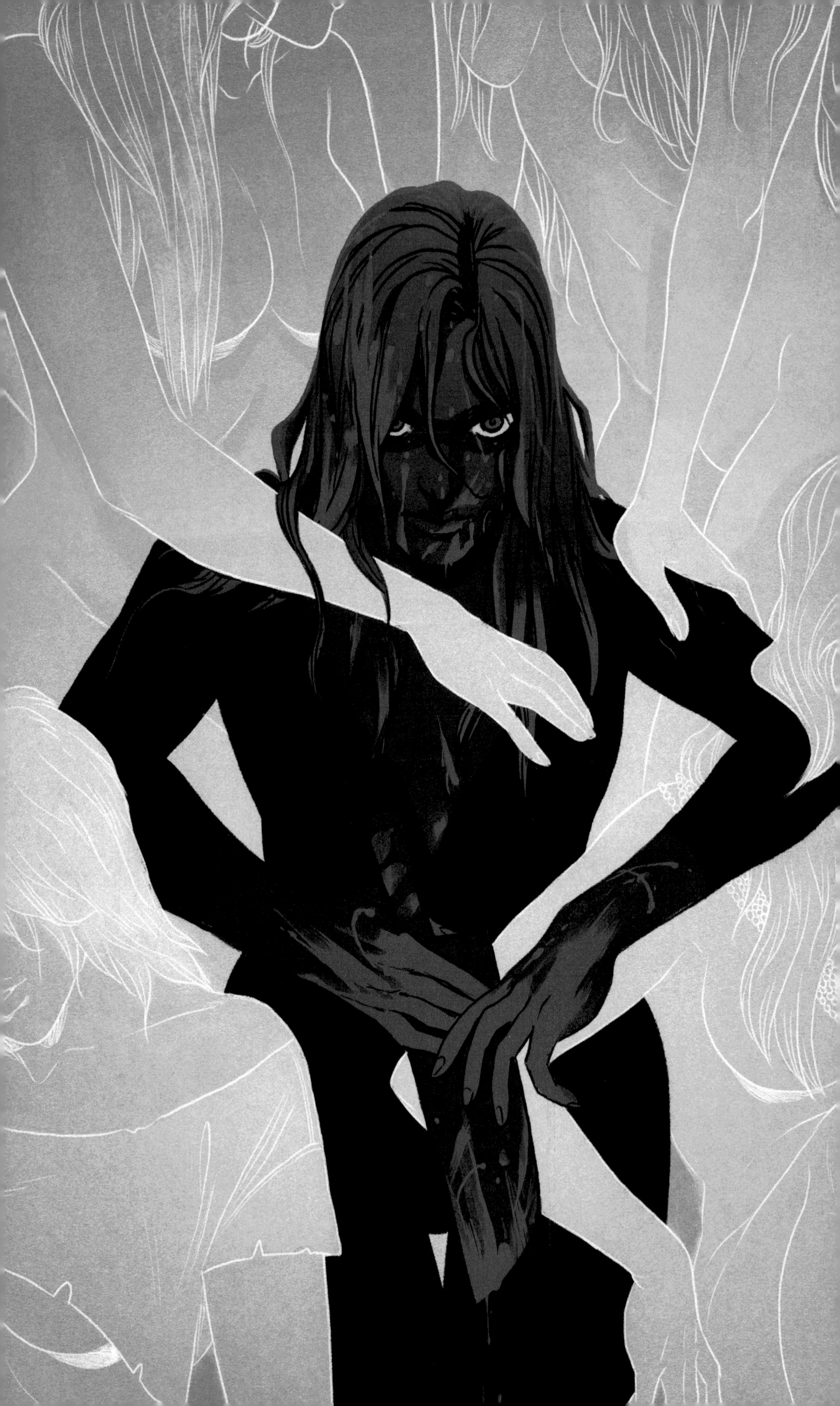

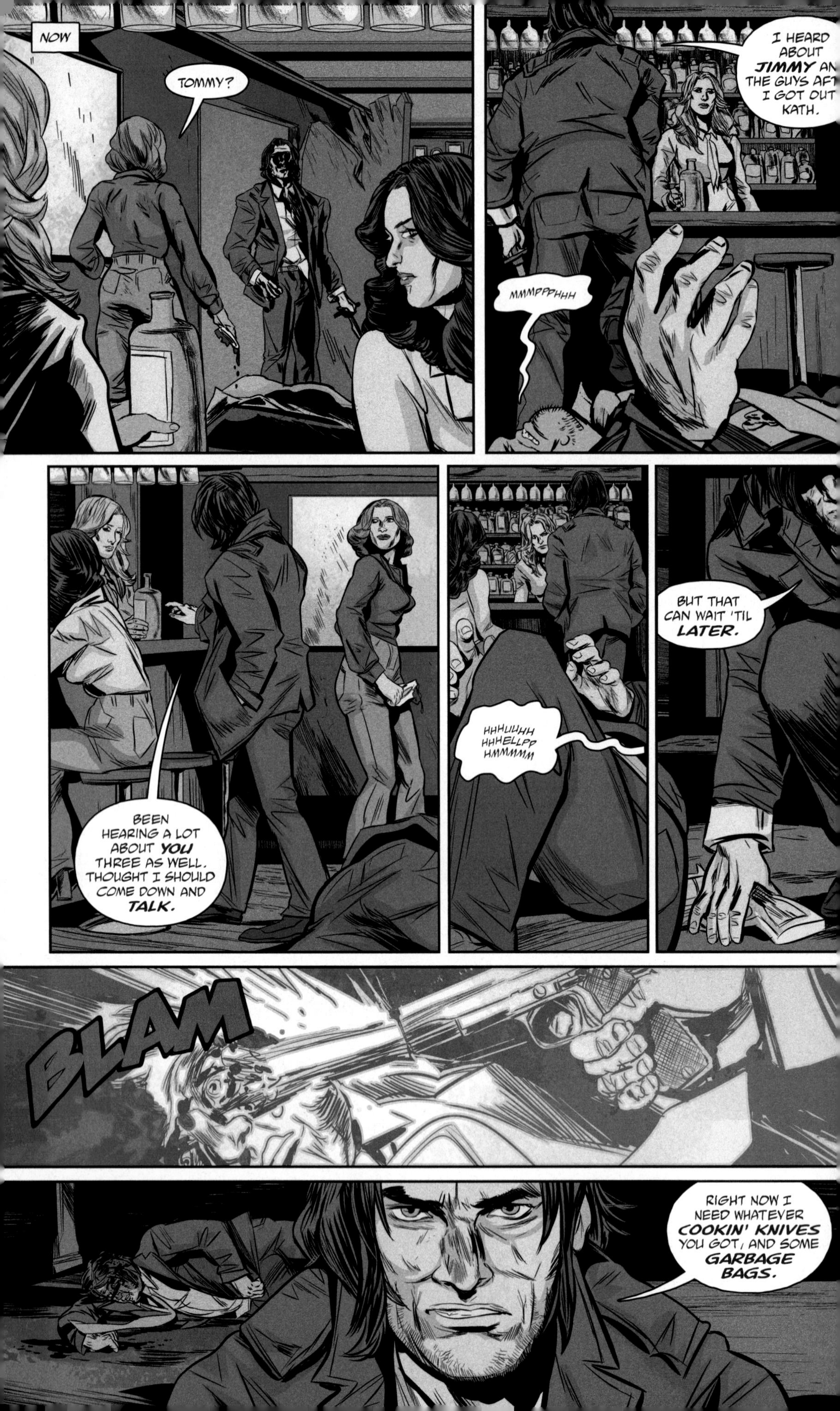
NOW
TOMMY?
I HEARD ABOUT JIMMY AN THE GUYS AFT I GOT OUT KATH.
MMMPPPHHH
BEEN HEARING A LOT ABOUT YOU THREE AS WELL. THOUGHT I SHOULD COME DOWN AND TALK.
HHHUUHH HHHELLPP HMMMMM
BUT THAT CAN WAIT 'TIL LATER.
BLAM
RIGHT NOW I NEED WHATEVER COOKIN' KNIVES YOU GOT, AND SOME GARBAGE BAGS.

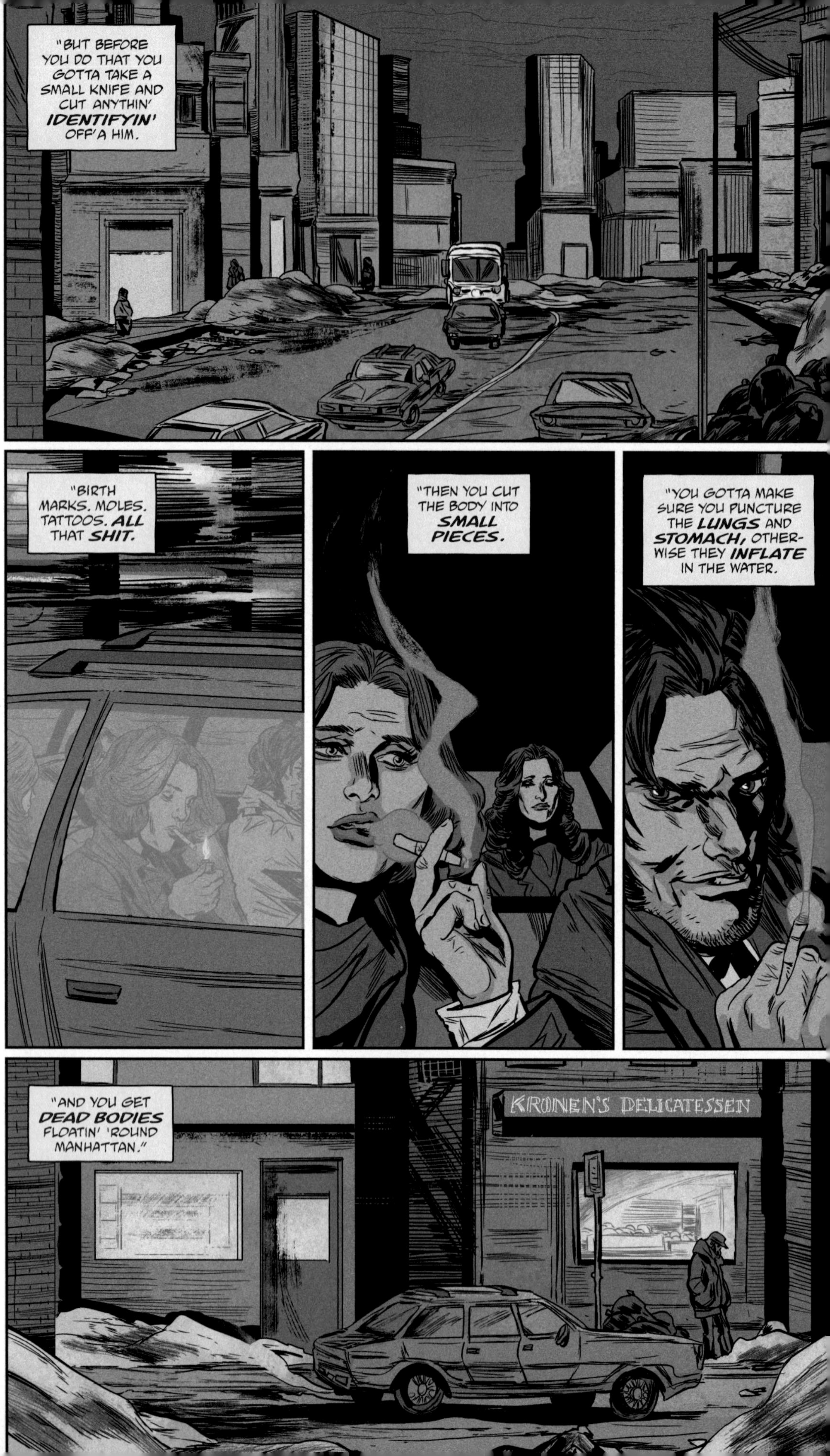
"BUT BEFORE YOU DO THAT YOU GOTTA TAKE A SMALL KNIFE AND CUT ANYTHIN' IDENTIFYIN' OFF'A HIM.
"BIRTH MARKS. MOLES. TATTOOS. ALL THAT SHIT.
"THEN YOU CUT THE BODY INTO SMALL PIECES.
"YOU GOTTA MAKE SURE YOU PUNCTURE THE LUNGS AND STOMACH, OTHER-WISE THEY INFLATE IN THE WATER.
"AND YOU GET DEAD BODIES FLOATIN' 'ROUND MANHATTAN."
KRONEN'S DELICATESSEN

"IF YOU DO IT RIGHT, NO ONE'LL EVER FIND THE BODY. AND NO *BODY* MEANS NO *INVESTIGATION.*"

SP*LASH.*

WHAT NOW?

WE GET THE FUCK *OUTTA* HERE AND CLEAN UP THE *BAR.*

I MEAN WITH *US.*

WAY I SEE IT--

--I WORK WITH *JIMMY.* HE AIN'T *HERE.* YOU GIRLS SEEM TO BE DOIN' OKAY...

SO LOOKS LIKE I'M WORKIN' WITH *YOU.*

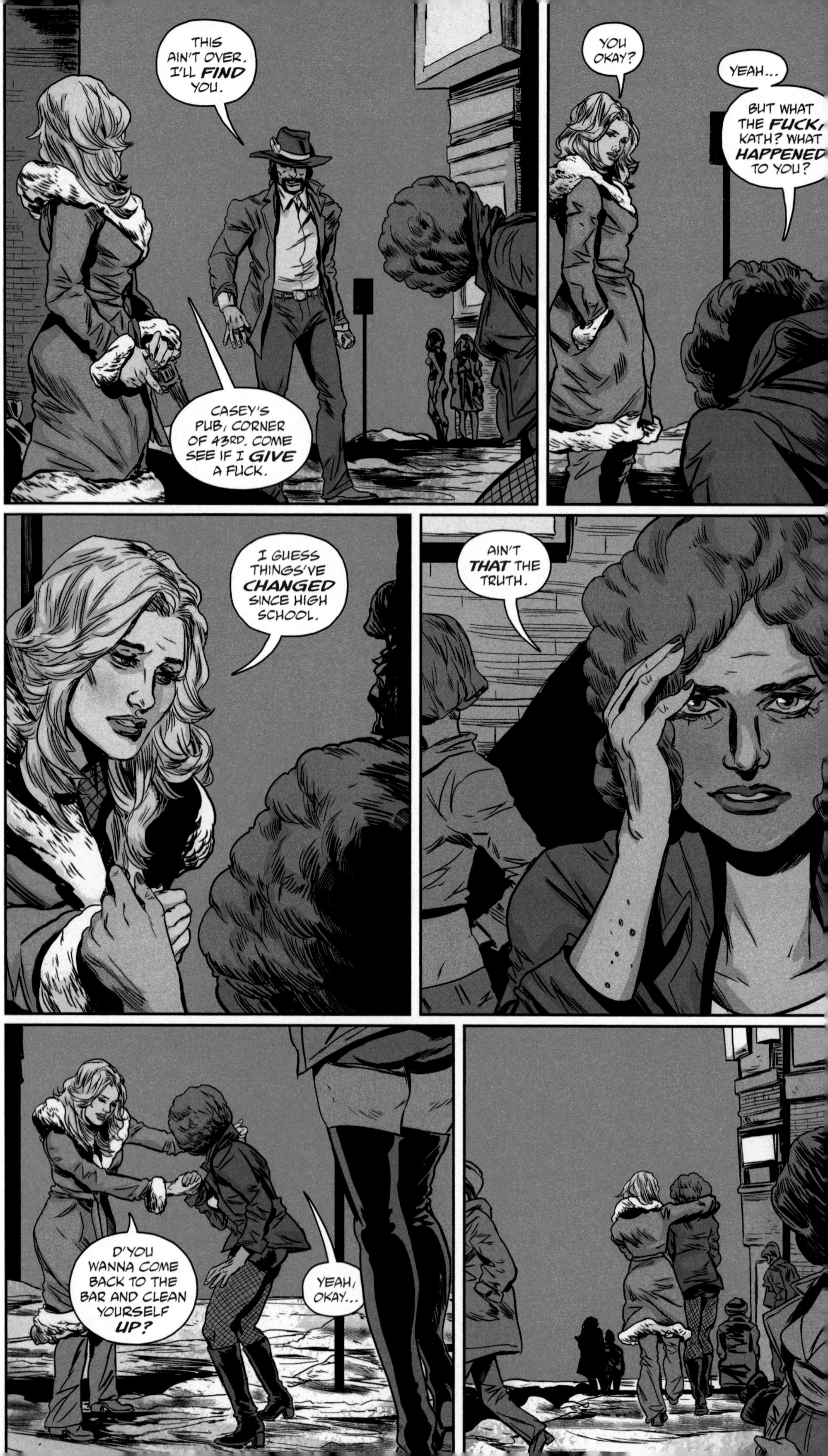
THIS AIN'T OVER. I'LL FIND YOU.
CASEY'S PUB, CORNER OF 43RD. COME SEE IF I GIVE A FUCK.
YOU OKAY?
YEAH...
BUT WHAT THE FUCK, KATH? WHAT HAPPENED TO YOU?
I GUESS THINGS'VE CHANGED SINCE HIGH SCHOOL.
AIN'T THAT THE TRUTH.
D'YOU WANNA COME BACK TO THE BAR AND CLEAN YOURSELF UP?
YEAH, OKAY...

DON'T MAKE ME FUCKIN' *ASK* FOR IT AGAIN, YOU *FAT FUCK.* I'LL CUT OUT YOUR FUCKIN' *EYE-BALLS* AND FILL THE HOLES WITH *BLEACH.*

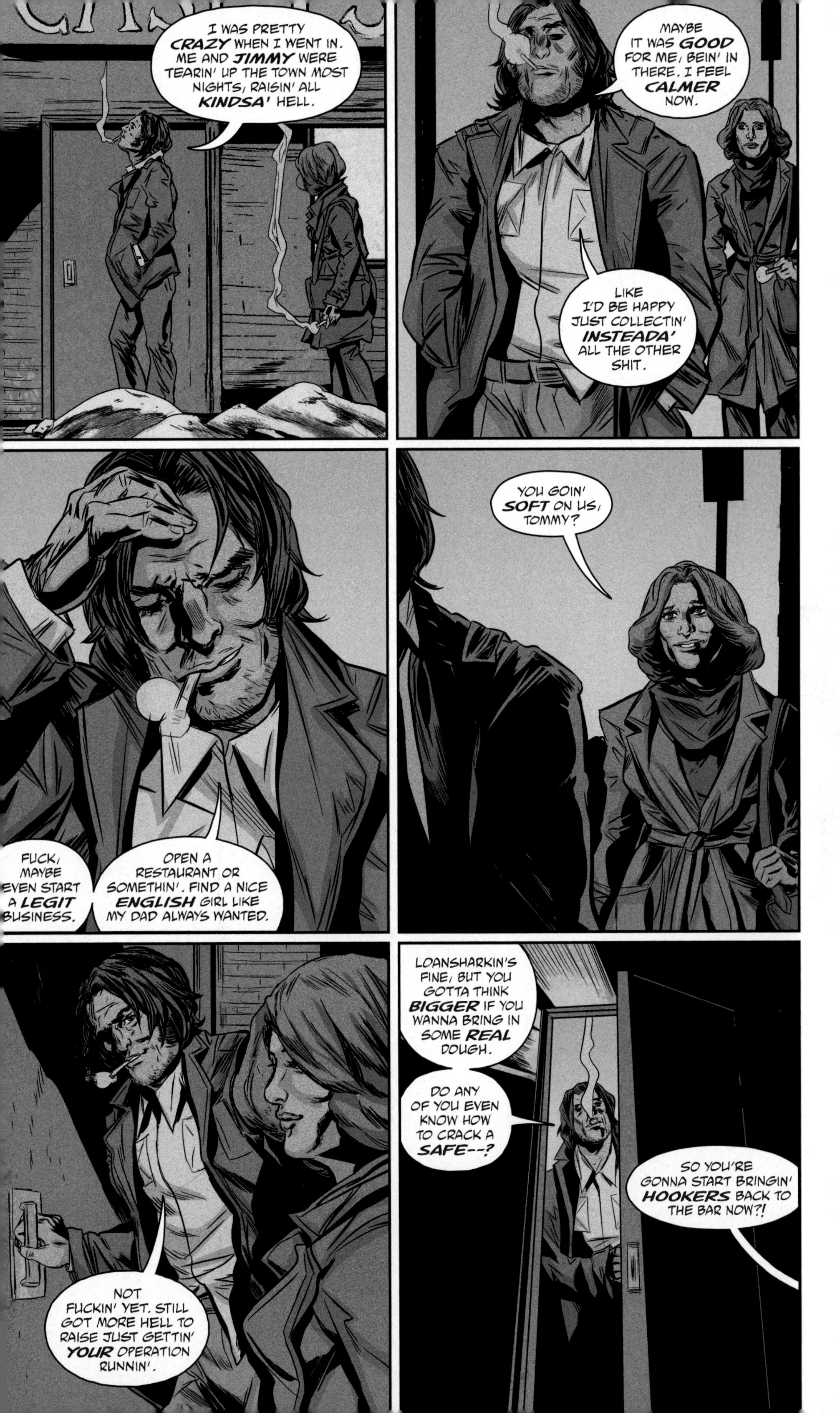
I WAS PRETTY CRAZY WHEN I WENT IN. ME AND JIMMY WERE TEARIN' UP THE TOWN MOST NIGHTS, RAISIN' ALL KINDSA' HELL.
MAYBE IT WAS GOOD FOR ME, BEIN' IN THERE. I FEEL CALMER NOW.
LIKE I'D BE HAPPY JUST COLLECTIN' INSTEADA' ALL THE OTHER SHIT.
FUCK, MAYBE EVEN START A LEGIT BUSINESS.
OPEN A RESTAURANT OR SOMETHIN'. FIND A NICE ENGLISH GIRL LIKE MY DAD ALWAYS WANTED.
YOU GOIN' SOFT ON US, TOMMY?
NOT FUCKIN' YET. STILL GOT MORE HELL TO RAISE JUST GETTIN' YOUR OPERATION RUNNIN'.
LOANSHARKIN'S FINE, BUT YOU GOTTA THINK BIGGER IF YOU WANNA BRING IN SOME REAL DOUGH.
DO ANY OF YOU EVEN KNOW HOW TO CRACK A SAFE--?
SO YOU'RE GONNA START BRINGIN' HOOKERS BACK TO THE BAR NOW?!

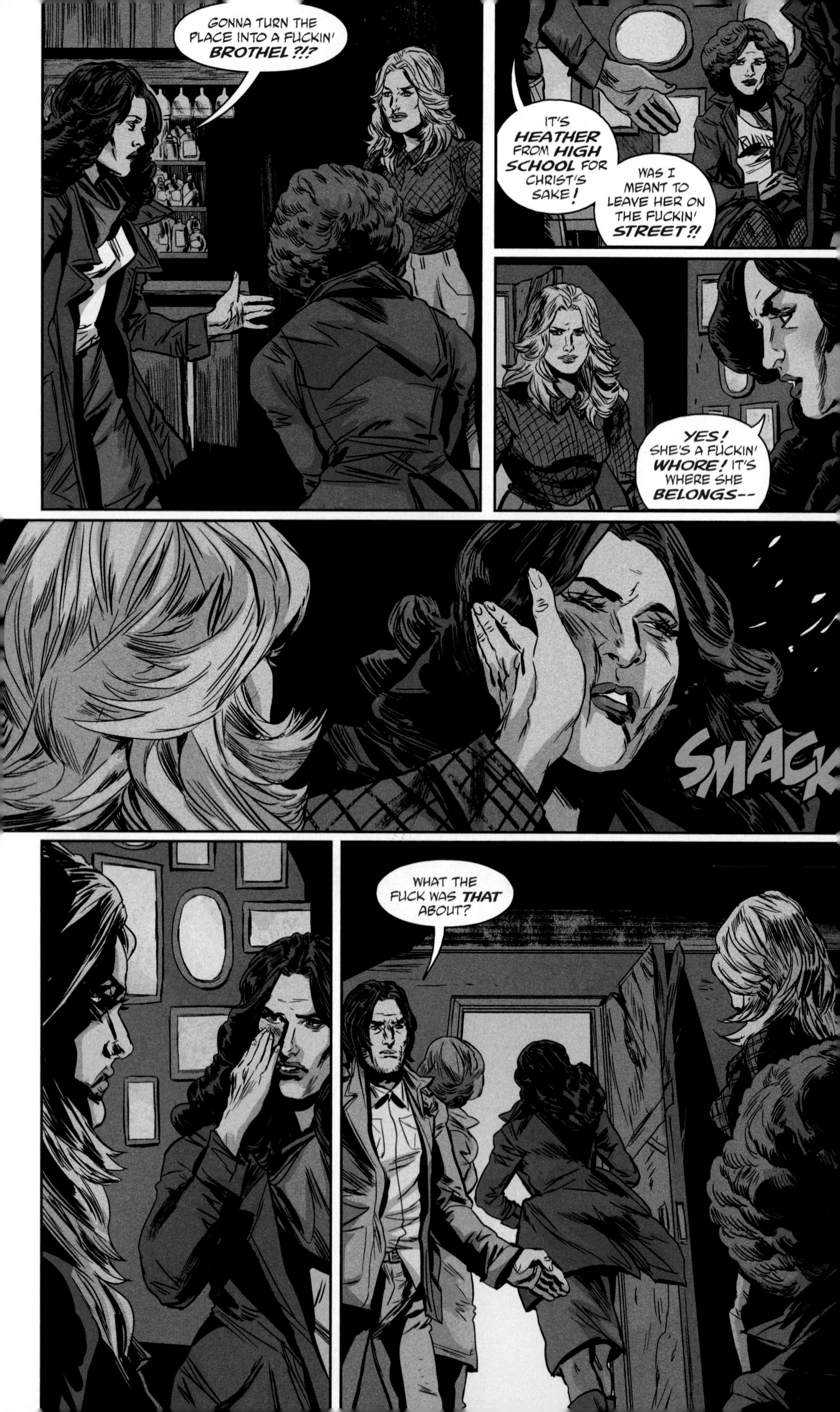
GONNA TURN THE PLACE INTO A FUCKIN' BROTHEL?!?
IT'S HEATHER FROM HIGH SCHOOL FOR CHRIST'S SAKE!
WAS I MEANT TO LEAVE HER ON THE FUCKIN' STREET?!
YES! SHE'S A FUCKIN' WHORE! IT'S WHERE SHE BELONGS--
SMACK
WHAT THE FUCK WAS THAT ABOUT?

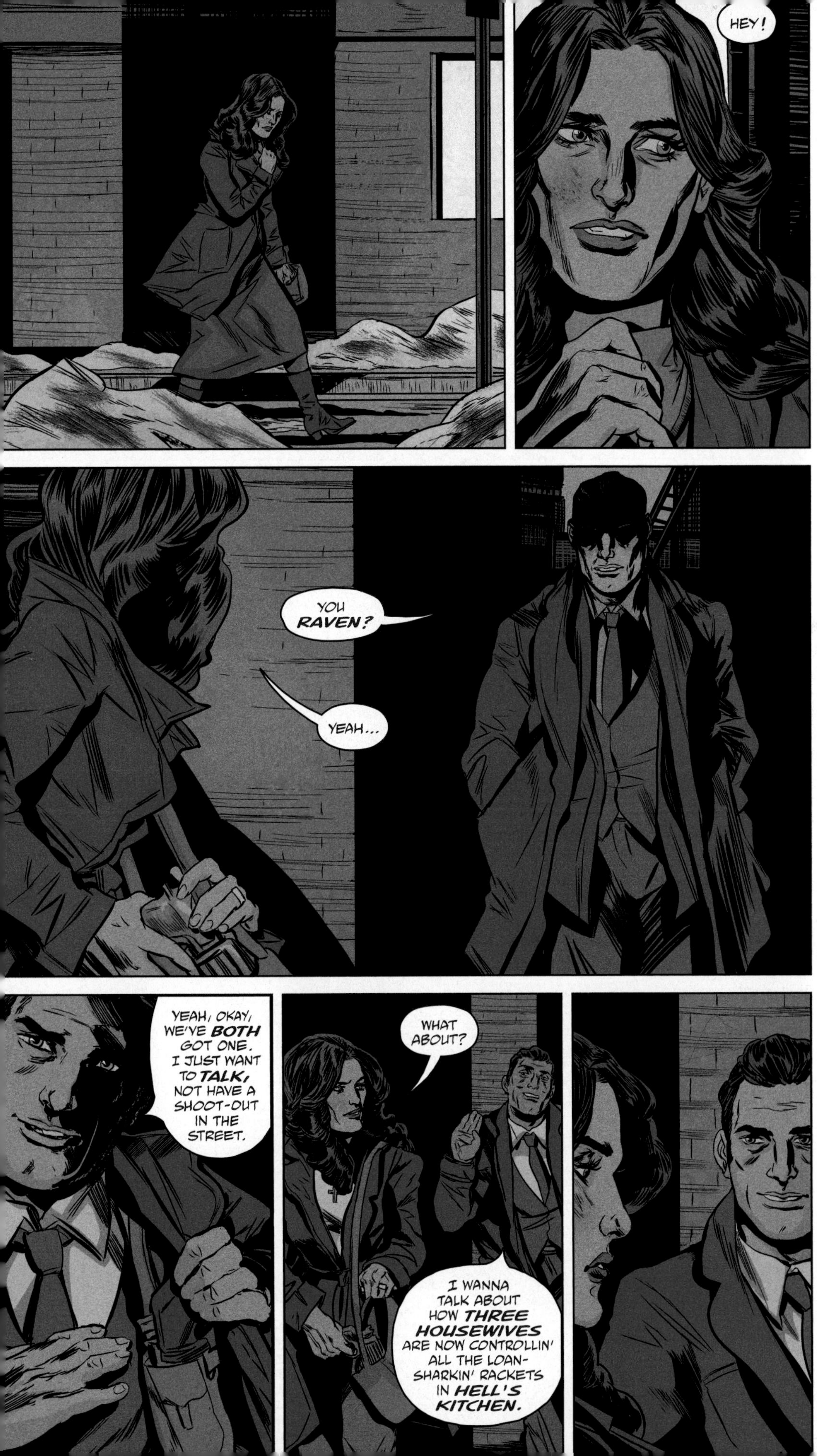
HEY!
YOU RAVEN?
YEAH...
YEAH, OKAY, WE'VE BOTH GOT ONE. I JUST WANT TO TALK, NOT HAVE A SHOOT-OUT IN THE STREET.
WHAT ABOUT?
I WANNA TALK ABOUT HOW THREE HOUSEWIVES ARE NOW CONTROLLIN' ALL THE LOAN-SHARKIN' RACKETS IN HELL'S KITCHEN.

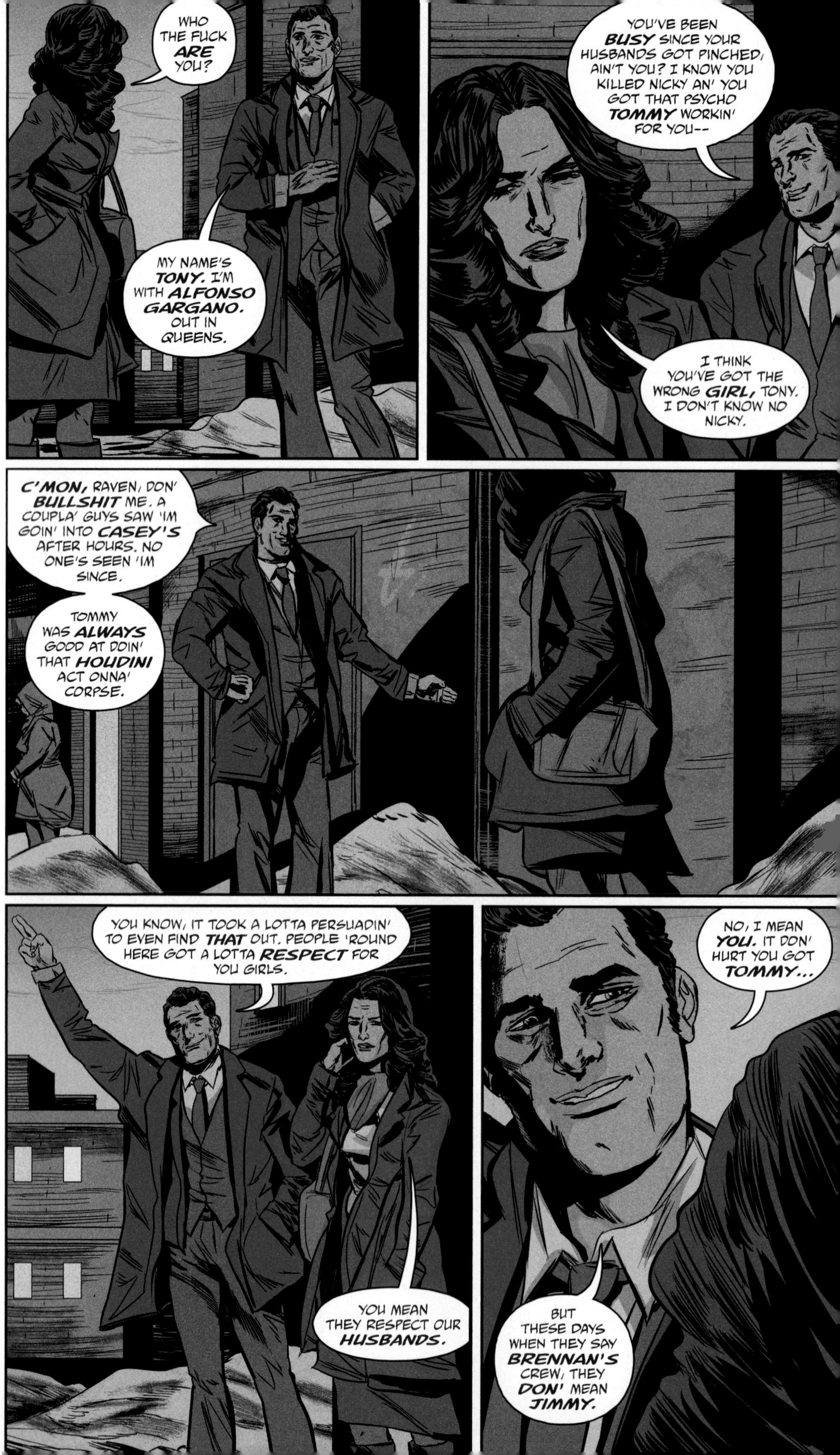
WHO THE FUCK ARE YOU?
MY NAME'S TONY. I'M WITH ALFONSO GARGANO. OUT IN QUEENS.
YOU'VE BEEN BUSY SINCE YOUR HUSBANDS GOT PINCHED, AIN'T YOU? I KNOW YOU KILLED NICKY AN' YOU GOT THAT PSYCHO TOMMY WORKIN' FOR YOU--
I THINK YOU'VE GOT THE WRONG GIRL, TONY. I DON'T KNOW NO NICKY.
C'MON, RAVEN, DON' BULLSHIT ME. A COUPLA' GUYS SAW 'IM GOIN' INTO CASEY'S AFTER HOURS. NO ONE'S SEEN 'IM SINCE.
TOMMY WAS ALWAYS GOOD AT DOIN' THAT HOUDINI ACT ONNA' CORPSE.
YOU KNOW, IT TOOK A LOTTA PERSUADIN' TO EVEN FIND THAT OUT. PEOPLE 'ROUND HERE GOT A LOTTA RESPECT FOR YOU GIRLS.
YOU MEAN THEY RESPECT OUR HUSBANDS.
NO, I MEAN YOU. IT DON' HURT YOU GOT TOMMY...
BUT THESE DAYS WHEN THEY SAY BRENNAN'S CREW, THEY DON' MEAN JIMMY.

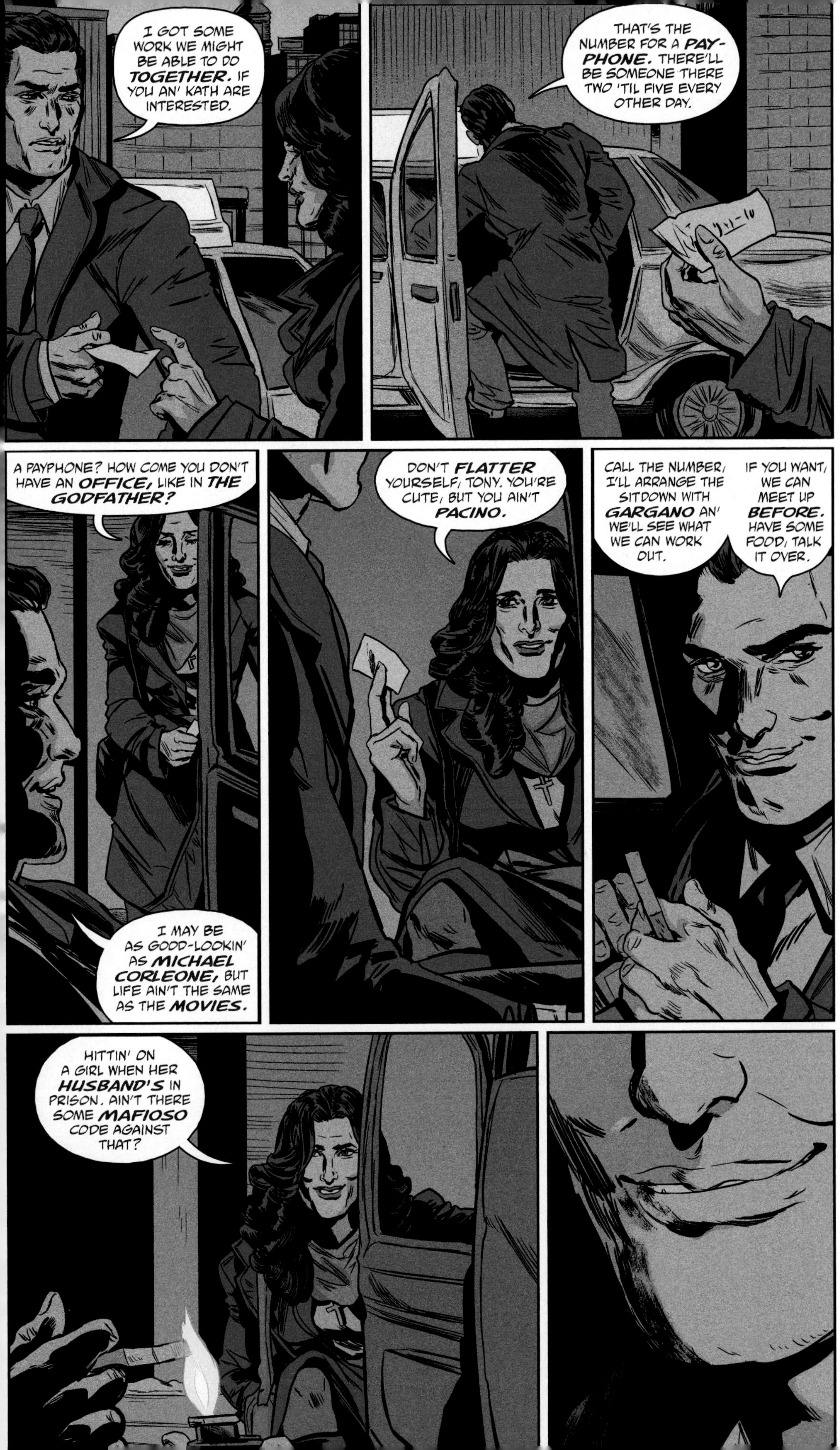
I GOT SOME WORK WE MIGHT BE ABLE TO DO TOGETHER. IF YOU AN' KATH ARE INTERESTED.
THAT'S THE NUMBER FOR A PAY-PHONE. THERE'LL BE SOMEONE THERE TWO 'TIL FIVE EVERY OTHER DAY.
A PAYPHONE? HOW COME YOU DON'T HAVE AN OFFICE, LIKE IN THE GODFATHER?
I MAY BE AS GOOD-LOOKIN' AS MICHAEL CORLEONE, BUT LIFE AIN'T THE SAME AS THE MOVIES.
DON'T FLATTER YOURSELF, TONY. YOU'RE CUTE, BUT YOU AIN'T PACINO.
CALL THE NUMBER, I'LL ARRANGE THE SITDOWN WITH GARGANO AN' WE'LL SEE WHAT WE CAN WORK OUT.
IF YOU WANT, WE CAN MEET UP BEFORE. HAVE SOME FOOD, TALK IT OVER.
HITTIN' ON A GIRL WHEN HER HUSBAND'S IN PRISON. AIN'T THERE SOME MAFIOSO CODE AGAINST THAT?

THIS AIN'T SOME *TRAP*, IS IT? GET REVENGE FOR TAKIN' OUT ONE OF YOUR *PEOPLE?*

YEAH, *FRANKY.* THE *BLACK SHEEP* OF THE CASTELLANO FAMILY. SOME *FUCK* PUT 'IM INNA *COMA.*

I DON' KNOW WHO DID IT, BUT I KNOW THAT FUCK *NICKY* WAS INVOLVED.

WHO, *NICKY?* HE WAS A TWO-BIT HUSTLER AN' A *SCUMBAG.* HE WASN'T CONNECTED.

HONESTLY, YOU DID ME A *FAVOR.* I THINK HE GOT MY BROTHER INTO SOME *SHIT* A WHILE BACK.

YOUR *BROTHER?*

ANYWAY, ENOUGH DWELLIN' ON THE *BAD* SHIT IN LIFE. WHAT'S THAT *IRISH* WORD YOU GOT FOR THAT?

MAUDLIN?

YEAH... ENOUGH *MAUDLIN...*

CALL ME!

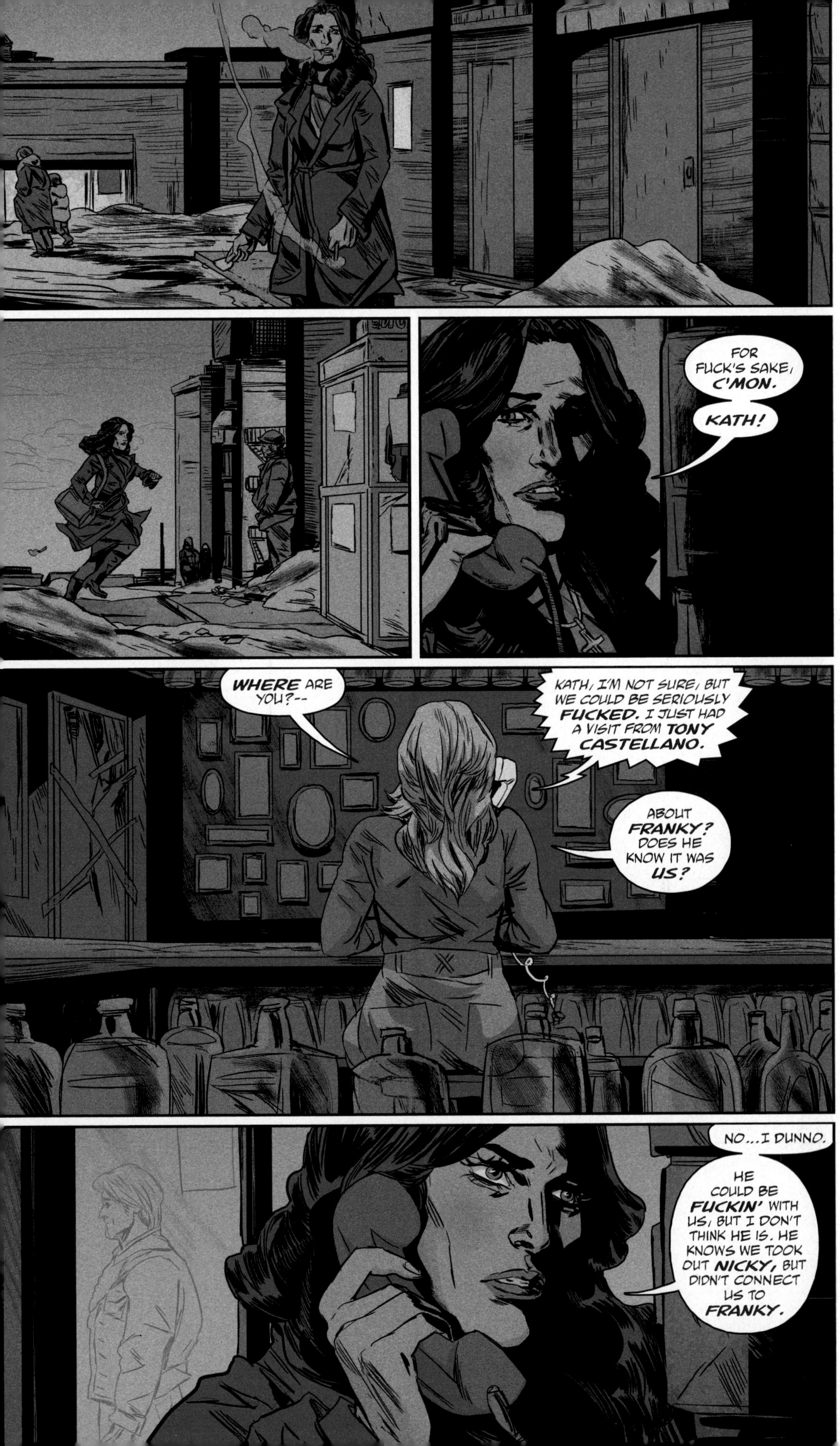
FOR FUCK'S SAKE, C'MON.
KATH!
WHERE ARE YOU?--
KATH, I'M NOT SURE, BUT WE COULD BE SERIOUSLY FUCKED. I JUST HAD A VISIT FROM TONY CASTELLANO.
ABOUT FRANKY? DOES HE KNOW IT WAS US?
NO...I DUNNO.
HE COULD BE FUCKIN' WITH US, BUT I DON'T THINK HE IS. HE KNOWS WE TOOK OUT NICKY, BUT DIDN'T CONNECT US TO FRANKY.

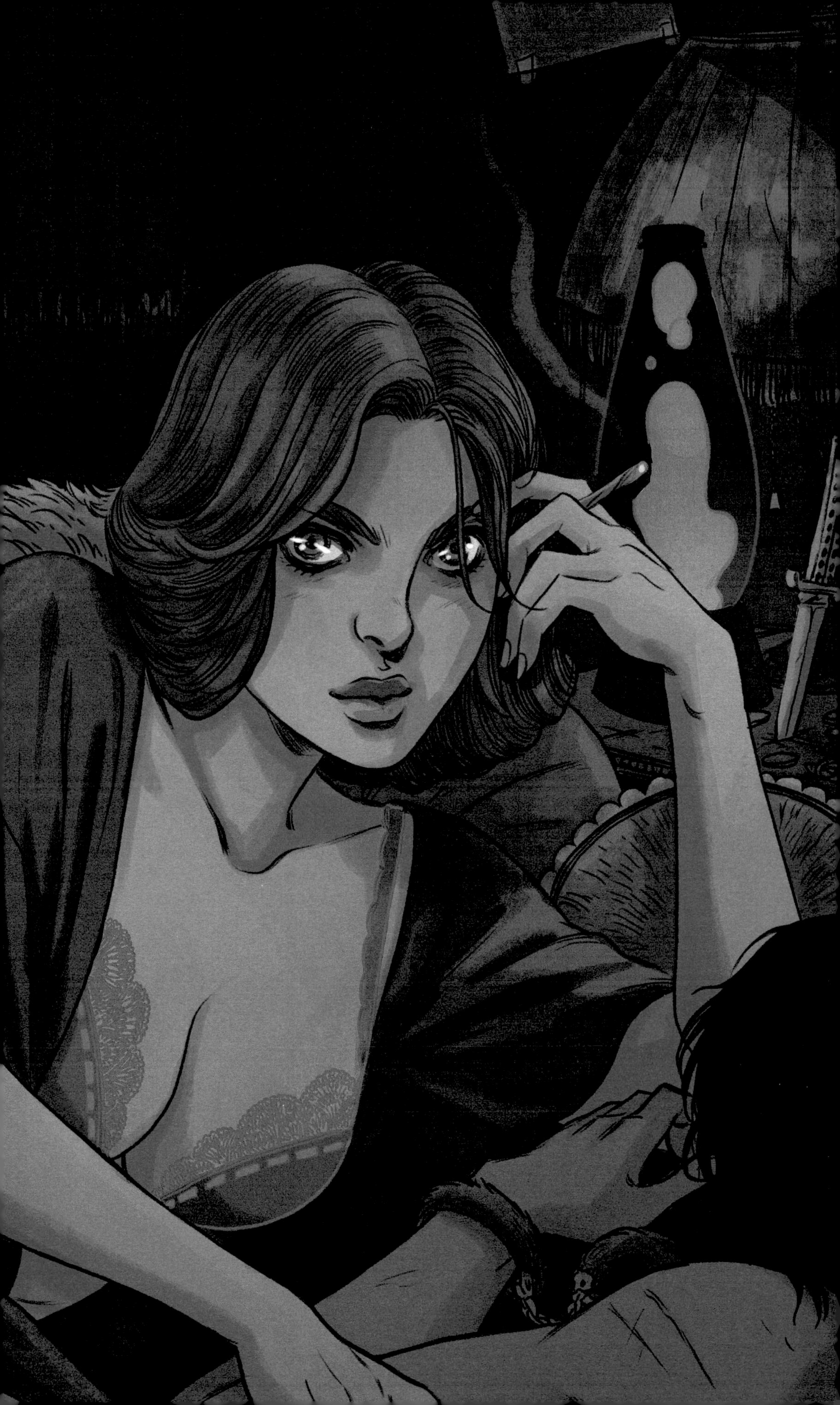

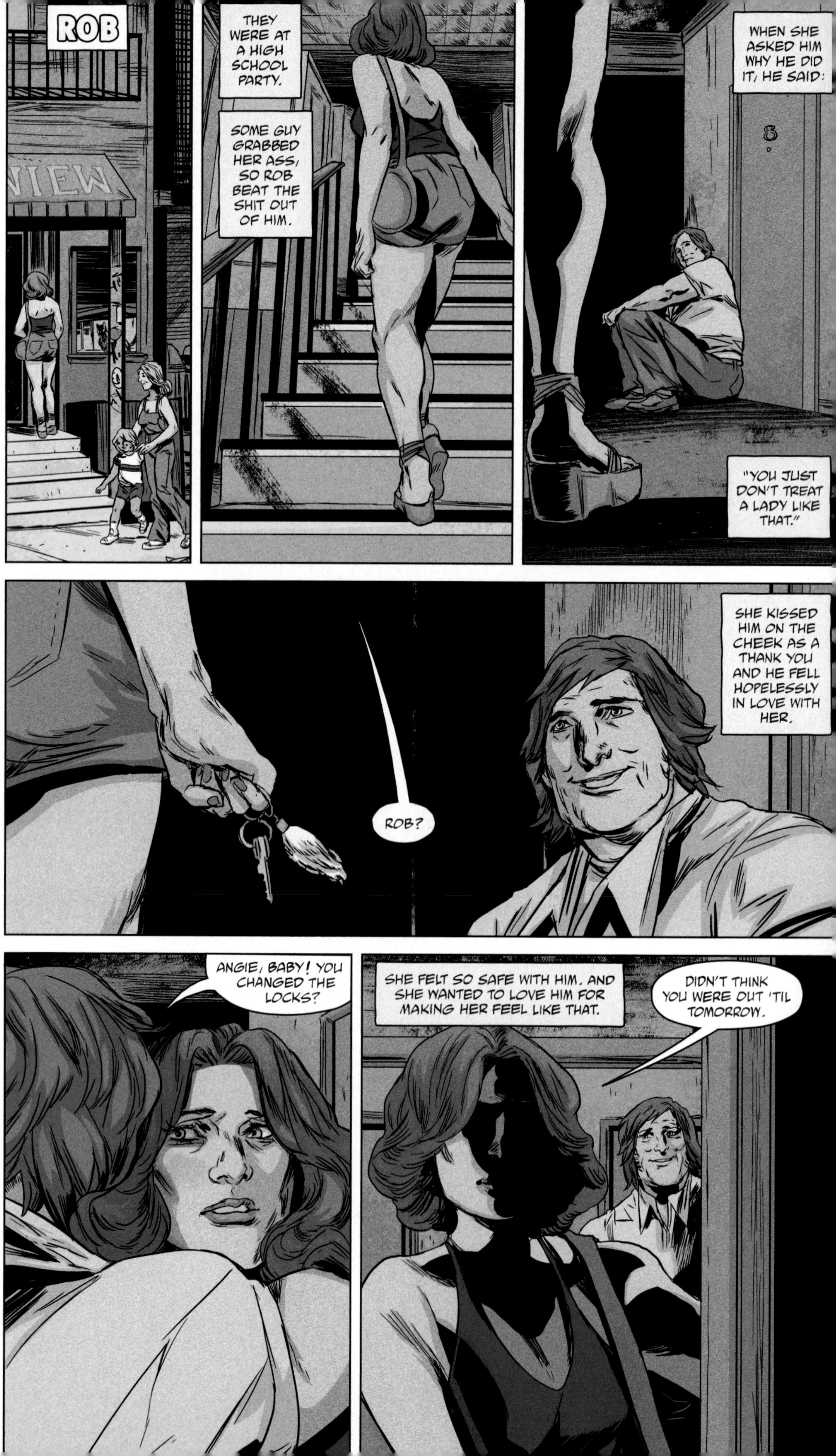

ROB
THEY WERE AT A HIGH SCHOOL PARTY.
SOME GUY GRABBED HER ASS, SO ROB BEAT THE SHIT OUT OF HIM.
WHEN SHE ASKED HIM WHY HE DID IT, HE SAID:
"YOU JUST DON'T TREAT A LADY LIKE THAT."
SHE KISSED HIM ON THE CHEEK AS A THANK YOU AND HE FELL HOPELESSLY IN LOVE WITH HER.
ROB?
ANGIE, BABY! YOU CHANGED THE LOCKS?
SHE FELT SO SAFE WITH HIM. AND SHE WANTED TO LOVE HIM FOR MAKING HER FEEL LIKE THAT.
DIDN'T THINK YOU WERE OUT 'TIL TOMORROW.

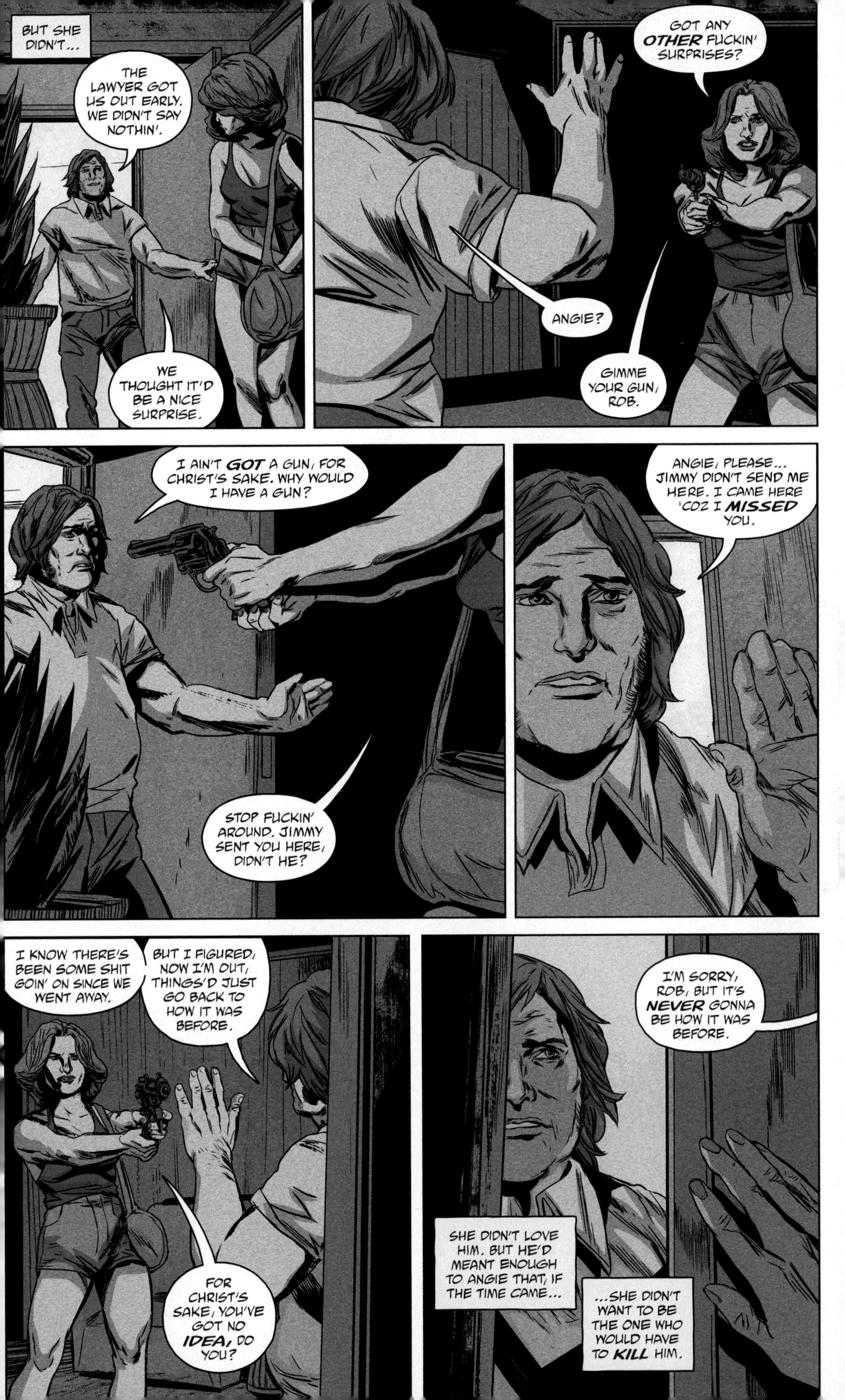
BUT SHE DIDN'T...
THE LAWYER GOT US OUT EARLY. WE DIDN'T SAY NOTHIN'.
WE THOUGHT IT'D BE A NICE SURPRISE.
GOT ANY OTHER FUCKIN' SURPRISES?
ANGIE?
GIMME YOUR GUN, ROB.
I AIN'T GOT A GUN, FOR CHRIST'S SAKE. WHY WOULD I HAVE A GUN?
STOP FUCKIN' AROUND. JIMMY SENT YOU HERE, DIDN'T HE?
ANGIE, PLEASE... JIMMY DIDN'T SEND ME HERE. I CAME HERE 'COZ I MISSED YOU.
I KNOW THERE'S BEEN SOME SHIT GOIN' ON SINCE WE WENT AWAY.
BUT I FIGURED, NOW I'M OUT, THINGS'D JUST GO BACK TO HOW IT WAS BEFORE.
FOR CHRIST'S SAKE, YOU'VE GOT NO IDEA, DO YOU?
I'M SORRY, ROB, BUT IT'S NEVER GONNA BE HOW IT WAS BEFORE.
SHE DIDN'T LOVE HIM. BUT HE'D MEANT ENOUGH TO ANGIE THAT, IF THE TIME CAME...
...SHE DIDN'T WANT TO BE THE ONE WHO WOULD HAVE TO KILL HIM.

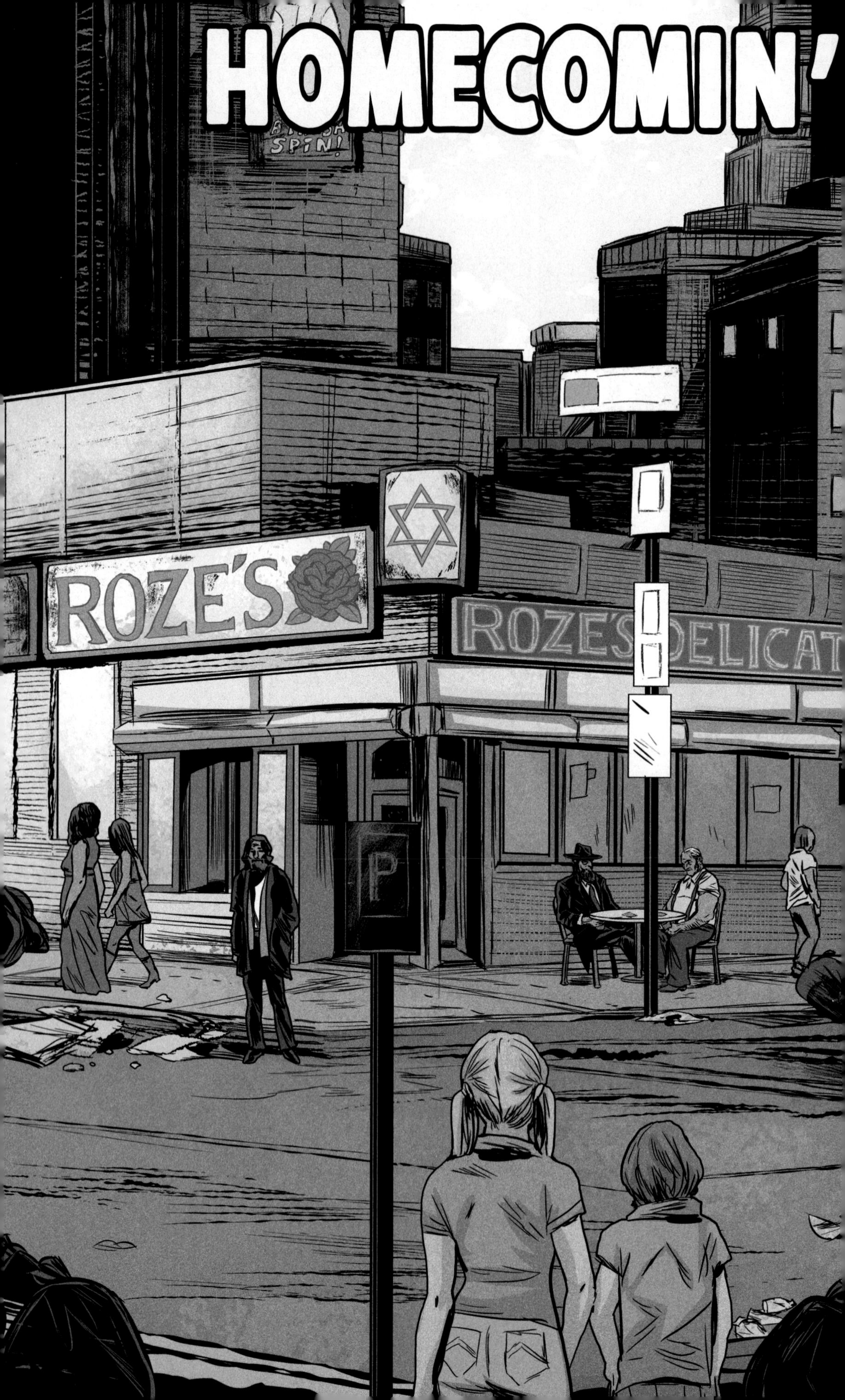
HOMECOMIN'
SPIN!
ROZE'S
ROZE'S DELICAT
P

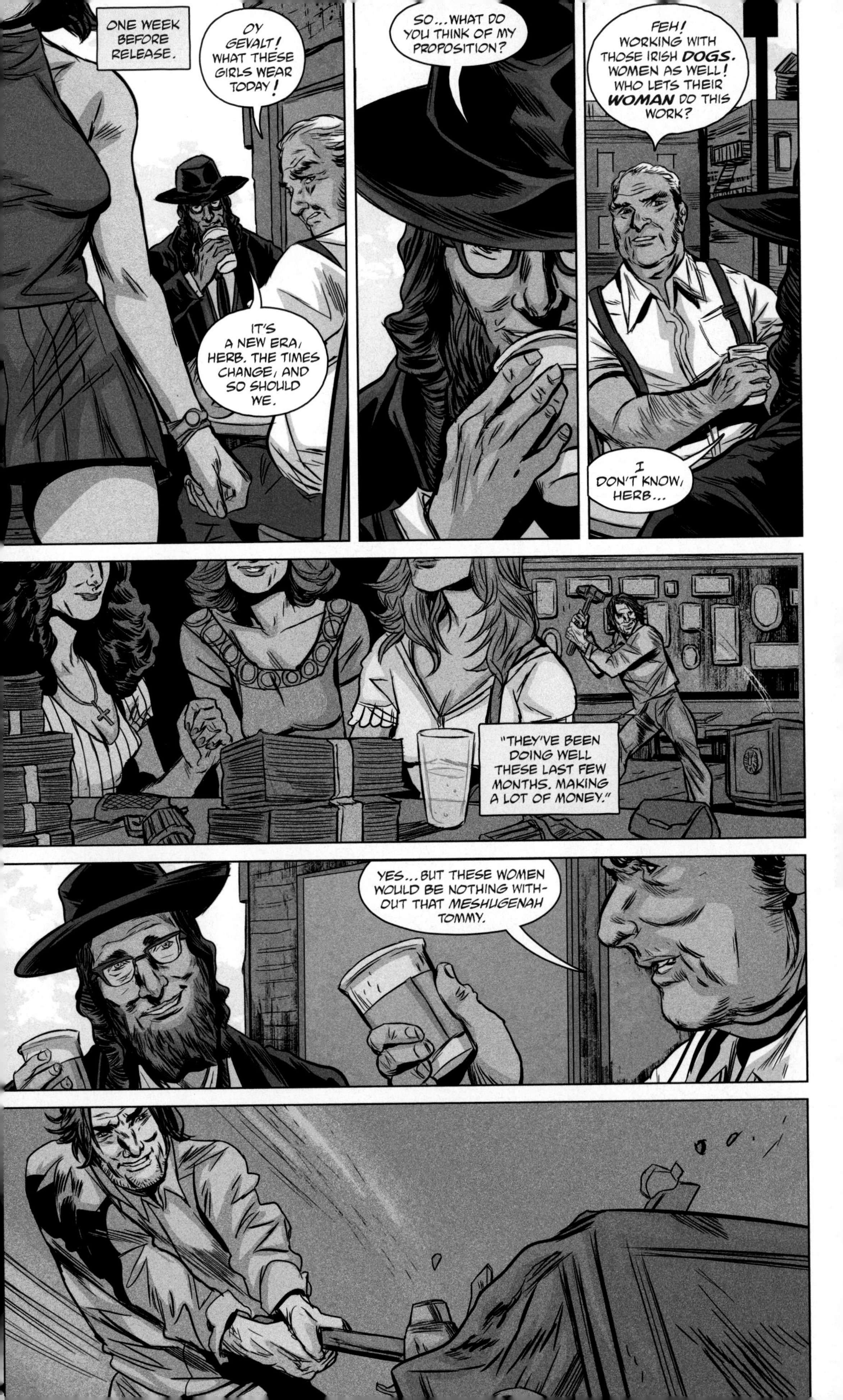
ONE WEEK BEFORE RELEASE.
OY GEVALT! WHAT THESE GIRLS WEAR TODAY!
IT'S A NEW ERA, HERB. THE TIMES CHANGE, AND SO SHOULD WE.
SO... WHAT DO YOU THINK OF MY PROPOSITION?
FEH! WORKING WITH THOSE IRISH DOGS. WOMEN AS WELL! WHO LETS THEIR WOMAN DO THIS WORK?
I DON'T KNOW, HERB...
"THEY'VE BEEN DOING WELL THESE LAST FEW MONTHS. MAKING A LOT OF MONEY."
YES... BUT THESE WOMEN WOULD BE NOTHING WITH-OUT THAT MESHUGENAH TOMMY.

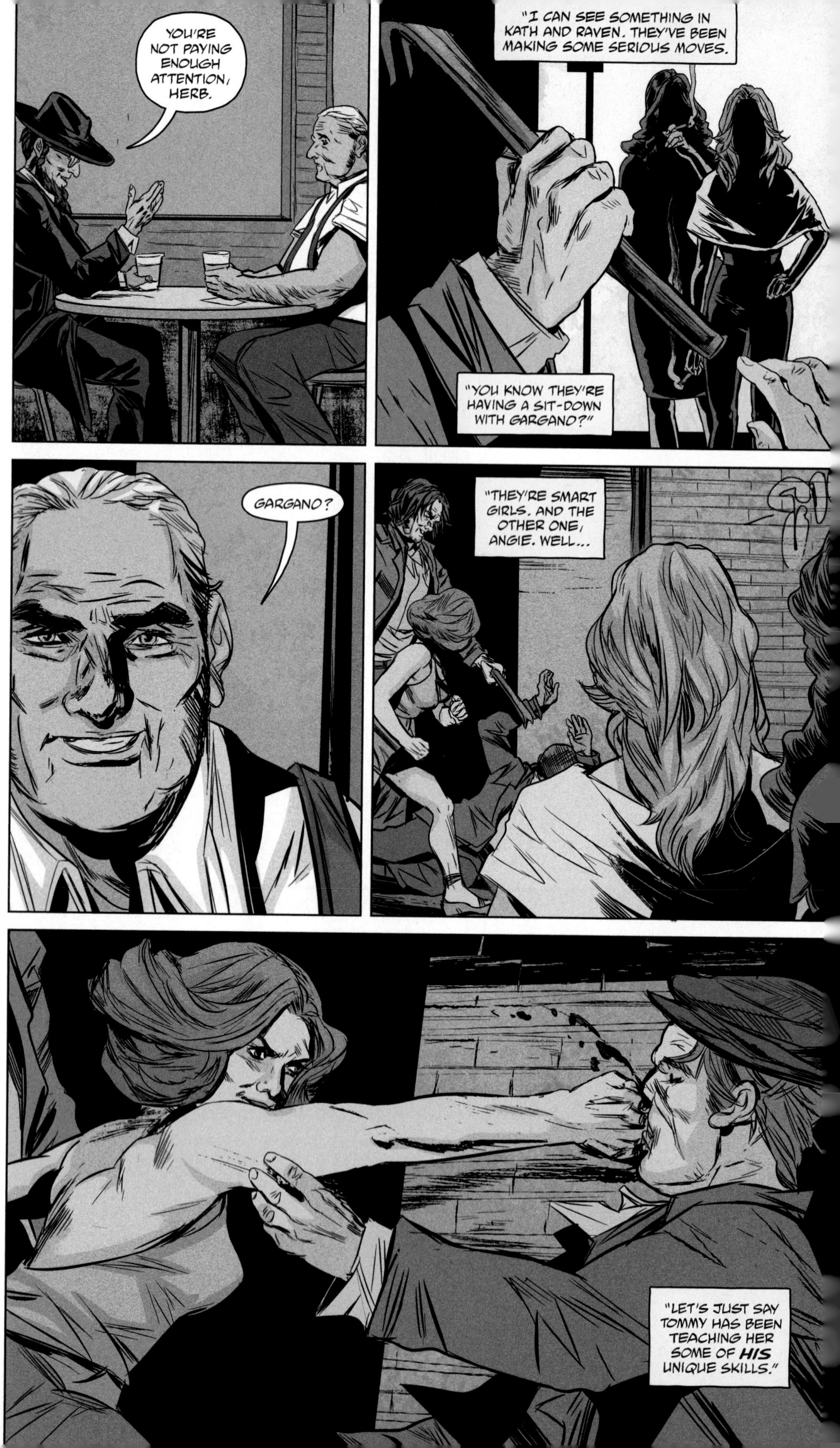
YOU'RE NOT PAYING ENOUGH ATTENTION, HERB.
"I CAN SEE SOMETHING IN KATH AND RAVEN. THEY'VE BEEN MAKING SOME SERIOUS MOVES.
"YOU KNOW THEY'RE HAVING A SIT-DOWN WITH GARGANO?"
GARGANO?
"THEY'RE SMART GIRLS. AND THE OTHER ONE, ANGIE. WELL...
"LET'S JUST SAY TOMMY HAS BEEN TEACHING HER SOME OF **HIS** UNIQUE SKILLS."

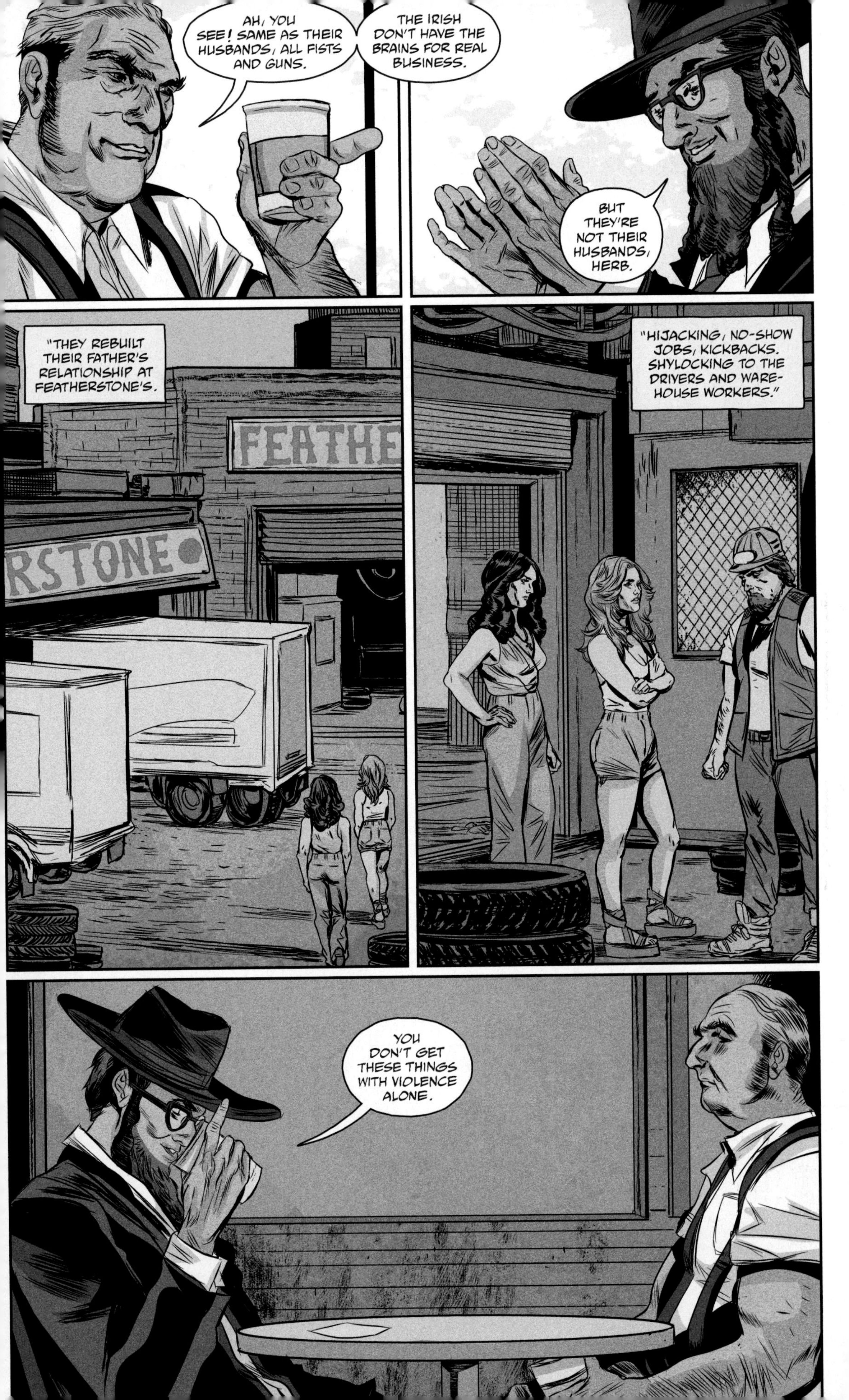
AH, YOU SEE! SAME AS THEIR HUSBANDS, ALL FISTS AND GUNS.
THE IRISH DON'T HAVE THE BRAINS FOR REAL BUSINESS.
BUT THEY'RE NOT THEIR HUSBANDS, HERB.
"THEY REBUILT THEIR FATHER'S RELATIONSHIP AT FEATHERSTONE'S.
FEATHE
RSTONE
"HIJACKING, NO-SHOW JOBS, KICKBACKS. SHYLOCKING TO THE DRIVERS AND WARE-HOUSE WORKERS."
YOU DON'T GET THESE THINGS WITH VIOLENCE ALONE.

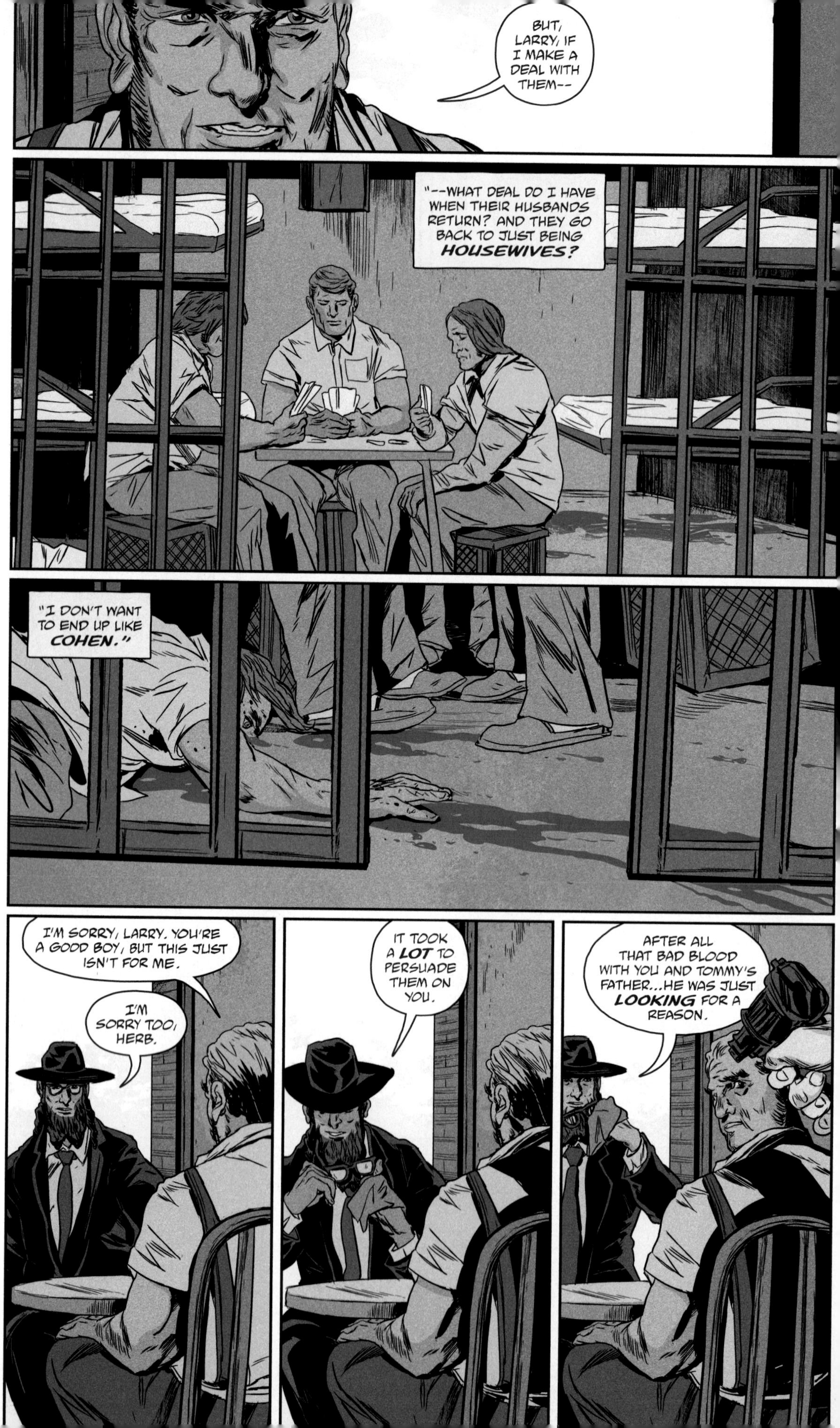
BUT, LARRY, IF I MAKE A DEAL WITH THEM--
"--WHAT DEAL DO I HAVE WHEN THEIR HUSBANDS RETURN? AND THEY GO BACK TO JUST BEING HOUSEWIVES?
"I DON'T WANT TO END UP LIKE COHEN."
I'M SORRY, LARRY. YOU'RE A GOOD BOY, BUT THIS JUST ISN'T FOR ME.
I'M SORRY TOO, HERB.
IT TOOK A LOT TO PERSUADE THEM ON YOU.
AFTER ALL THAT BAD BLOOD WITH YOU AND TOMMY'S FATHER...HE WAS JUST LOOKING FOR A REASON.

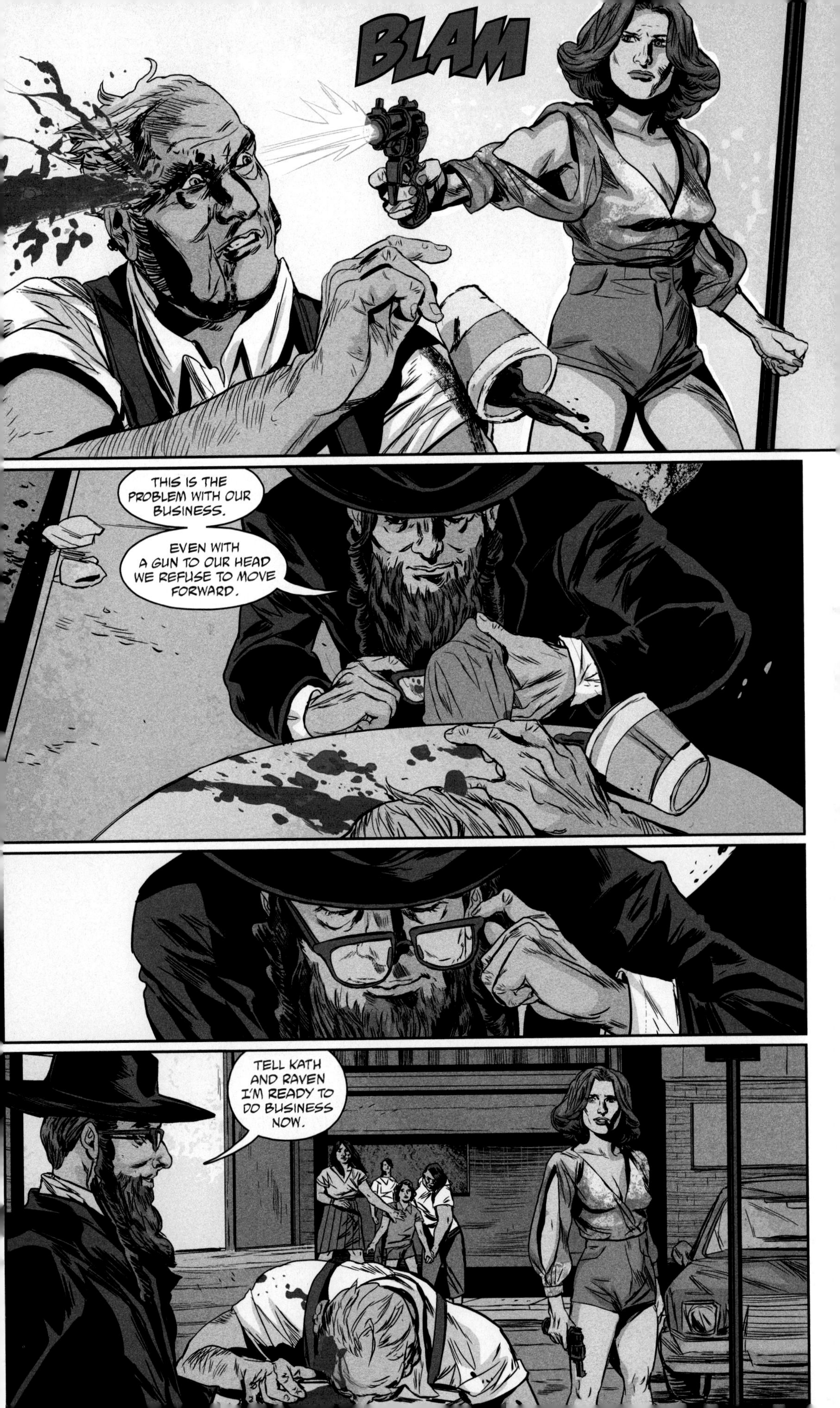
BLAM
THIS IS THE PROBLEM WITH OUR BUSINESS.
EVEN WITH A GUN TO OUR HEAD WE REFUSE TO MOVE FORWARD.
TELL KATH AND RAVEN I'M READY TO DO BUSINESS NOW.

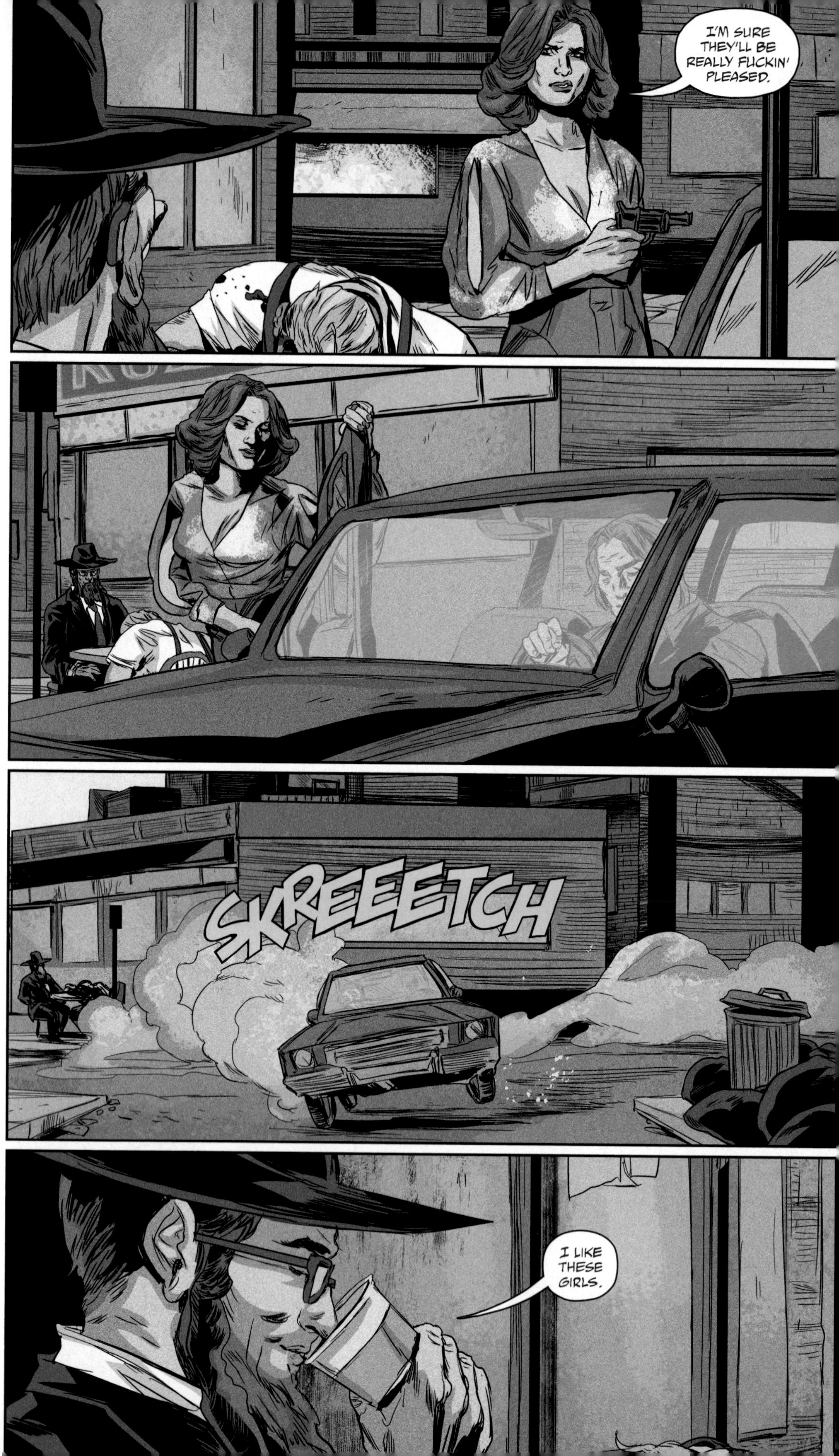
I'M SURE THEY'LL BE REALLY FUCKIN' PLEASED.
SKREEETCH
I LIKE THESE GIRLS.

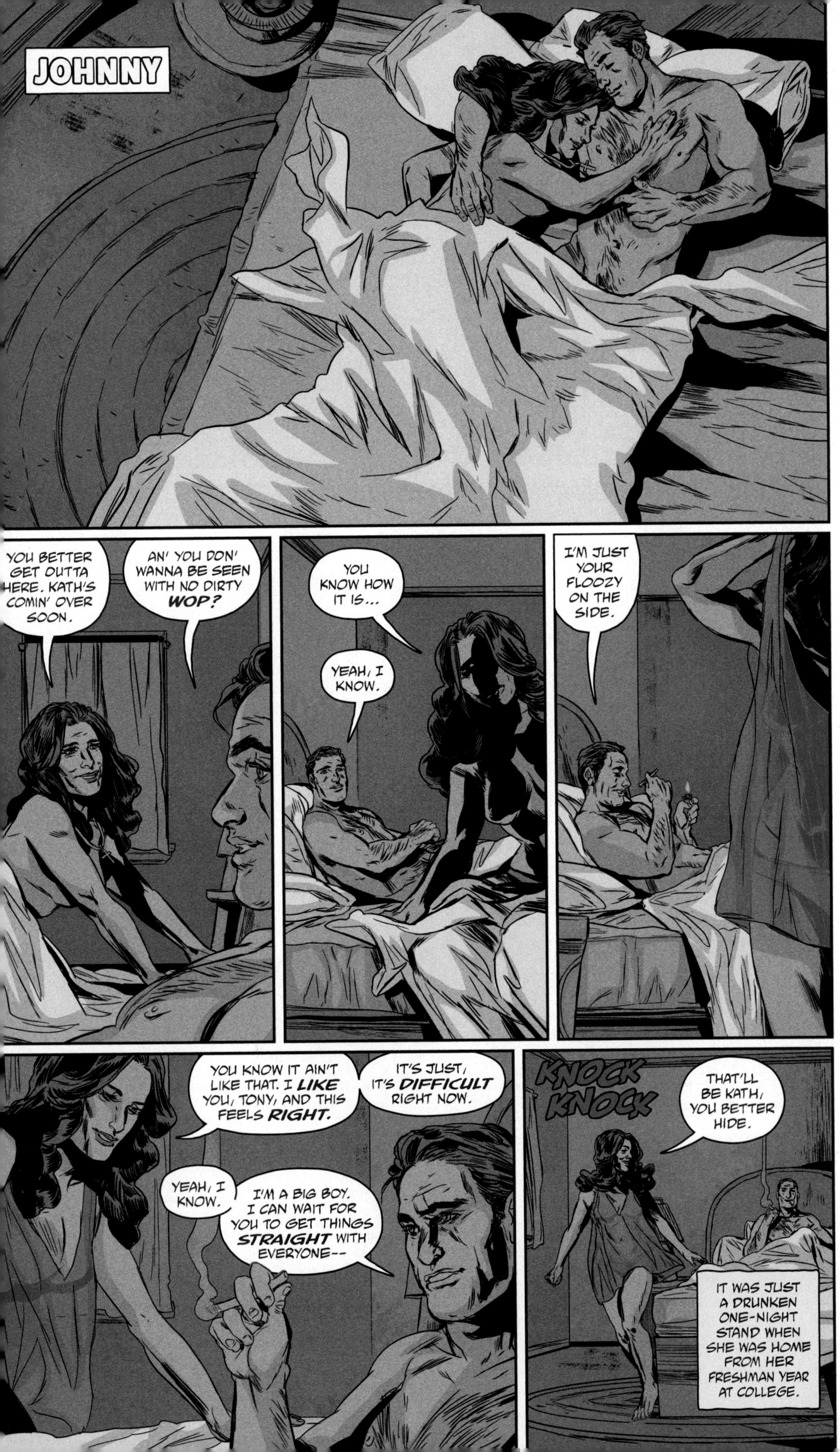
JOHNNY
YOU BETTER GET OUTTA HERE. KATH'S COMIN' OVER SOON.
AN' YOU DON' WANNA BE SEEN WITH NO DIRTY WOP?
YOU KNOW HOW IT IS...
YEAH, I KNOW.
I'M JUST YOUR FLOOZY ON THE SIDE.
YOU KNOW IT AIN'T LIKE THAT. I LIKE YOU, TONY, AND THIS FEELS RIGHT.
IT'S JUST, IT'S DIFFICULT RIGHT NOW.
YEAH, I KNOW.
I'M A BIG BOY. I CAN WAIT FOR YOU TO GET THINGS STRAIGHT WITH EVERYONE--
KNOCK KNOCK
THAT'LL BE KATH, YOU BETTER HIDE.
IT WAS JUST A DRUNKEN ONE-NIGHT STAND WHEN SHE WAS HOME FROM HER FRESHMAN YEAR AT COLLEGE.

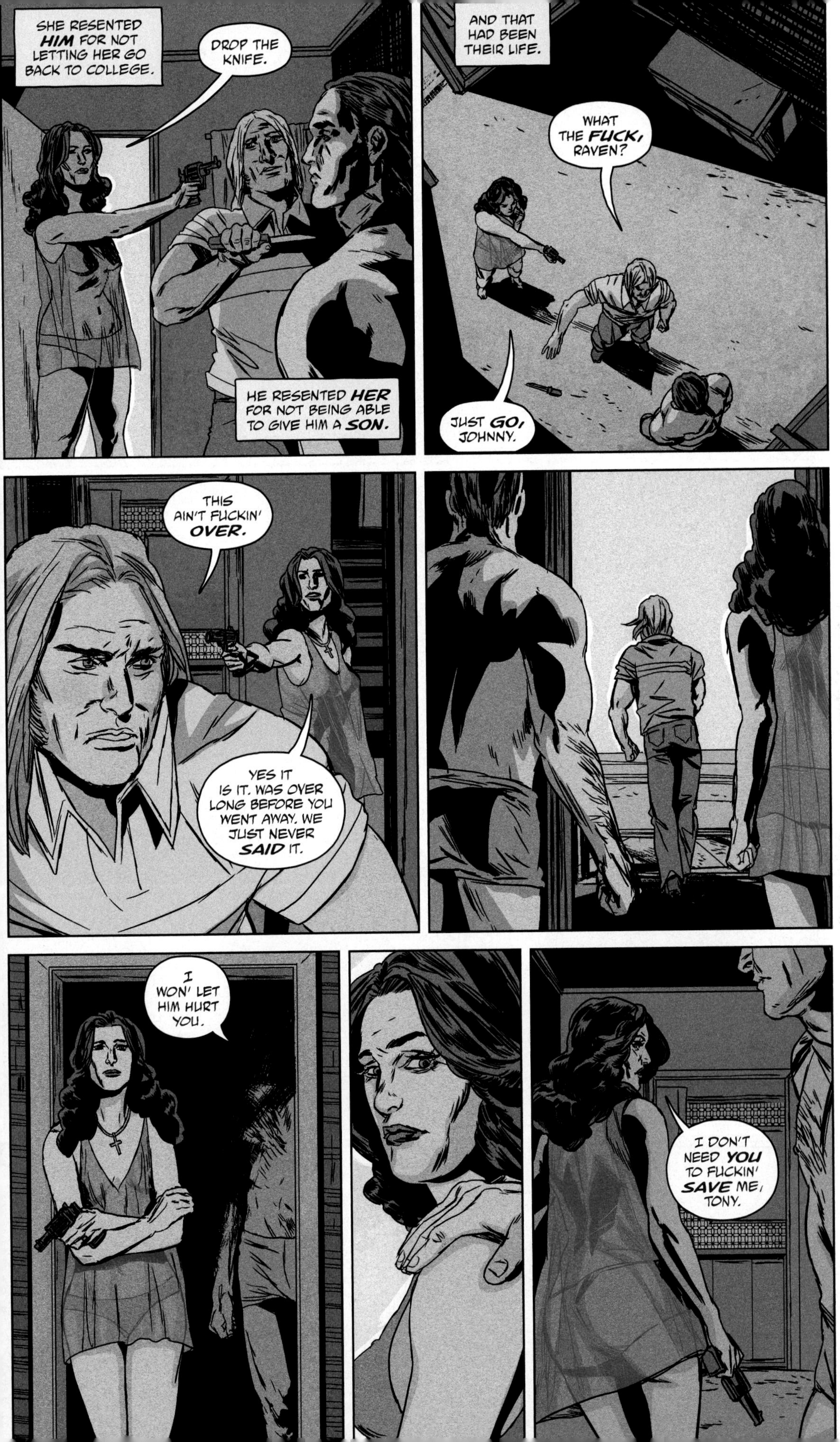
SHE RESENTED HIM FOR NOT LETTING HER GO BACK TO COLLEGE.
DROP THE KNIFE.
HE RESENTED HER FOR NOT BEING ABLE TO GIVE HIM A SON.
AND THAT HAD BEEN THEIR LIFE.
WHAT THE FUCK, RAVEN?
JUST GO, JOHNNY.
THIS AIN'T FUCKIN' OVER.
YES IT IS IT. WAS OVER LONG BEFORE YOU WENT AWAY. WE JUST NEVER SAID IT.
I WON' LET HIM HURT YOU.
I DON'T NEED YOU TO FUCKIN' SAVE ME, TONY.

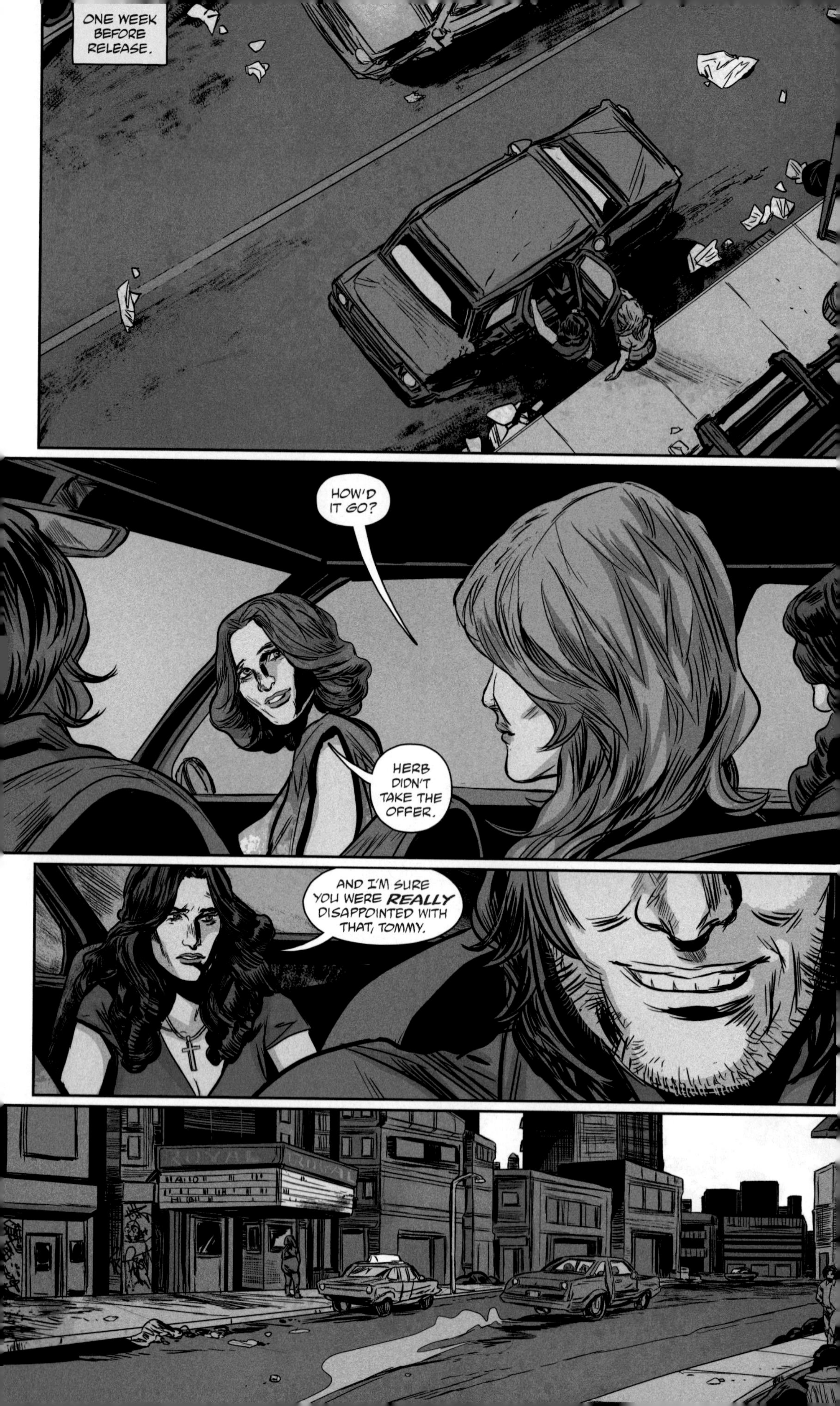
ONE WEEK BEFORE RELEASE.
HOW'D IT GO?
HERB DIDN'T TAKE THE OFFER.
AND I'M SURE YOU WERE REALLY DISAPPOINTED WITH THAT, TOMMY.

YOU EVER DONE BUSINESS WITH THESE GUYS, TOMMY?

I COULD NEVER GET WITH ALL THAT ASS-KISSING, MAFIA CODE CRAP.

GARGANO? NAH. I DEALT WITH WISEGUYS BEFORE, THOUGH.

IT'S ALL BULLSHIT. THEY'RE ALWAYS SCREWIN' EACH OTHER OVER AND KILLIN' EACH OTHER WITHOUT THE BIG BOSS'S SAY-SO.

DO A DEAL WITH HIM, YEAH. BUT DON'T EVER FUCKIN' TRUST HIM.

IF SCREWIN' YOU HELPS HIM, HE'LL SCREW YOU.

MATRANGA'S
MUSICAL INSTRUMENTS

I'D STILL FEEL BETTER IF YOU CAME IN WITH US.

IT'S YOUR THING, NOT MINE. YOU DON'T NEED ME.

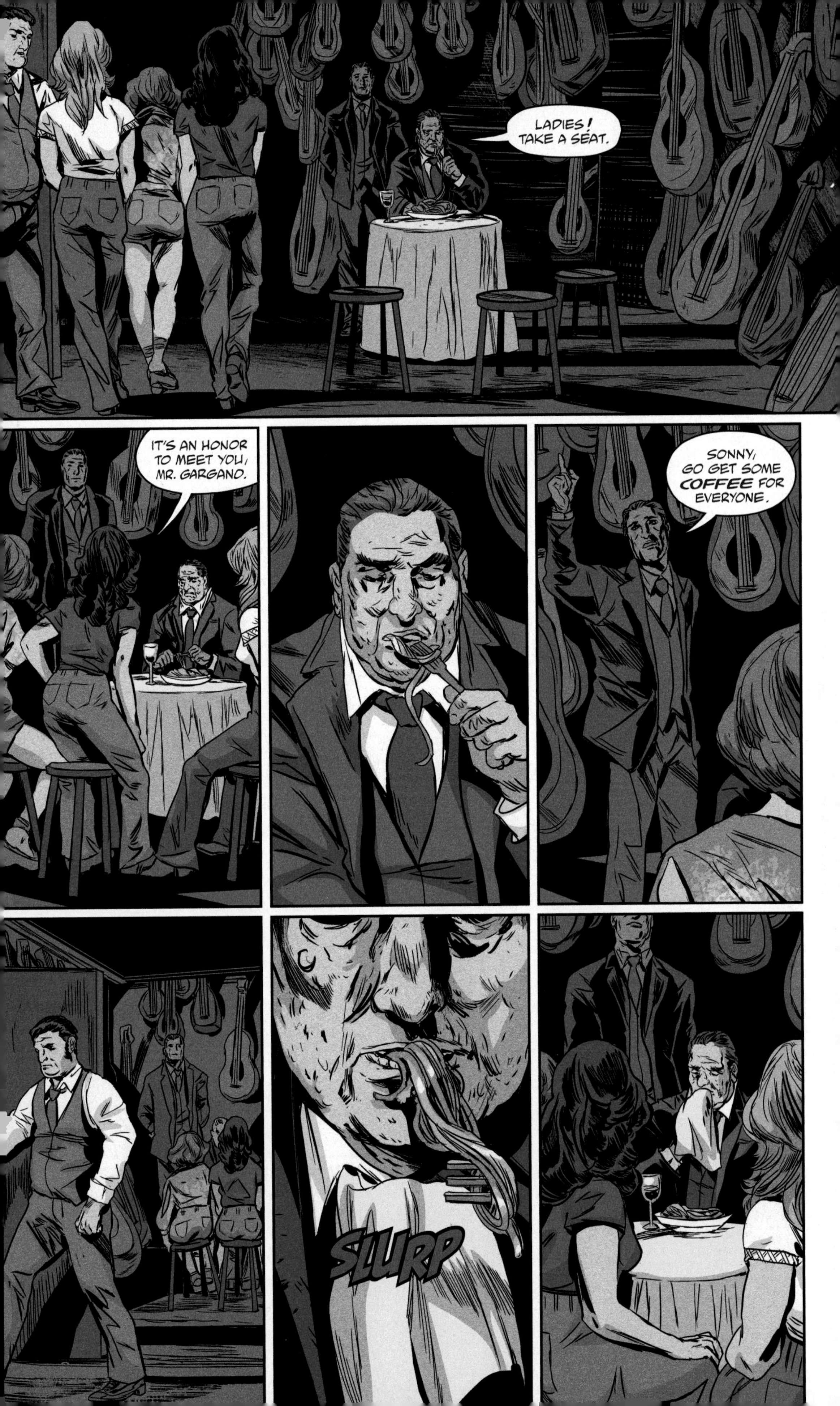
LADIES! TAKE A SEAT.
IT'S AN HONOR TO MEET YOU, MR. GARGANO.
SONNY, GO GET SOME COFFEE FOR EVERYONE.
SLURP

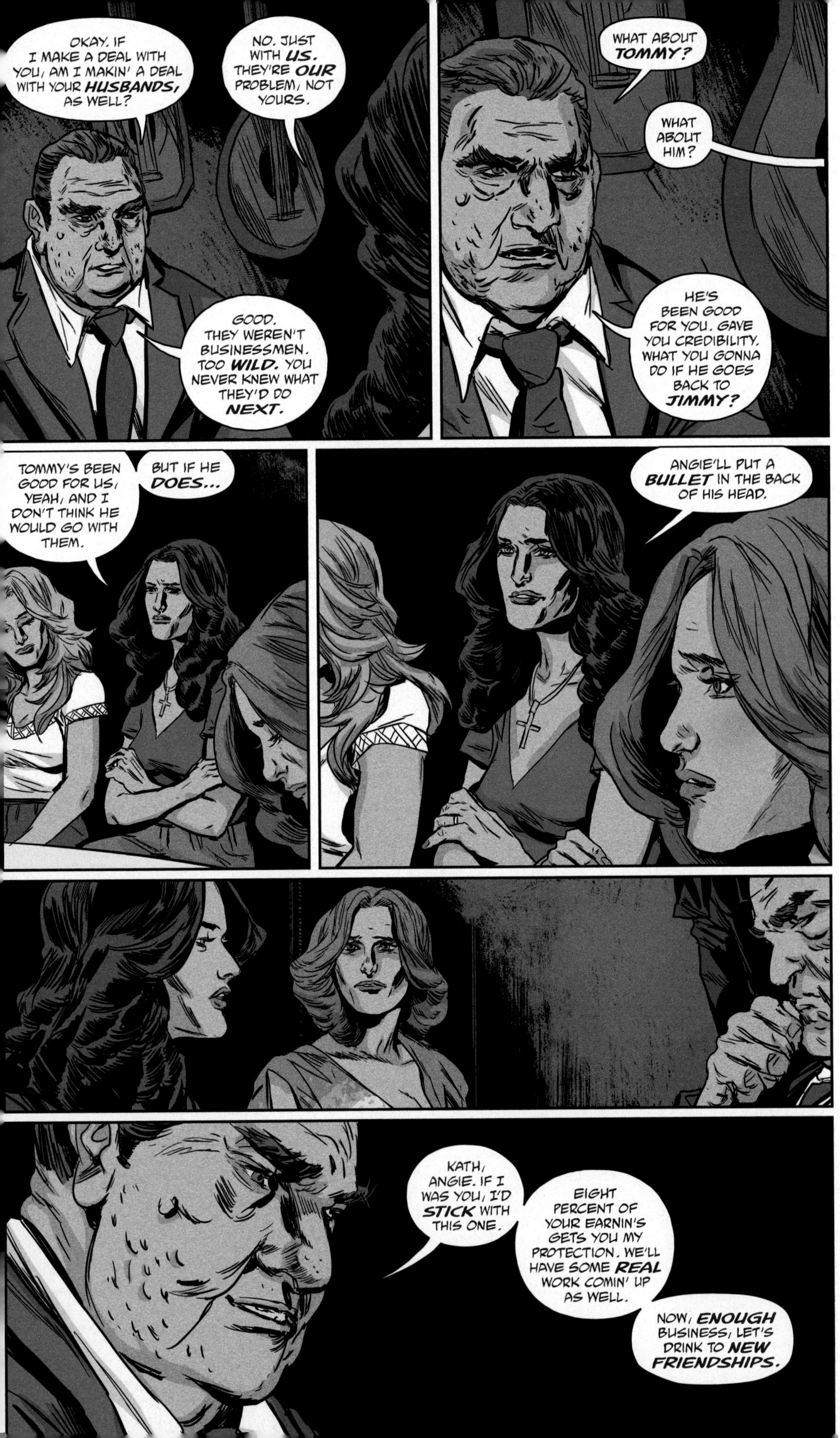

OKAY. IF I MAKE A DEAL WITH YOU, AM I MAKIN' A DEAL WITH YOUR HUSBANDS, AS WELL?
NO. JUST WITH US. THEY'RE OUR PROBLEM, NOT YOURS.
GOOD. THEY WEREN'T BUSINESSMEN. TOO WILD. YOU NEVER KNEW WHAT THEY'D DO NEXT.
WHAT ABOUT TOMMY?
WHAT ABOUT HIM?
HE'S BEEN GOOD FOR YOU. GAVE YOU CREDIBILITY. WHAT YOU GONNA DO IF HE GOES BACK TO JIMMY?
TOMMY'S BEEN GOOD FOR US, YEAH, AND I DON'T THINK HE WOULD GO WITH THEM.
BUT IF HE DOES...
ANGIE'LL PUT A BULLET IN THE BACK OF HIS HEAD.
KATH, ANGIE. IF I WAS YOU, I'D STICK WITH THIS ONE.
EIGHT PERCENT OF YOUR EARNIN'S GETS YOU MY PROTECTION. WE'LL HAVE SOME REAL WORK COMIN' UP AS WELL.
NOW, ENOUGH BUSINESS, LET'S DRINK TO NEW FRIENDSHIPS.

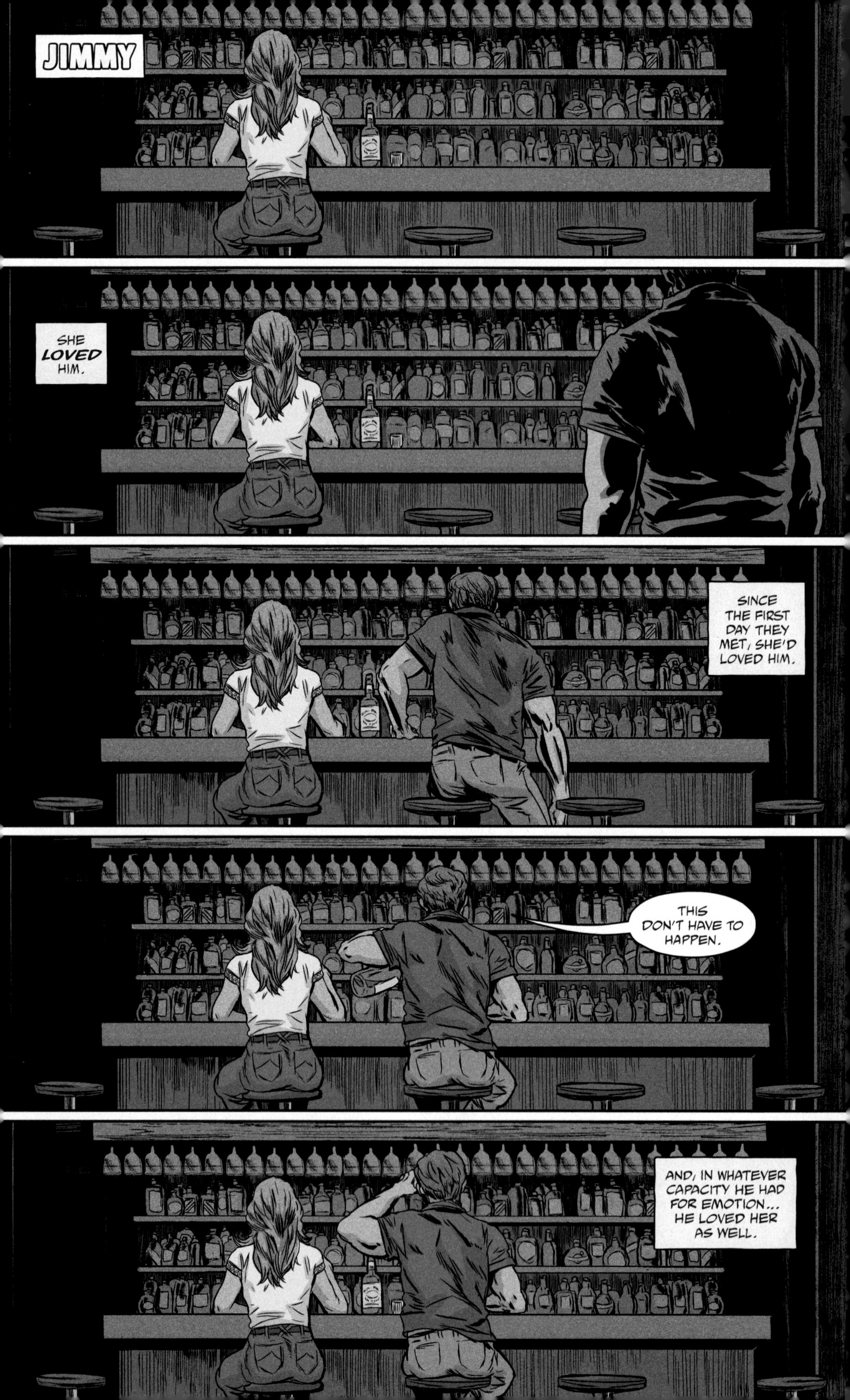
JIMMY
SHE LOVED HIM.
SINCE THE FIRST DAY THEY MET, SHE'D LOVED HIM.
THIS DON'T HAVE TO HAPPEN.
AND, IN WHATEVER CAPACITY HE HAD FOR EMOTION... HE LOVED HER AS WELL.

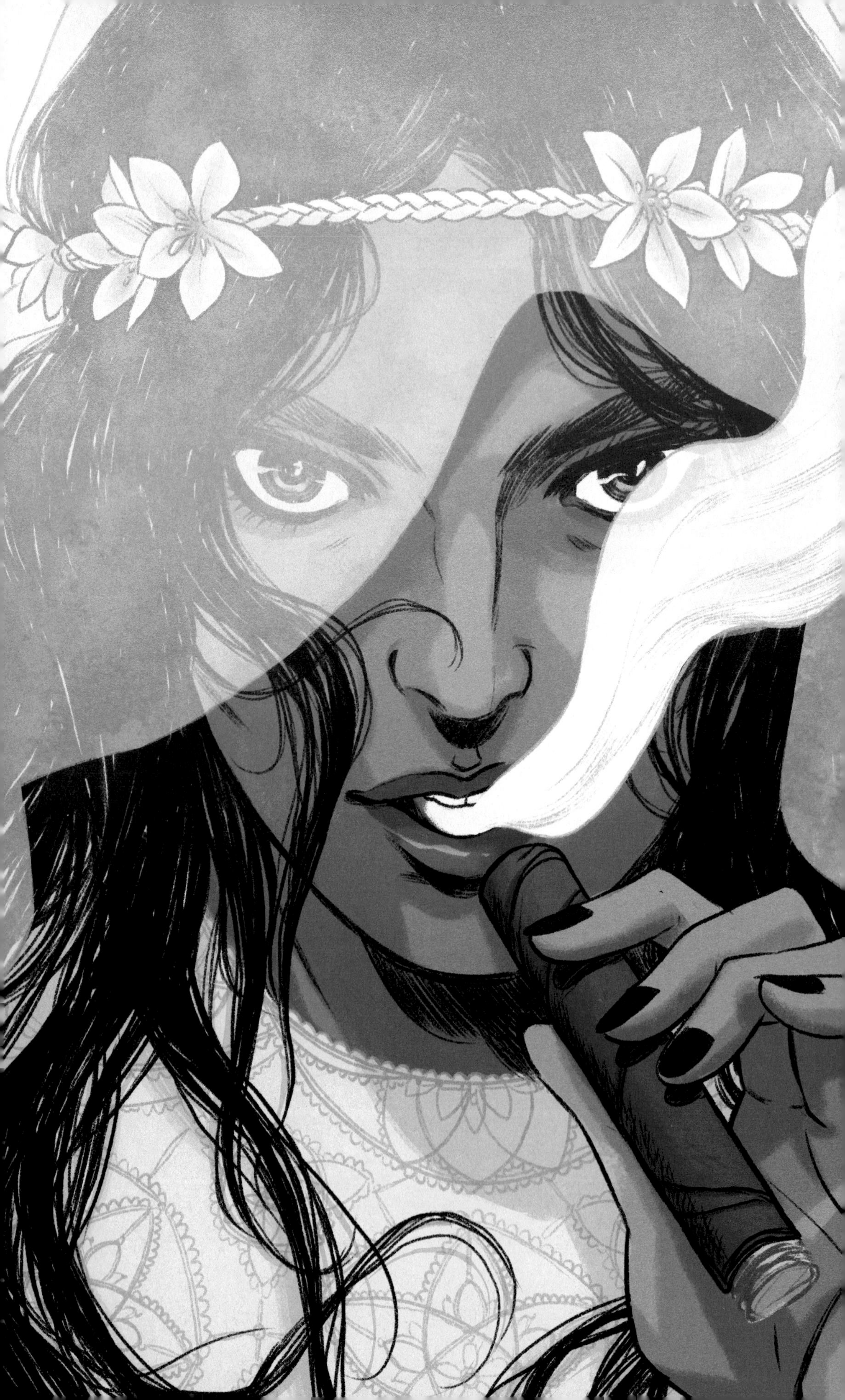

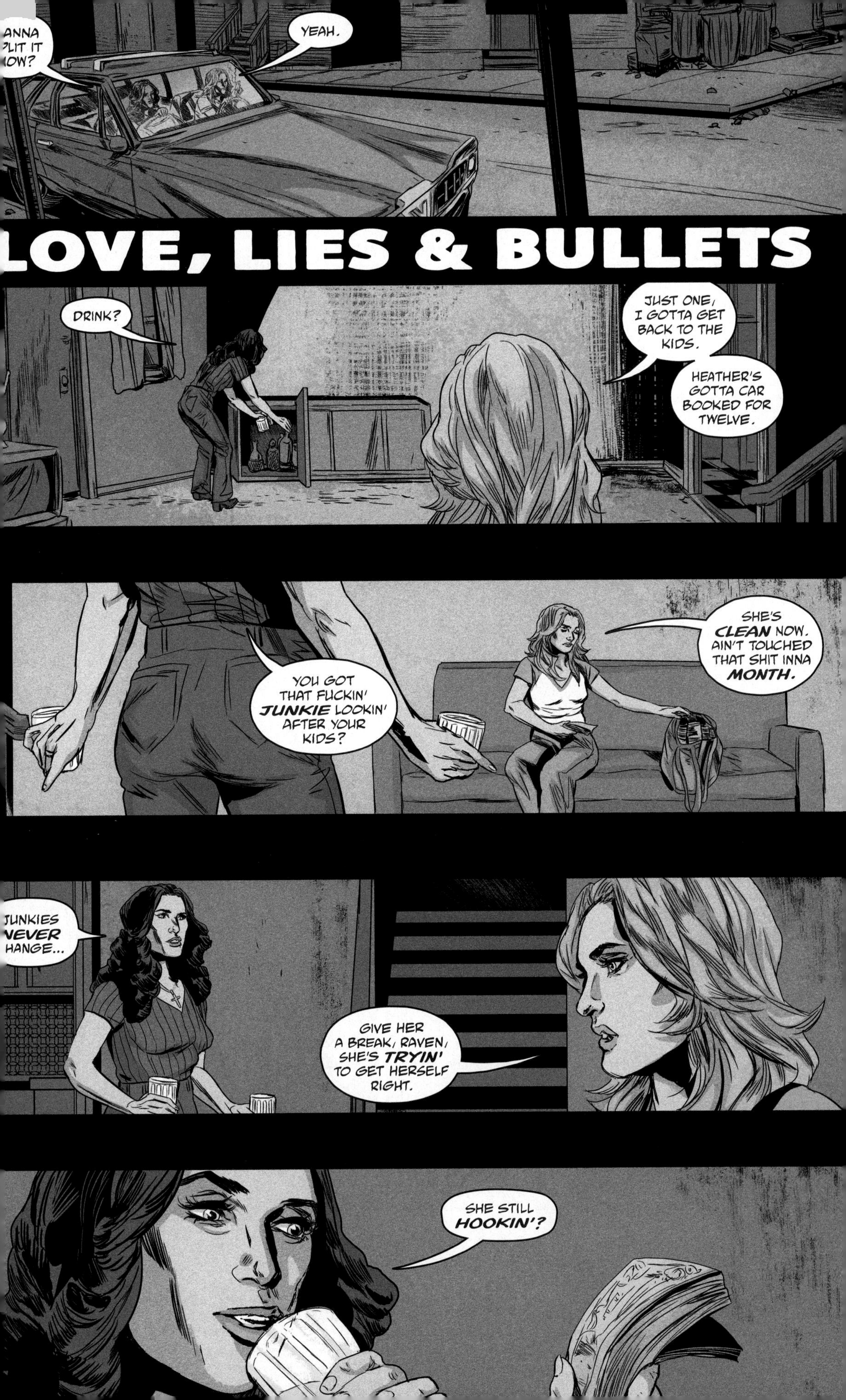
ANNA
PLIT IT
OW?
YEAH.
LOVE, LIES & BULLETS
DRINK?
JUST ONE, I GOTTA GET BACK TO THE KIDS.
HEATHER'S GOTTA CAR BOOKED FOR TWELVE.
YOU GOT THAT FUCKIN' JUNKIE LOOKIN' AFTER YOUR KIDS?
SHE'S CLEAN NOW. AIN'T TOUCHED THAT SHIT INNA MONTH.
JUNKIES NEVER HANGE...
GIVE HER A BREAK, RAVEN, SHE'S TRYIN' TO GET HERSELF RIGHT.
SHE STILL HOOKIN'?

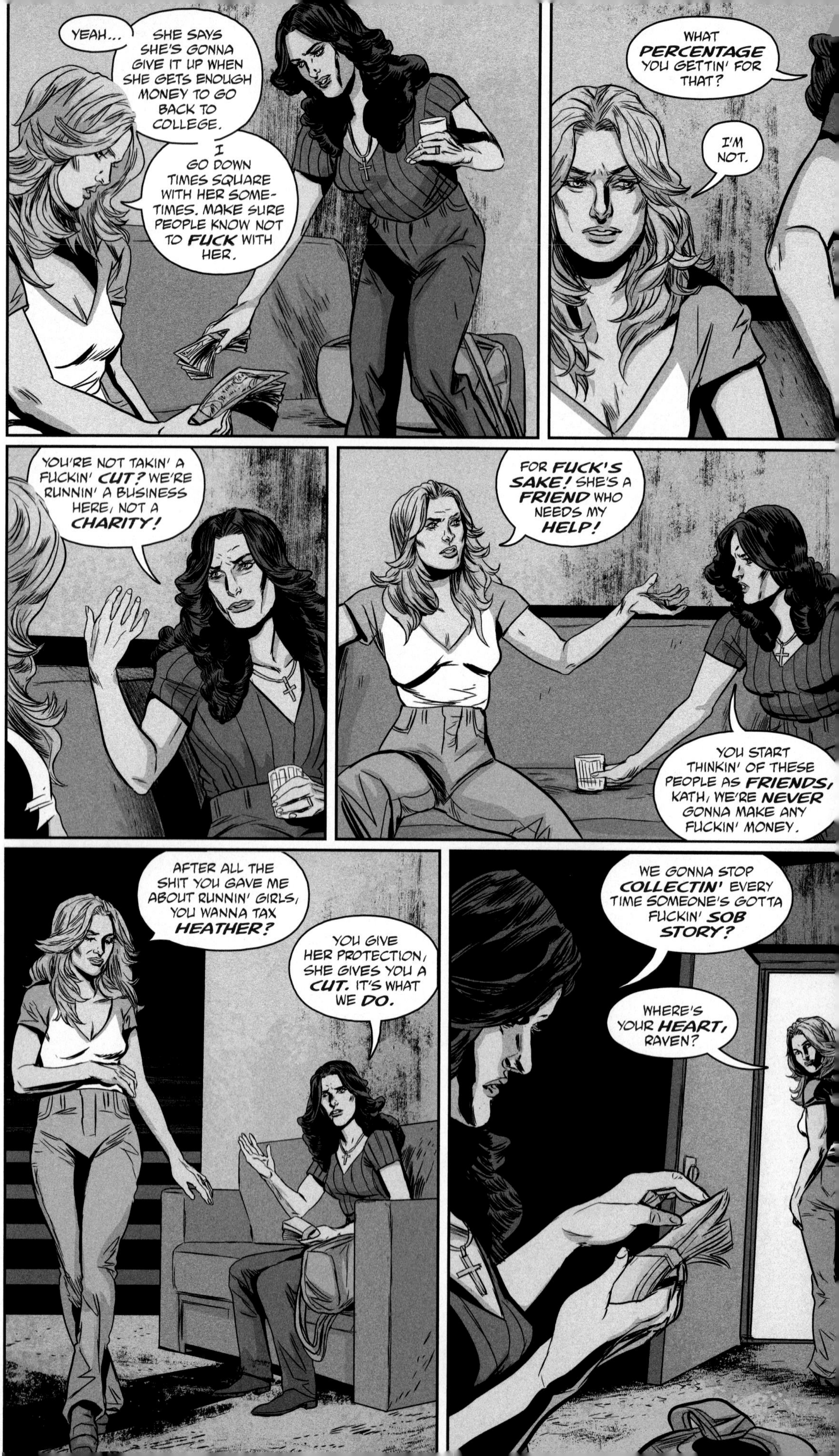
YEAH...
SHE SAYS SHE'S GONNA GIVE IT UP WHEN SHE GETS ENOUGH MONEY TO GO BACK TO COLLEGE.
I GO DOWN TIMES SQUARE WITH HER SOME-TIMES. MAKE SURE PEOPLE KNOW NOT TO FUCK WITH HER.
WHAT PERCENTAGE YOU GETTIN' FOR THAT?
I'M NOT.
YOU'RE NOT TAKIN' A FUCKIN' CUT? WE'RE RUNNIN' A BUSINESS HERE, NOT A CHARITY!
FOR FUCK'S SAKE! SHE'S A FRIEND WHO NEEDS MY HELP!
YOU START THINKIN' OF THESE PEOPLE AS FRIENDS, KATH, WE'RE NEVER GONNA MAKE ANY FUCKIN' MONEY.
AFTER ALL THE SHIT YOU GAVE ME ABOUT RUNNIN' GIRLS, YOU WANNA TAX HEATHER?
YOU GIVE HER PROTECTION, SHE GIVES YOU A CUT. IT'S WHAT WE DO.
WE GONNA STOP COLLECTIN' EVERY TIME SOMEONE'S GOTTA FUCKIN' SOB STORY?
WHERE'S YOUR HEART, RAVEN?

DON'T GO **SOFT** ON ME, KATH.

YOU KNOW, YOU'RE TALKIN' PRETTY FUCKIN' **BIG** FOR SOMEONE WHO DIDN'T EVEN WANNA GET **INTO** THIS.

YEAH, BUT WE'RE FUCKIN' IN IT **NOW**, AIN'T WE? AND IF WE'RE GONNA DO IT, WE GOTTA DO IT **RIGHT**.

IF YOU CAN'T SEE THAT ANYMORE, MAYBE YOU SHOULD JUST GET **OUTTA** THIS THING. BEFORE THAT BIG FUCKIN' HEART OF YOURS **BREAKS**.

OH, **FUCK YOU** IF YOU BELIEVE THAT, RAVEN.

EVEN IN **THIS**, SOME THINGS ARE MORE IMPORTANT THAN MONEY.

SLAM

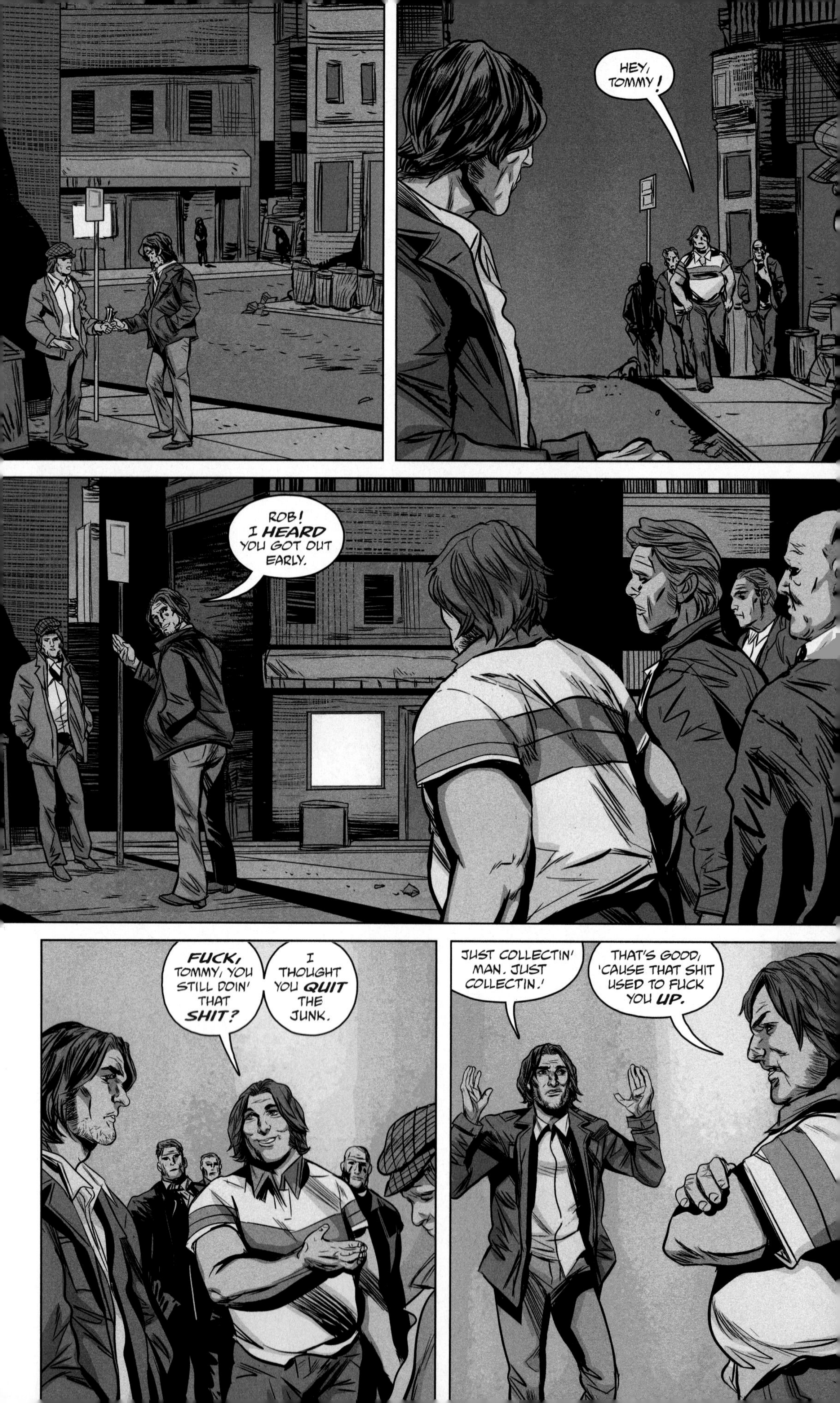
HEY, TOMMY!
ROB! I HEARD YOU GOT OUT EARLY.
FUCK, TOMMY, YOU STILL DOIN' THAT SHIT?
I THOUGHT YOU QUIT THE JUNK.
JUST COLLECTIN' MAN. JUST COLLECTIN.'
THAT'S GOOD, 'CAUSE THAT SHIT USED TO FUCK YOU UP.

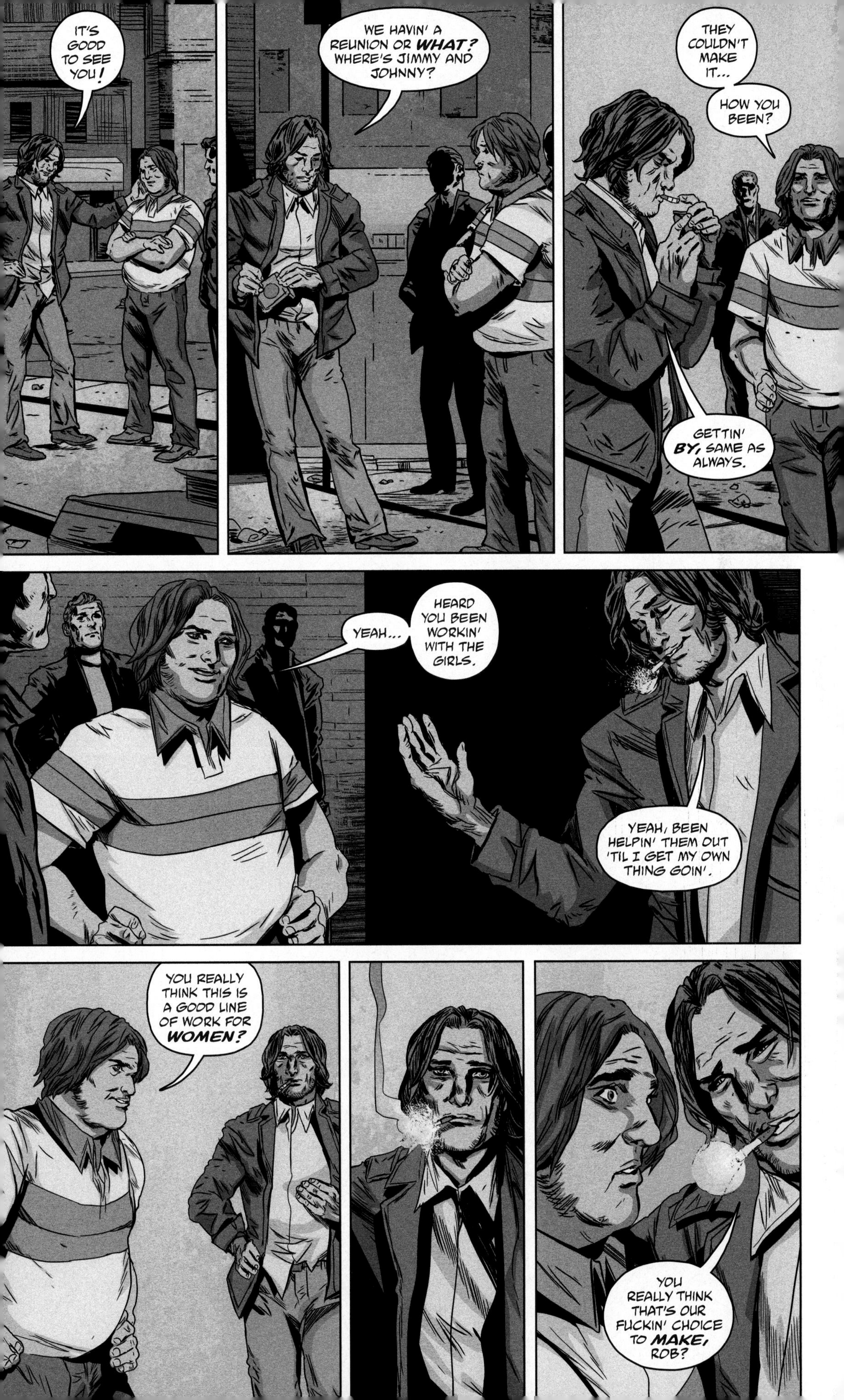
IT'S GOOD TO SEE YOU!
WE HAVIN' A REUNION OR WHAT? WHERE'S JIMMY AND JOHNNY?
THEY COULDN'T MAKE IT...
HOW YOU BEEN?
GETTIN' BY, SAME AS ALWAYS.
YEAH...
HEARD YOU BEEN WORKIN' WITH THE GIRLS.
YEAH, BEEN HELPIN' THEM OUT 'TIL I GET MY OWN THING GOIN'.
YOU REALLY THINK THIS IS A GOOD LINE OF WORK FOR WOMEN?
YOU REALLY THINK THAT'S OUR FUCKIN' CHOICE TO MAKE, ROB?

I DIDN'T KNOW I HAD TO PICK A SIDE.

OF COURSE YOU FUCKIN' DO!

ENOUGH OF THIS SHIT, TOMMY, WHO YOU WITH? US OR THEM?

WHAT YOU GONNA DO, TOMMY? TURN ON YOUR CREW AS WELL AS FUCK MY WIFE?

WHAT!? I AIN'T FUCKIN' ANGIE!

DON'T YOU FUCKIN' LIE TO ME! EVERYONE'S SEEN YOU TOGETHER.

YOU'RE THE SAME AS THAT FUCKIN' GREASEBALL CASTELLANO.

LOOK, ROB, I AIN'T LYING. ANGIE'S LIKE A SISTER--

CRAKK

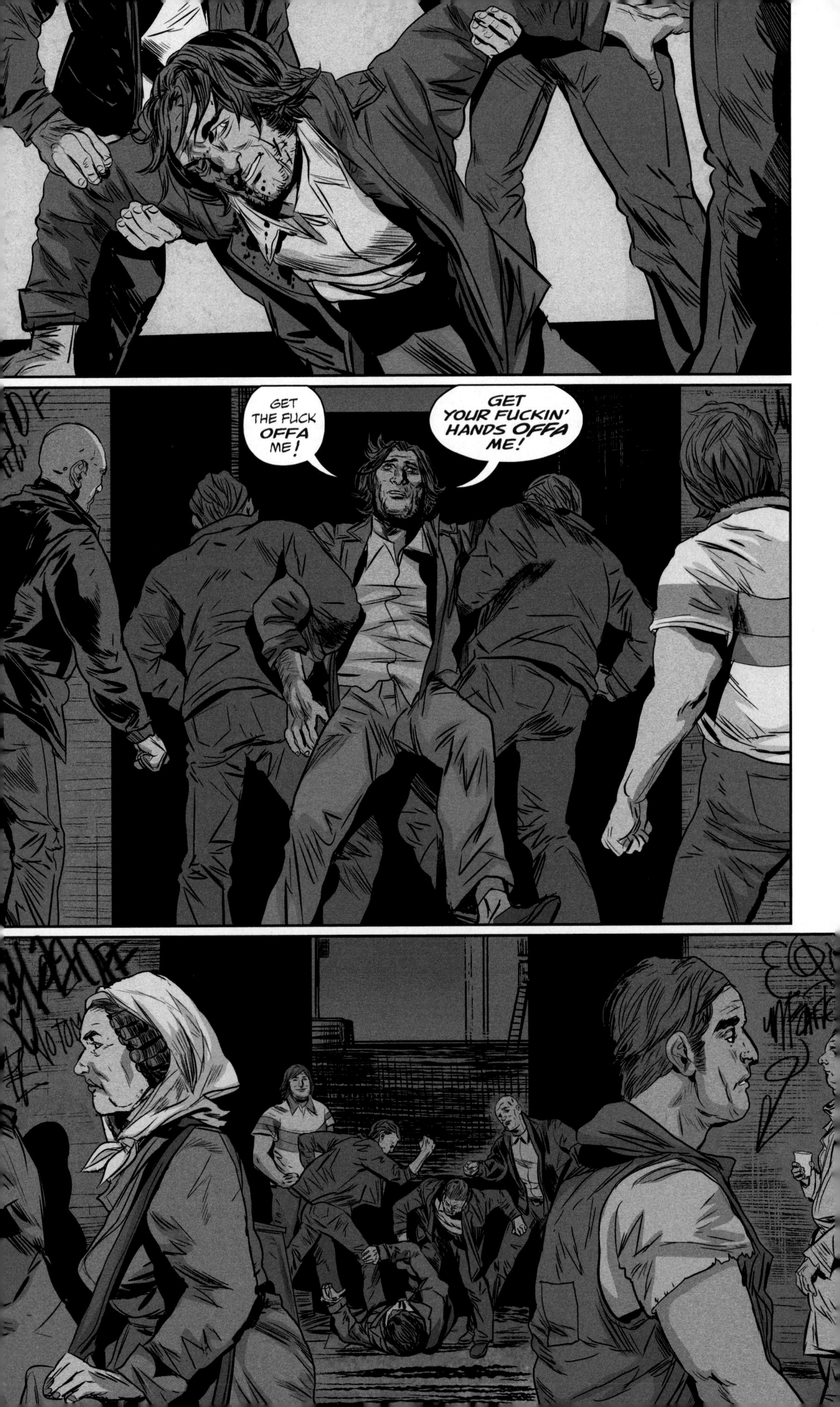
GET THE FUCK OFFA ME!
GET YOUR FUCKIN' HANDS OFFA ME!

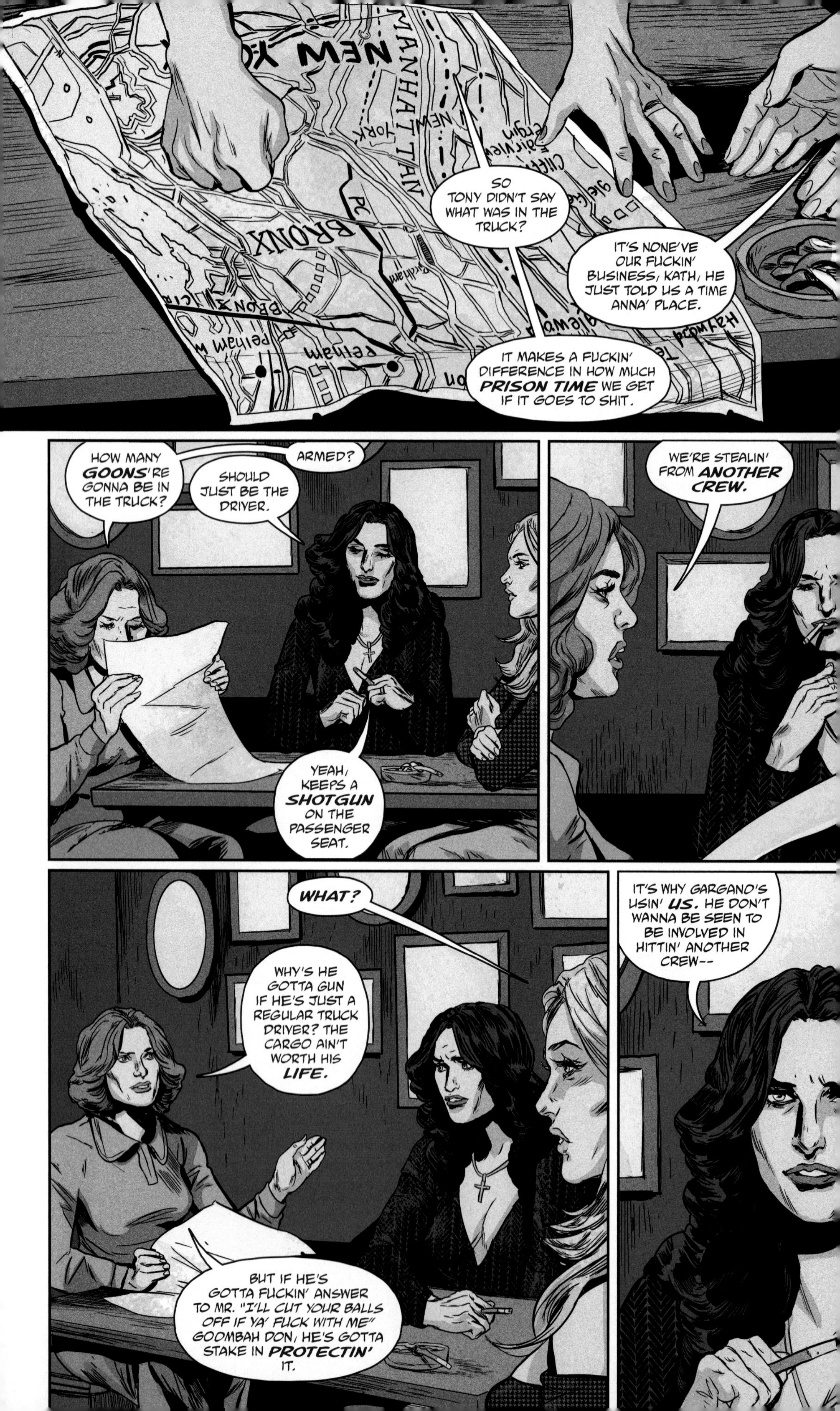
NEW YO
MANHATTAN
BRONX
SO TONY DIDN'T SAY WHAT WAS IN THE TRUCK?
IT'S NONE'VE OUR FUCKIN' BUSINESS, KATH, HE JUST TOLD US A TIME ANNA' PLACE.
IT MAKES A FUCKIN' DIFFERENCE IN HOW MUCH PRISON TIME WE GET IF IT GOES TO SHIT.
HOW MANY GOONS'RE GONNA BE IN THE TRUCK?
SHOULD JUST BE THE DRIVER.
ARMED?
YEAH, KEEPS A SHOTGUN ON THE PASSENGER SEAT.
WE'RE STEALIN' FROM ANOTHER CREW.
WHAT?
WHY'S HE GOTTA GUN IF HE'S JUST A REGULAR TRUCK DRIVER? THE CARGO AIN'T WORTH HIS LIFE.
BUT IF HE'S GOTTA FUCKIN' ANSWER TO MR. "I'LL CUT YOUR BALLS OFF IF YA' FUCK WITH ME" GOOMBAH DON, HE'S GOTTA STAKE IN PROTECTIN' IT.
IT'S WHY GARGANO'S USIN' US. HE DON'T WANNA BE SEEN TO BE INVOLVED IN HITTIN' ANOTHER CREW--

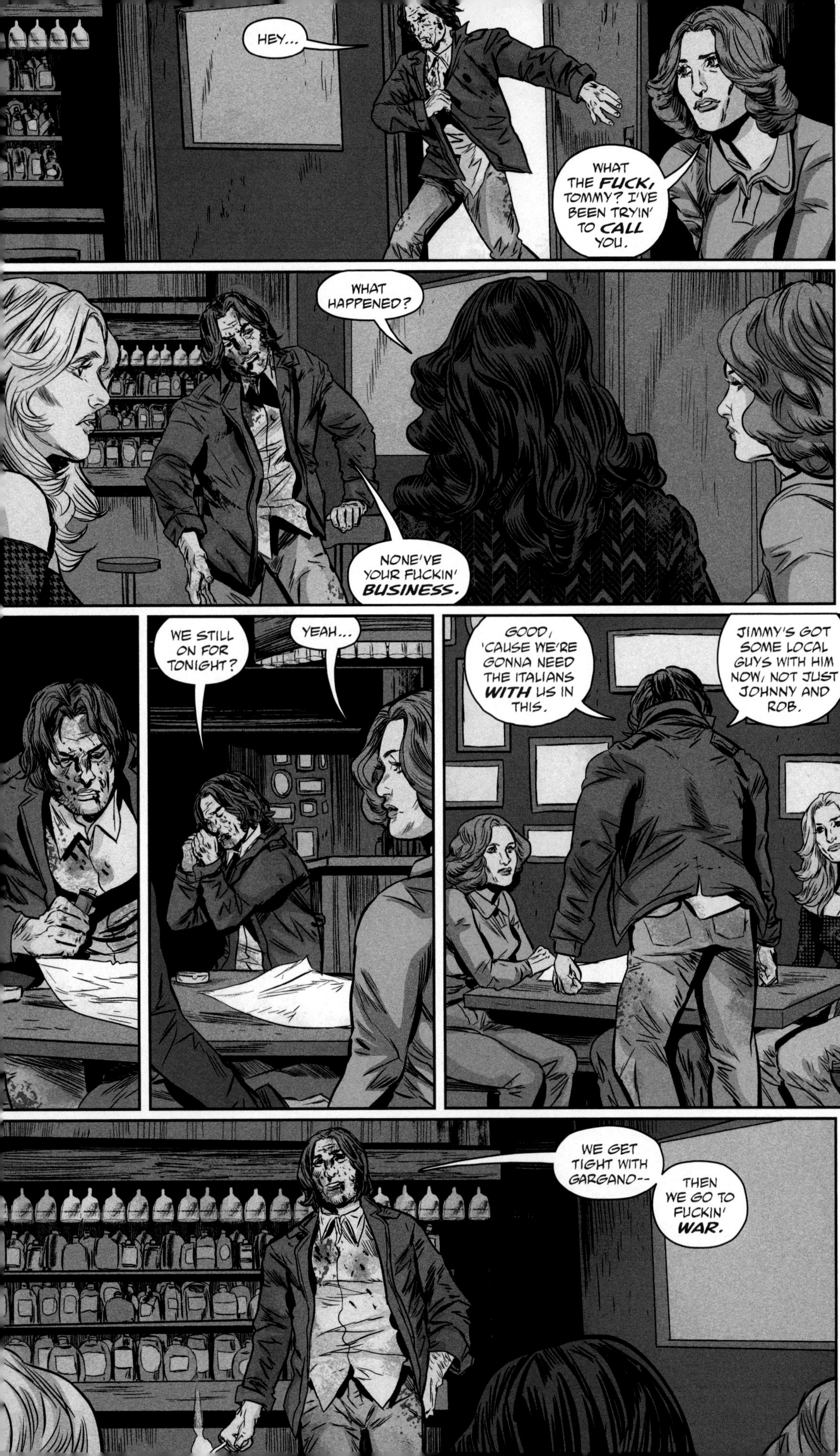
HEY...
WHAT THE FUCK, TOMMY? I'VE BEEN TRYIN' TO CALL YOU.
WHAT HAPPENED?
NONE'VE YOUR FUCKIN' BUSINESS.
WE STILL ON FOR TONIGHT?
YEAH...
GOOD, 'CAUSE WE'RE GONNA NEED THE ITALIANS WITH US IN THIS.
JIMMY'S GOT SOME LOCAL GUYS WITH HIM NOW, NOT JUST JOHNNY AND ROB.
WE GET TIGHT WITH GARGANO--
THEN WE GO TO FUCKIN' WAR.

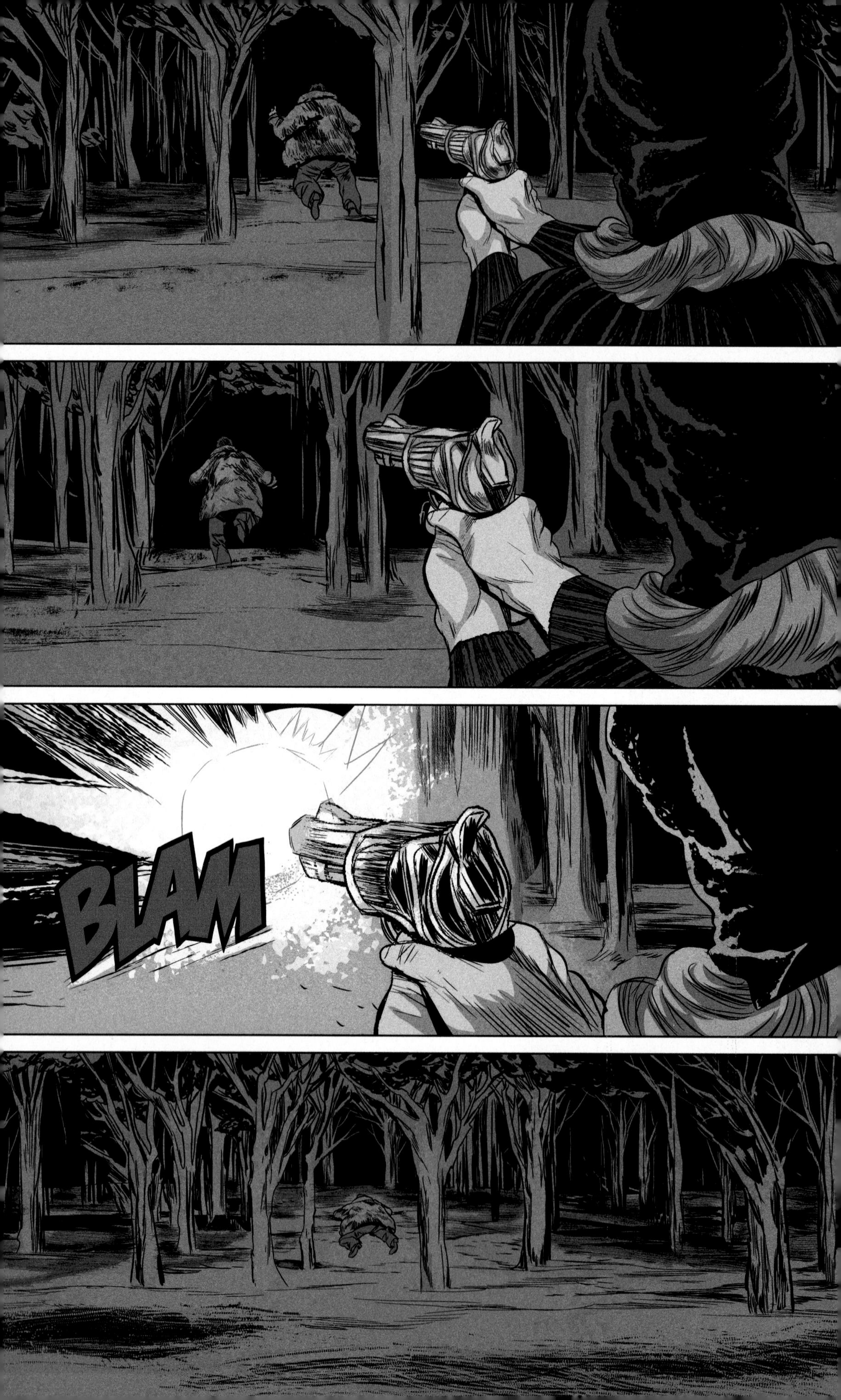
BLAM

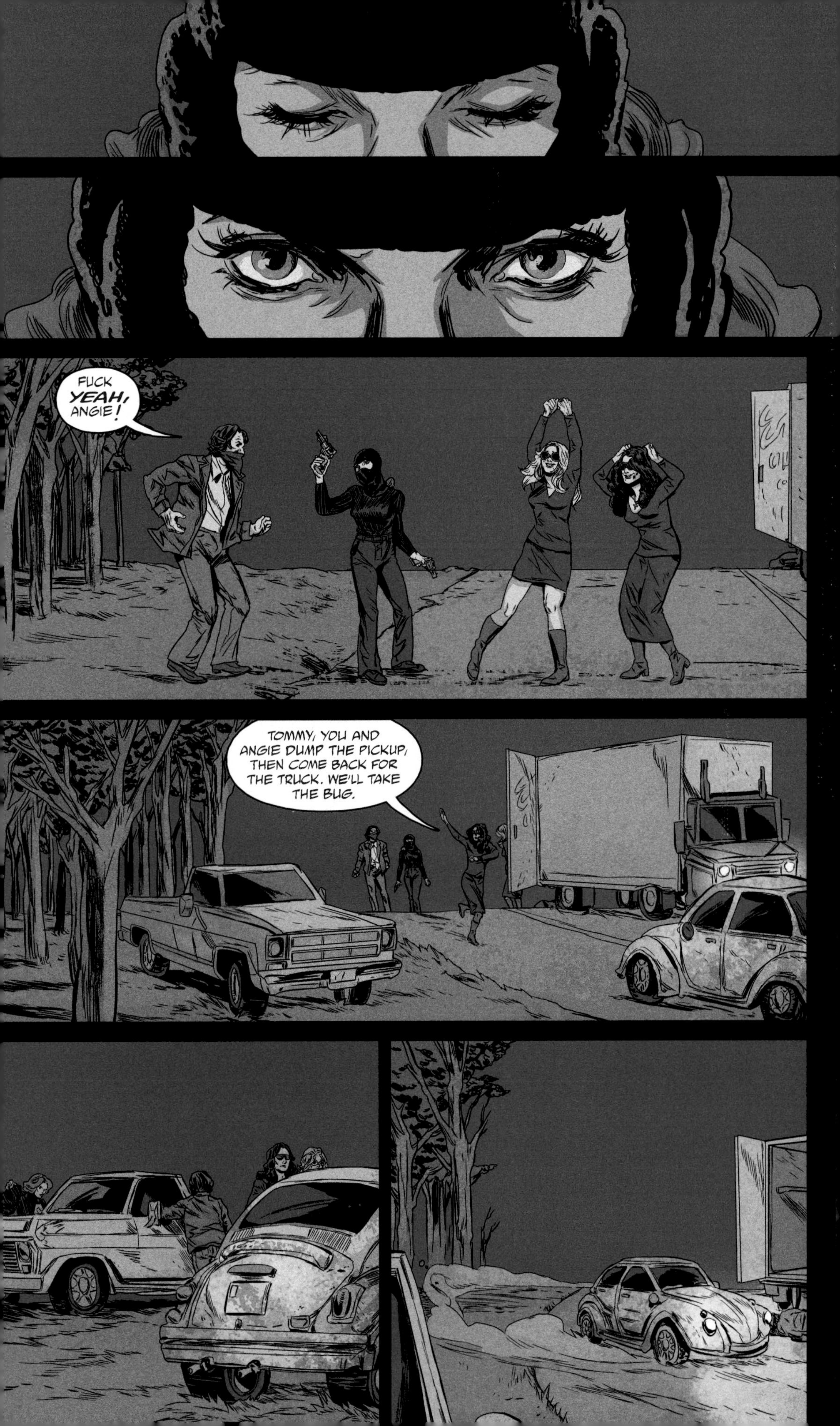
FUCK YEAH, ANGIE!
TOMMY, YOU AND ANGIE DUMP THE PICKUP, THEN COME BACK FOR THE TRUCK. WE'LL TAKE THE BUG.

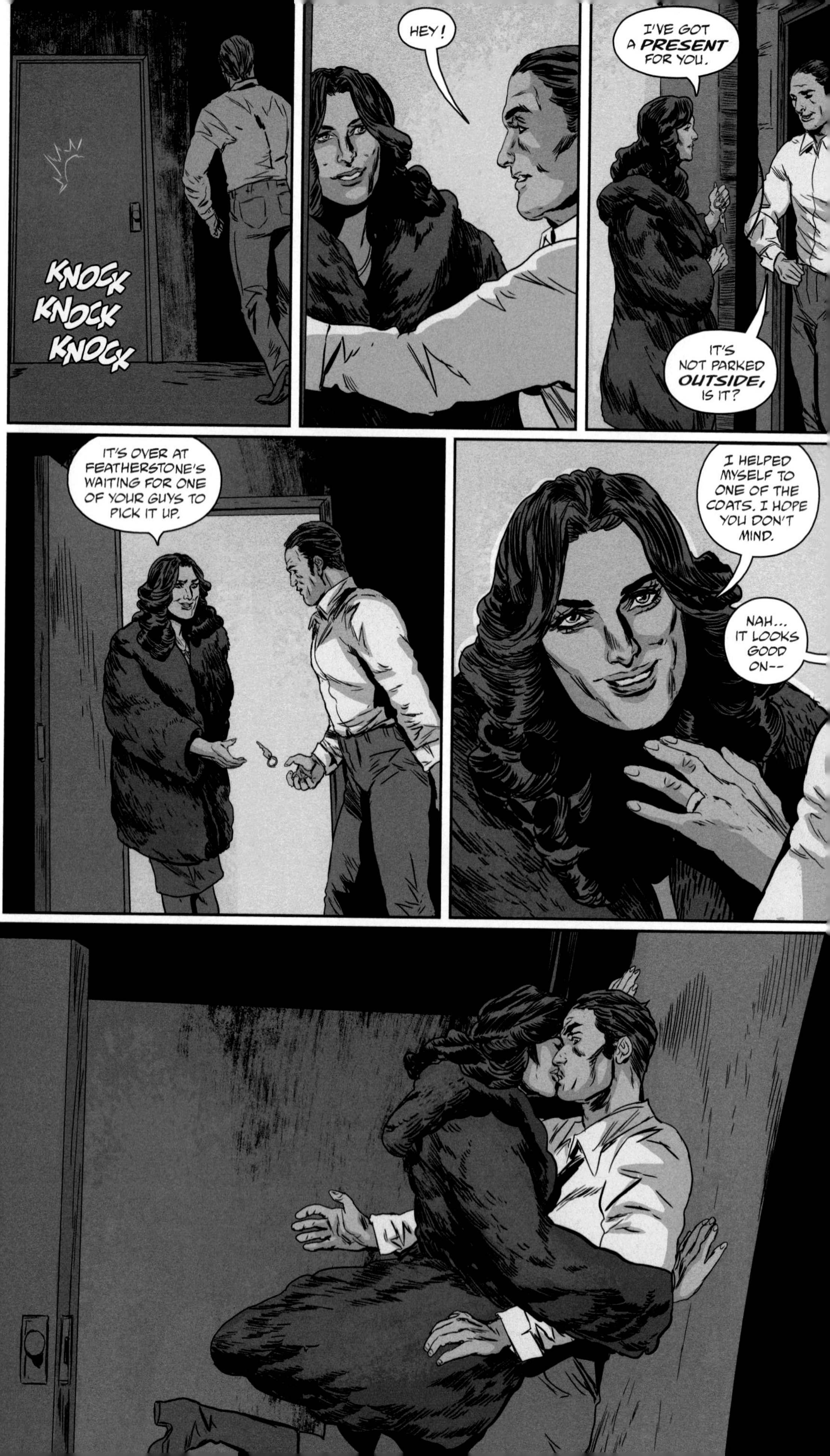
KNOCK
KNOCK
KNOCK
HEY!
I'VE GOT A PRESENT FOR YOU.
IT'S NOT PARKED OUTSIDE, IS IT?
IT'S OVER AT FEATHERSTONE'S WAITING FOR ONE OF YOUR GUYS TO PICK IT UP.
I HELPED MYSELF TO ONE OF THE COATS. I HOPE YOU DON'T MIND.
NAH... IT LOOKS GOOD ON--

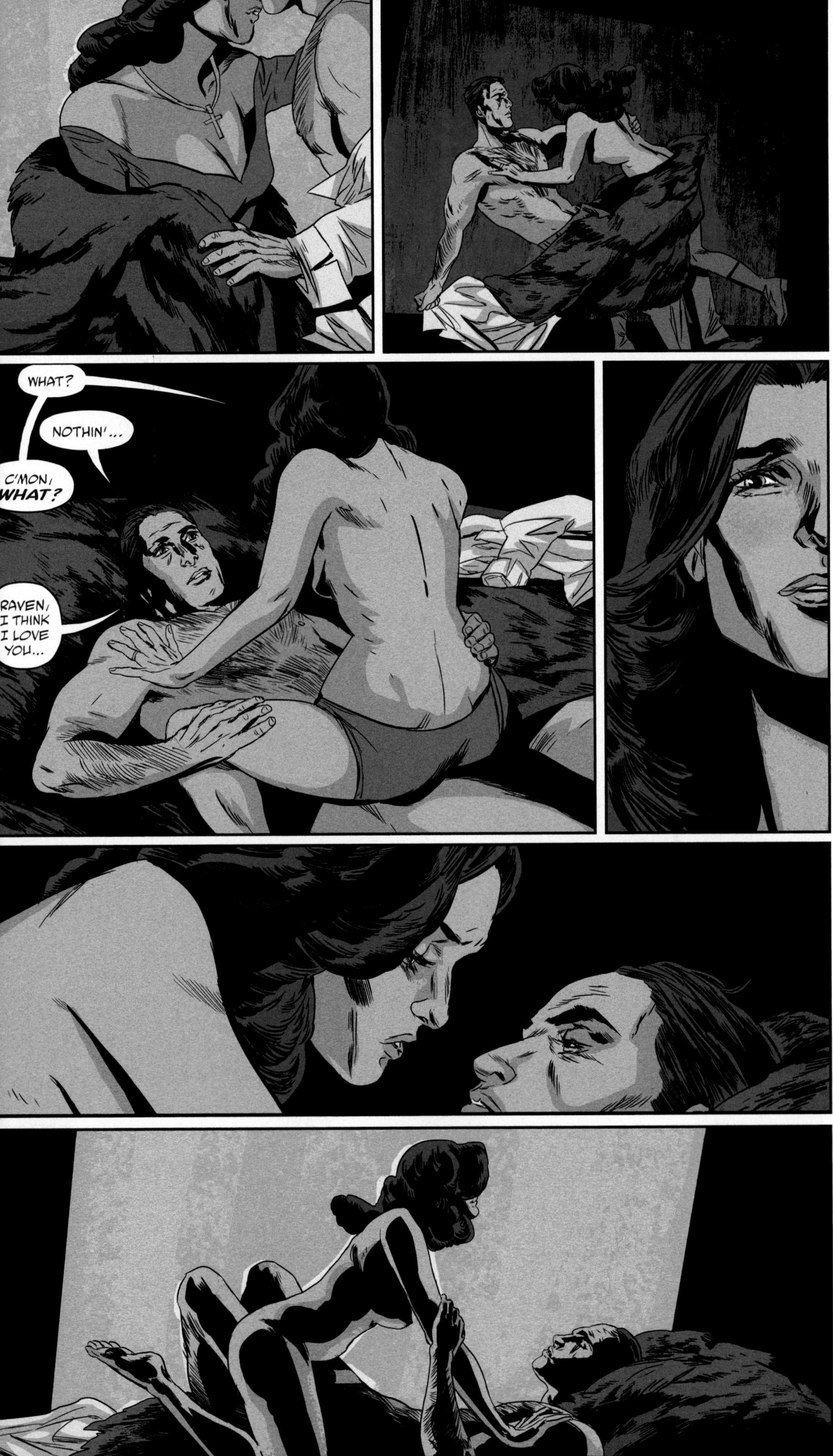
WHAT?
NOTHIN'...
C'MON, WHAT?
RAVEN, I THINK I LOVE YOU...

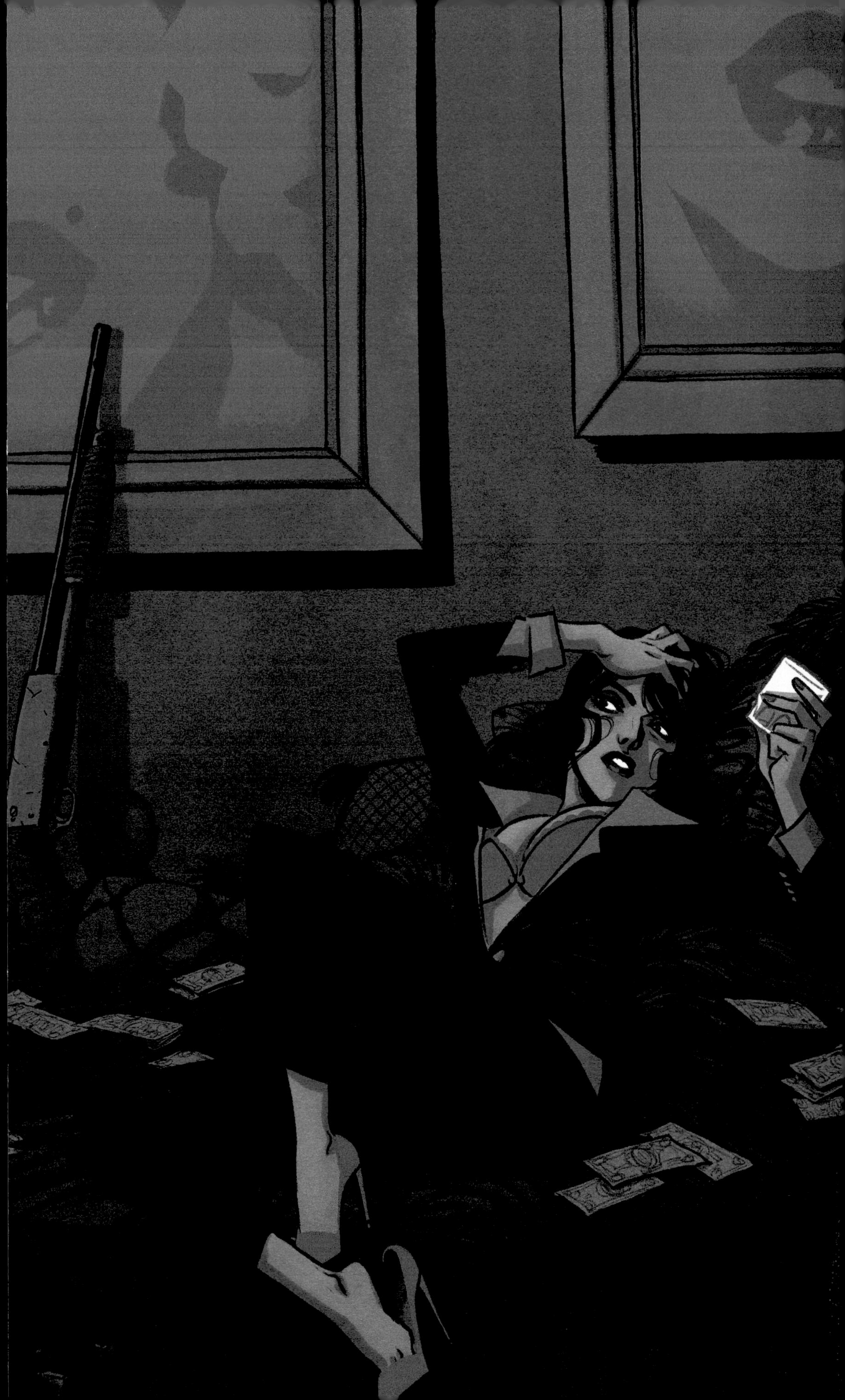

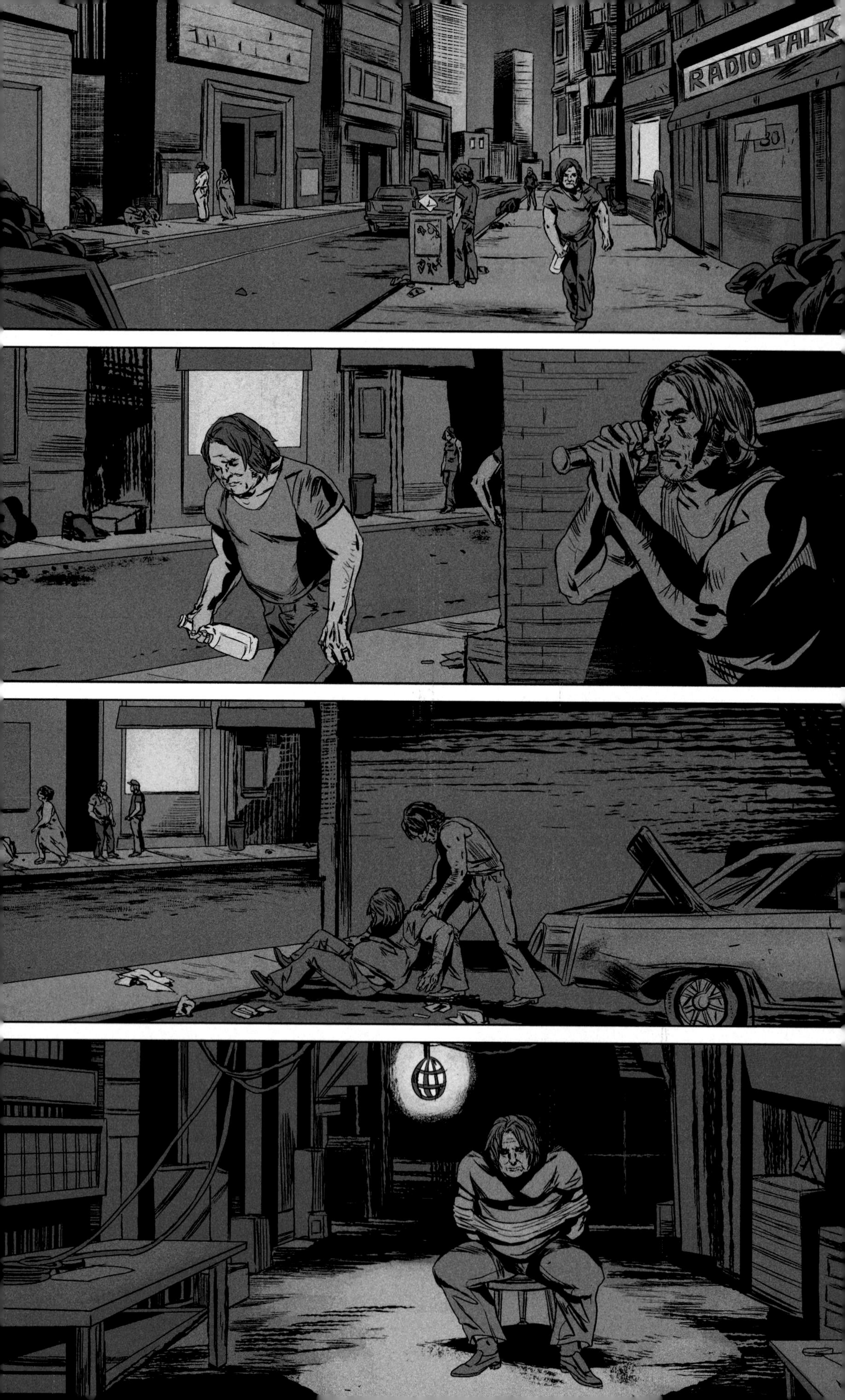
RADIO TALK
30

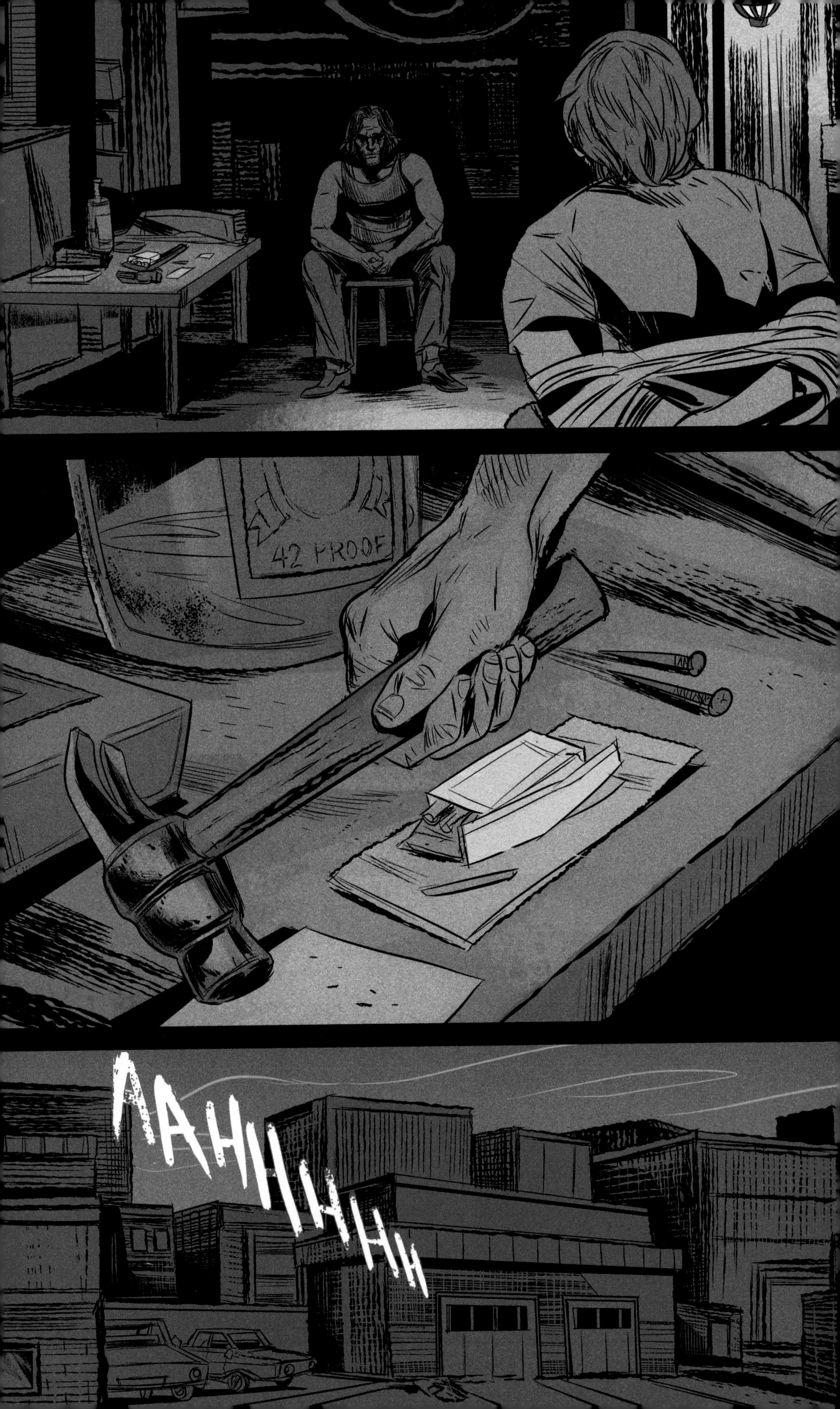
42 PROOF
AAHHHHHH

WHAT WE DO TO SURVIVE

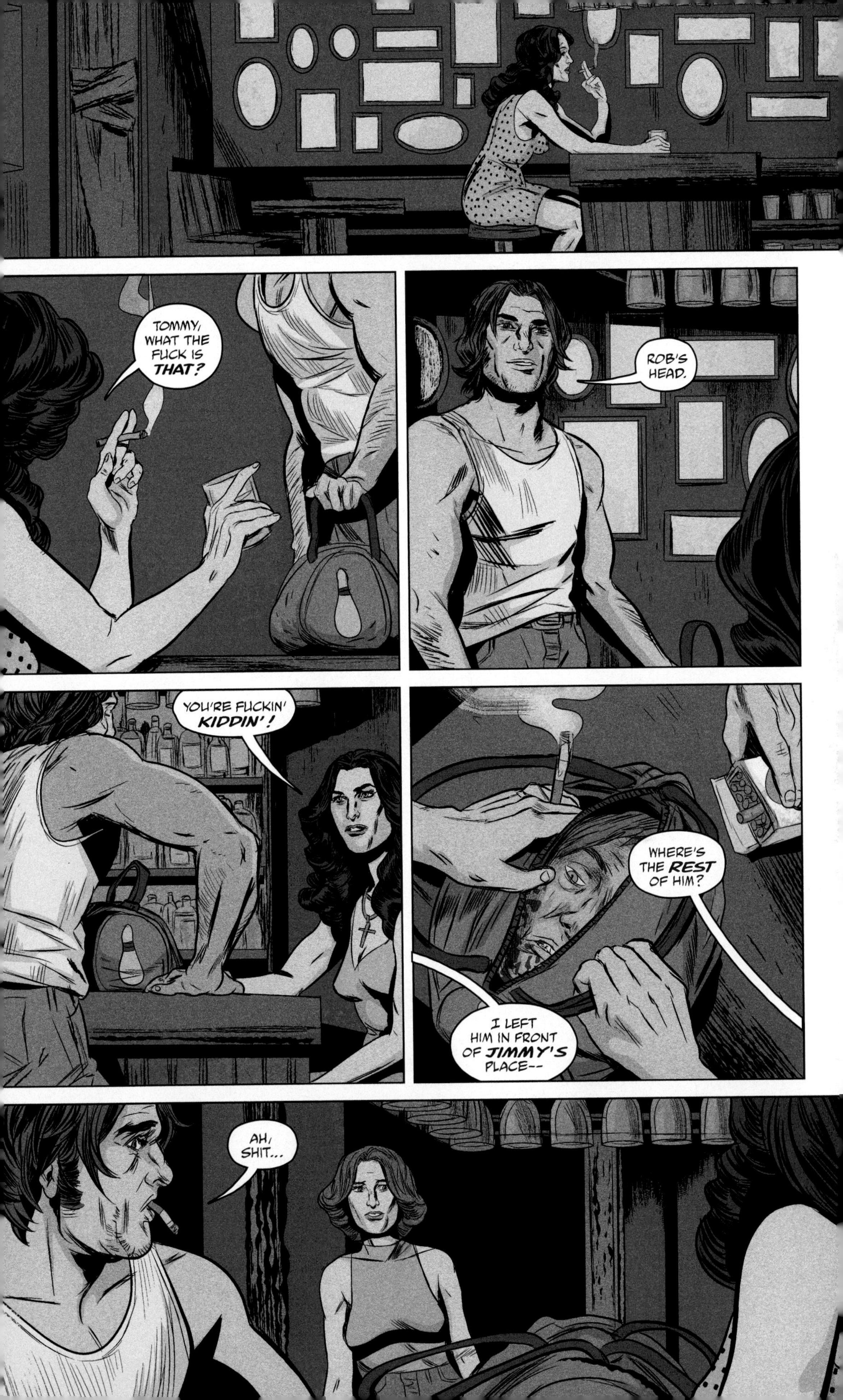

TOMMY, WHAT THE FUCK IS THAT?
ROB'S HEAD.
YOU'RE FUCKIN' KIDDIN'!
WHERE'S THE REST OF HIM?
I LEFT HIM IN FRONT OF JIMMY'S PLACE--
AH, SHIT...

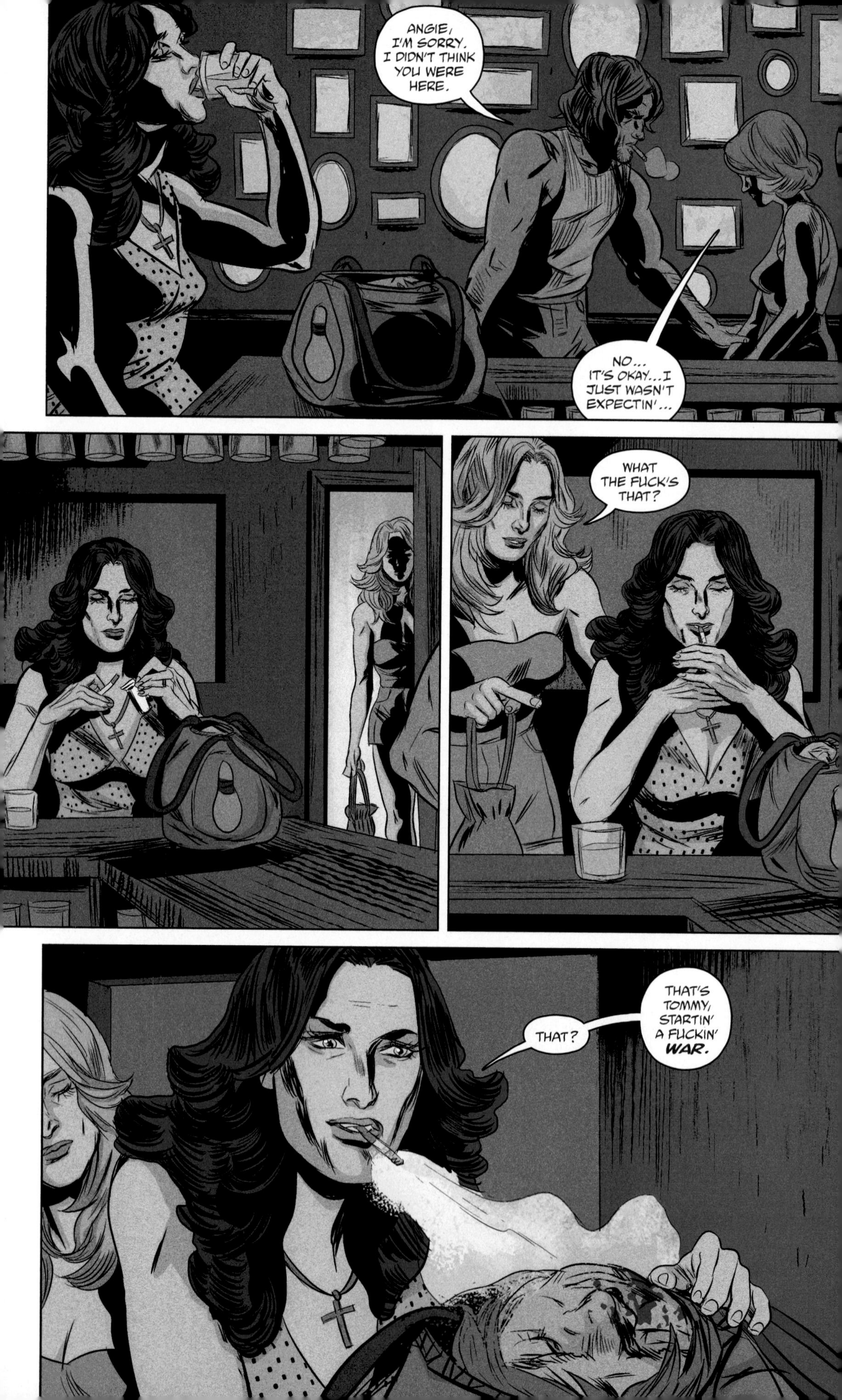
ANGIE, I'M SORRY. I DIDN'T THINK YOU WERE HERE.
NO... IT'S OKAY... I JUST WASN'T EXPECTIN'...
WHAT THE FUCK'S THAT?
THAT?
THAT'S TOMMY, STARTIN' A FUCKIN' **WAR.**

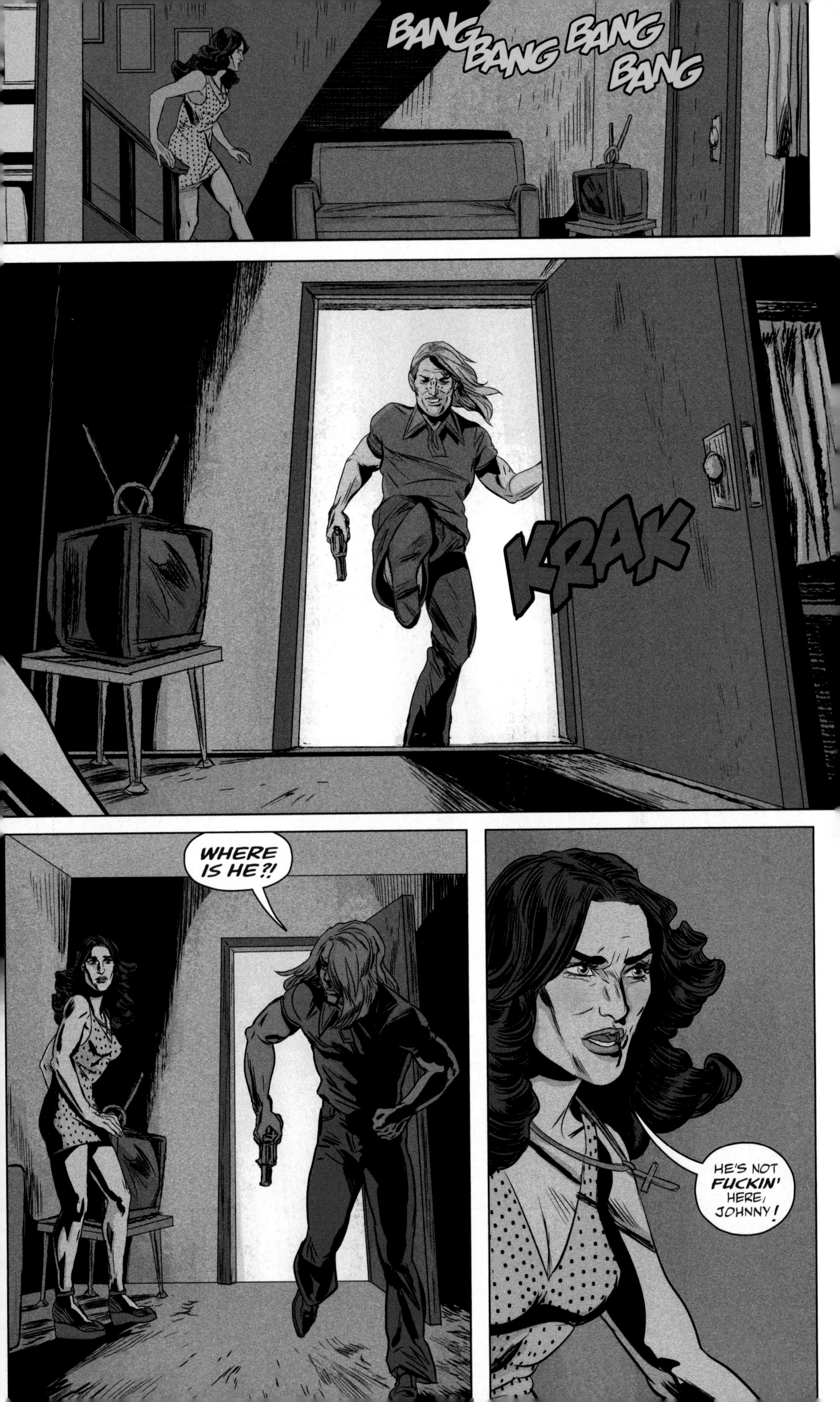
BANG BANG BANG BANG
KRAK
WHERE IS HE?!
HE'S NOT FUCKIN' HERE, JOHNNY!

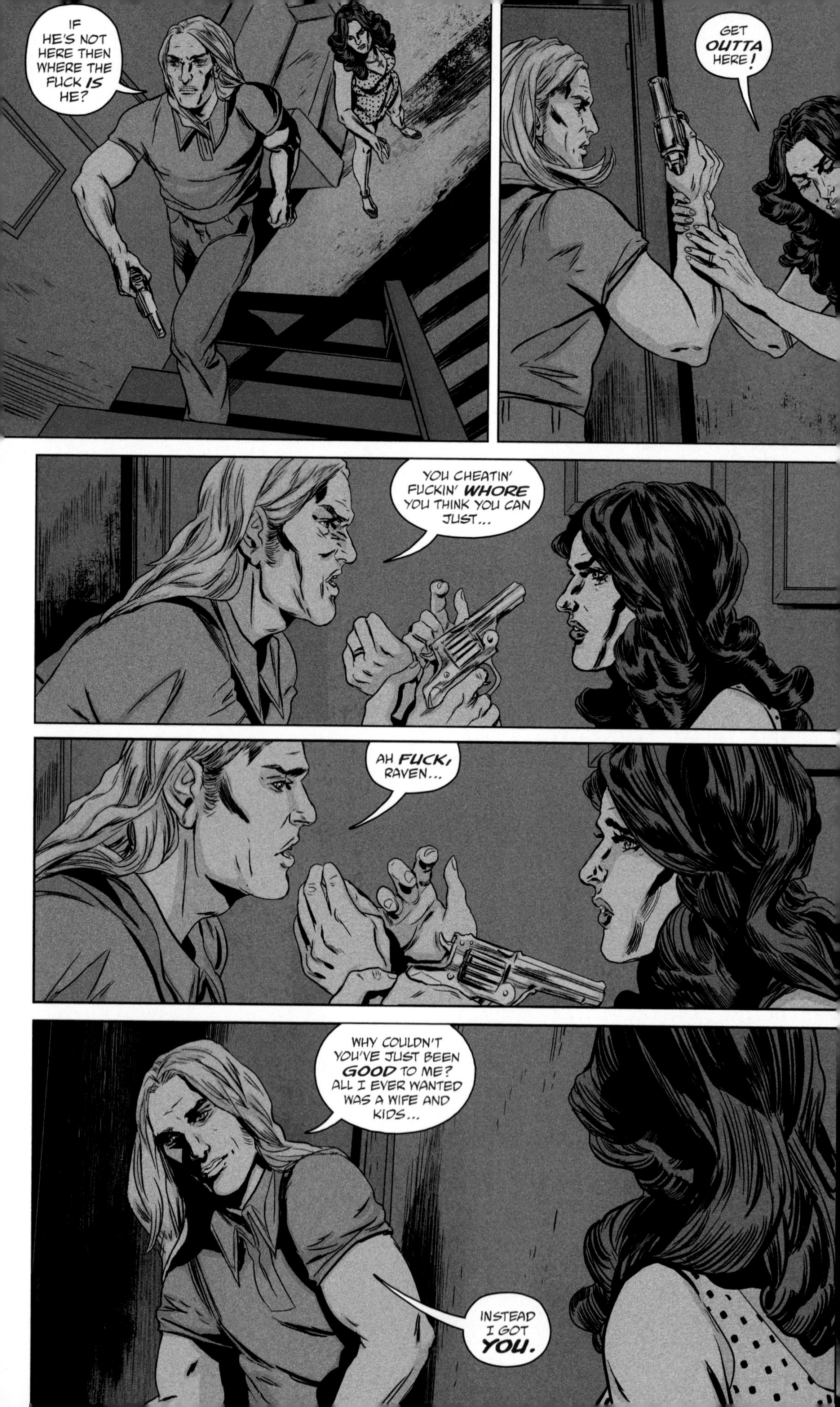
IF HE'S NOT HERE THEN WHERE THE FUCK IS HE?
GET OUTTA HERE!
YOU CHEATIN' FUCKIN' WHORE YOU THINK YOU CAN JUST...
AH FUCK, RAVEN...
WHY COULDN'T YOU'VE JUST BEEN GOOD TO ME? ALL I EVER WANTED WAS A WIFE AND KIDS...
INSTEAD I GOT YOU.

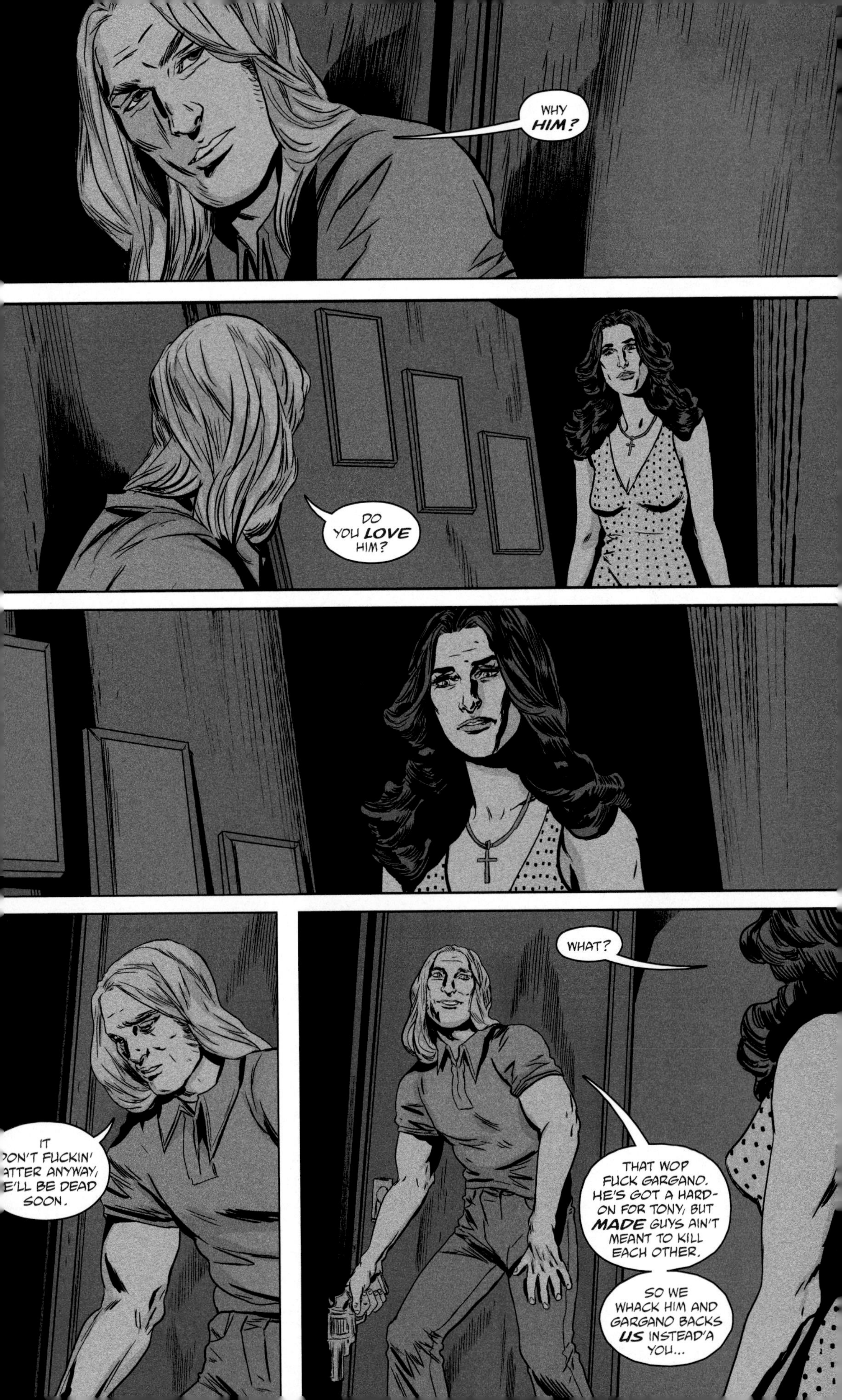
WHY HIM?
DO YOU LOVE HIM?
IT ON'T FUCKIN' ATTER ANYWAY, E'LL BE DEAD SOON.
WHAT?
THAT WOP FUCK GARGANO. HE'S GOT A HARD-ON FOR TONY, BUT MADE GUYS AIN'T MEANT TO KILL EACH OTHER.
SO WE WHACK HIM AND GARGANO BACKS US INSTEAD'A YOU...

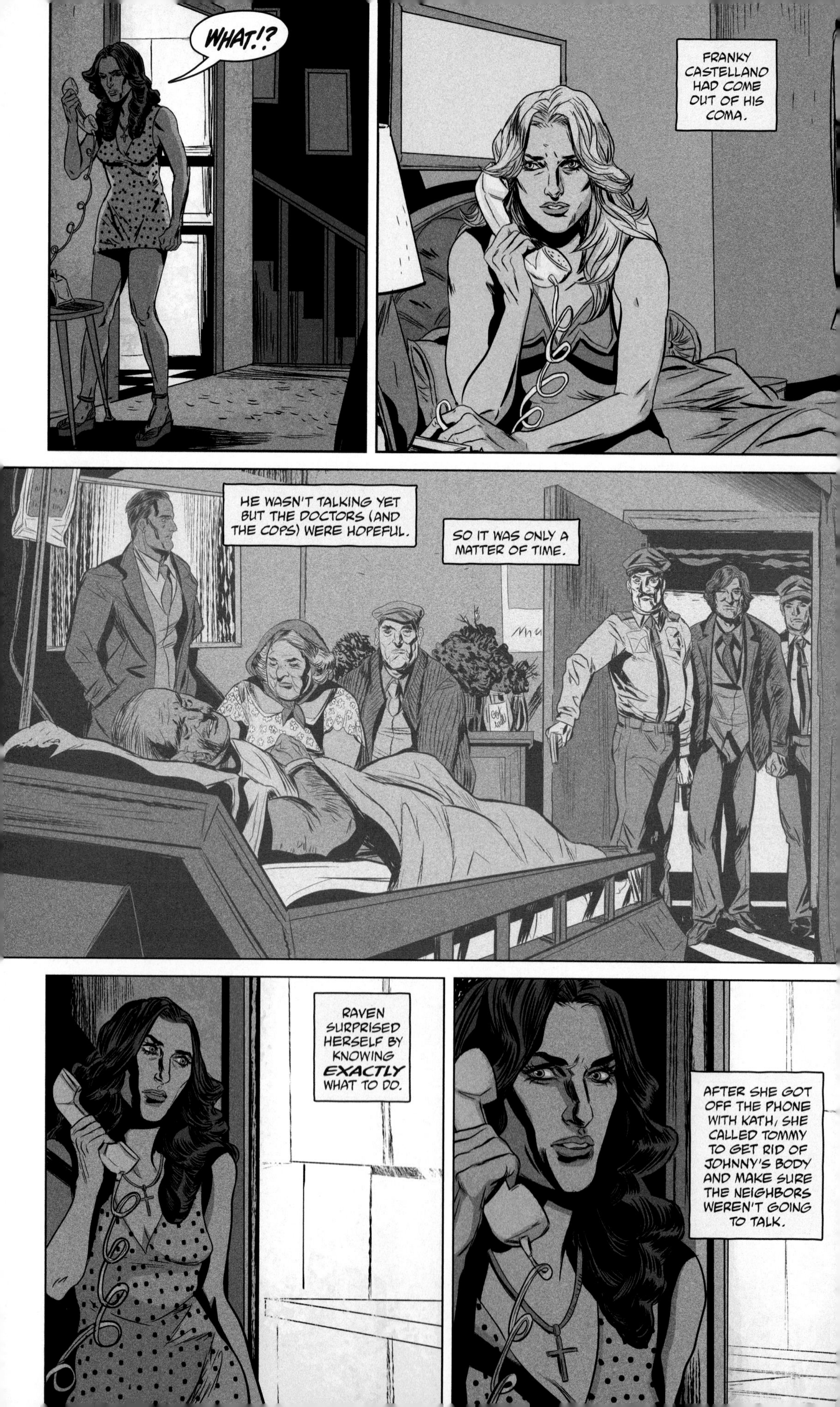
WHAT!?
FRANKY CASTELLANO HAD COME OUT OF HIS COMA.
HE WASN'T TALKING YET BUT THE DOCTORS (AND THE COPS) WERE HOPEFUL.
SO IT WAS ONLY A MATTER OF TIME.
RAVEN SURPRISED HERSELF BY KNOWING *EXACTLY* WHAT TO DO.
AFTER SHE GOT OFF THE PHONE WITH KATH, SHE CALLED TOMMY TO GET RID OF JOHNNY'S BODY AND MAKE SURE THE NEIGHBORS WEREN'T GOING TO TALK.

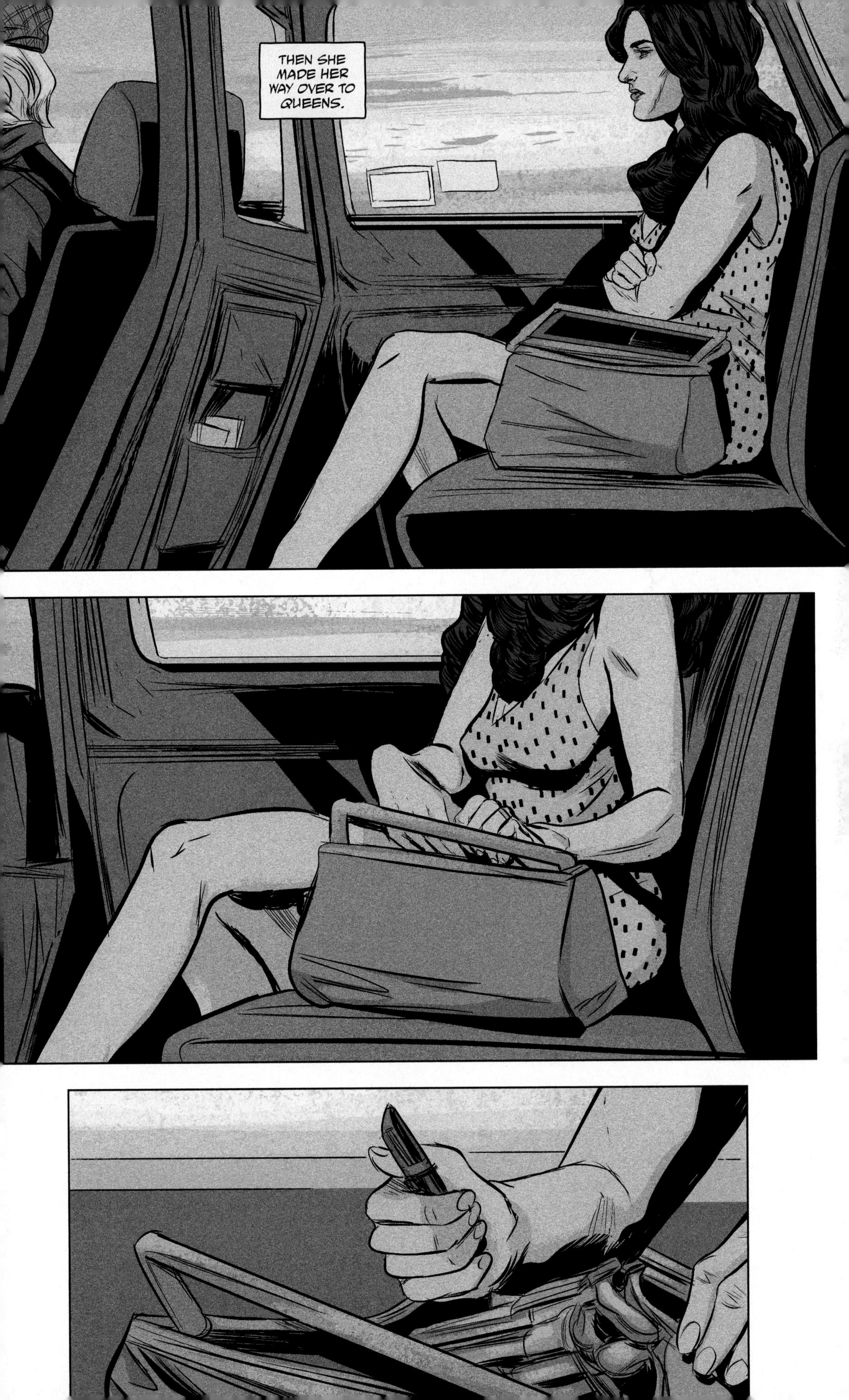
THEN SHE MADE HER WAY OVER TO QUEENS.

"BUT FROM NOW ON, IN THIS THING, I ONLY TALK TO YOU. KATH *TALKS* BIG, BUT SHE AIN'T GOT THE *HEART* FOR IT."

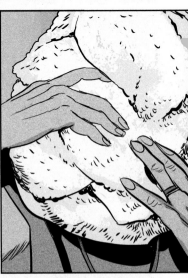

"BUT YOU, RAVEN. YOU WERE *BORN* TO DO THIS."

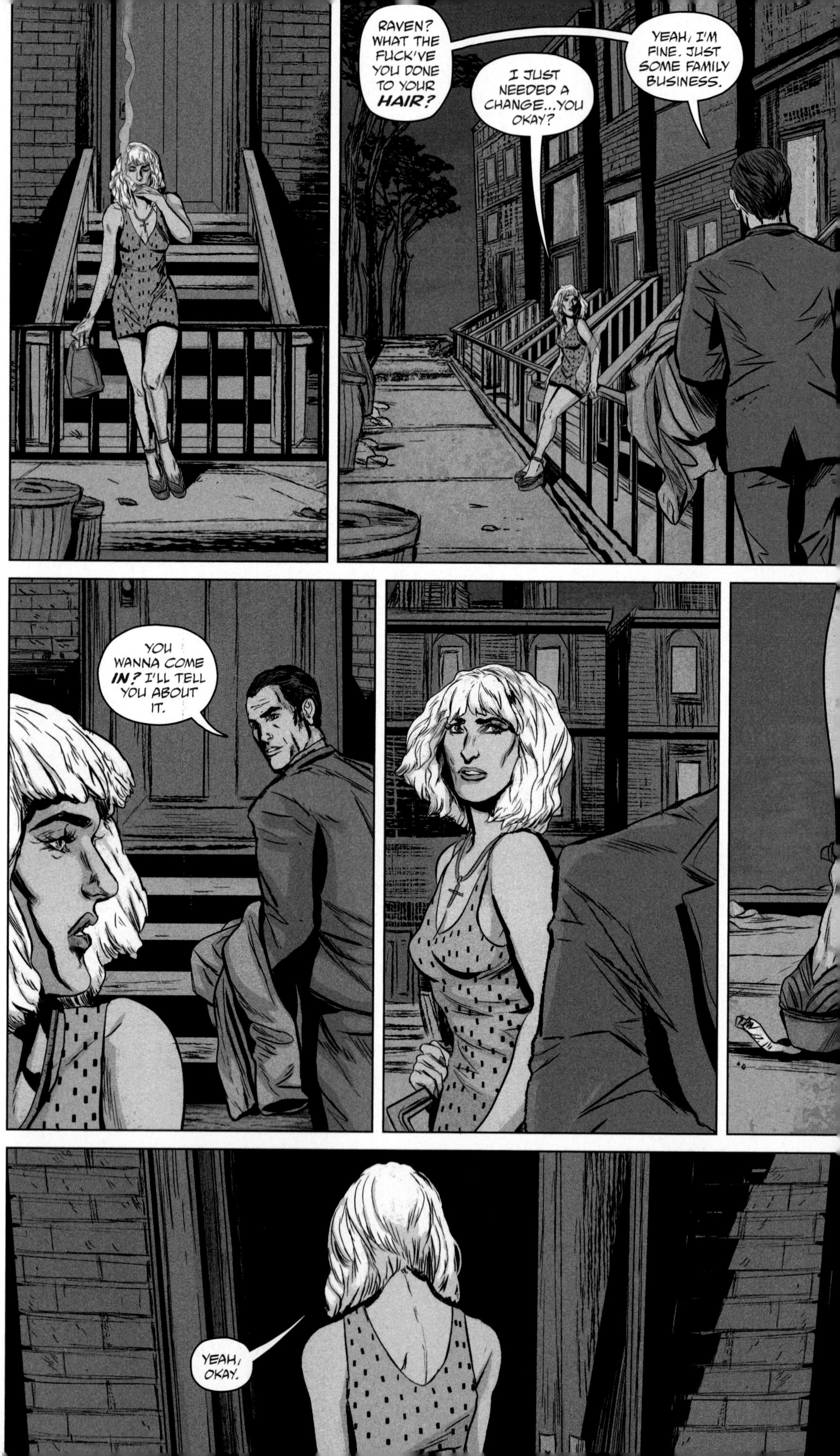
RAVEN? WHAT THE FUCK'VE YOU DONE TO YOUR HAIR?
I JUST NEEDED A CHANGE...YOU OKAY?
YEAH, I'M FINE. JUST SOME FAMILY BUSINESS.
YOU WANNA COME IN? I'LL TELL YOU ABOUT IT.
YEAH, OKAY.

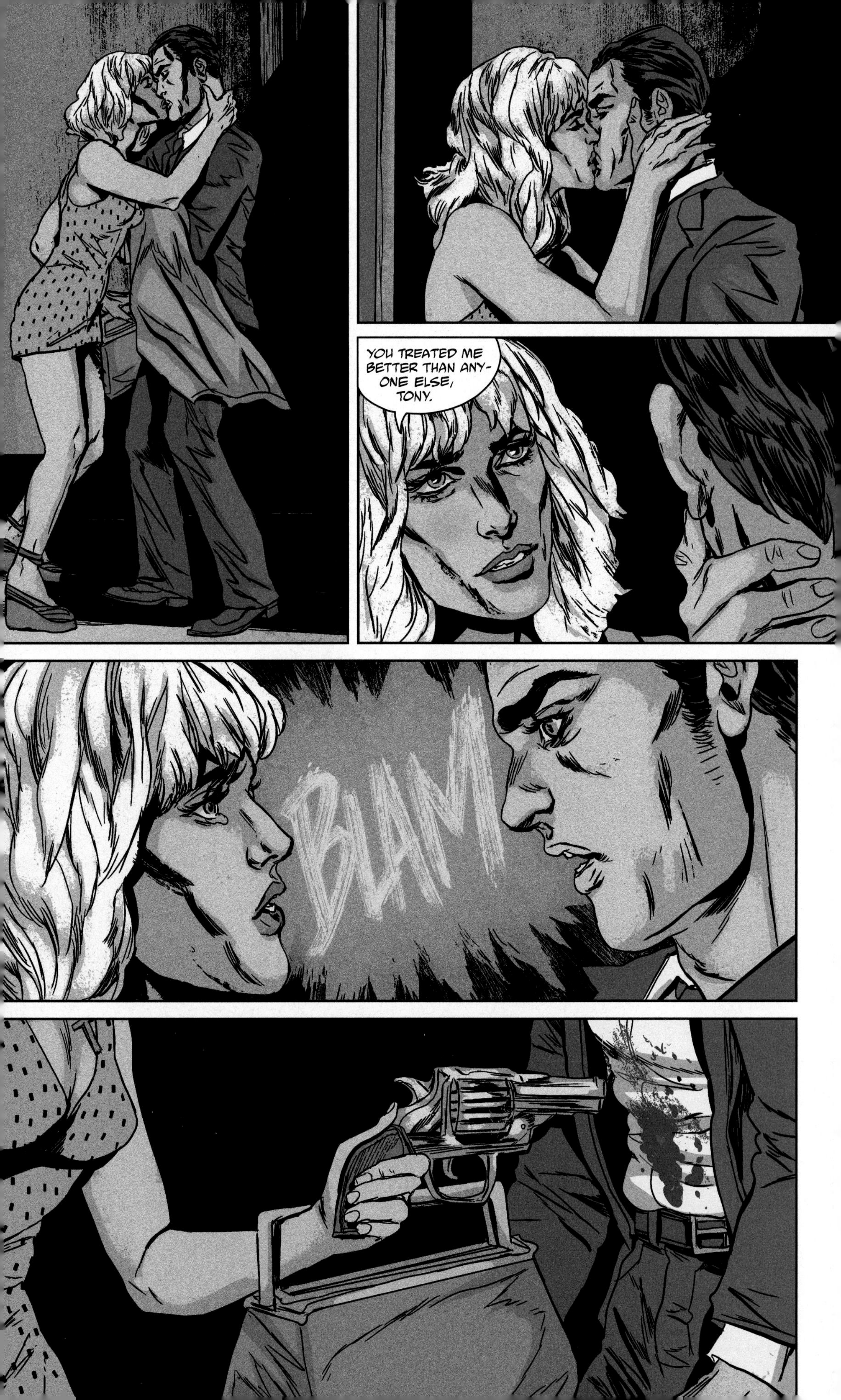
YOU TREATED ME BETTER THAN ANY-ONE ELSE, TONY.
BLAM

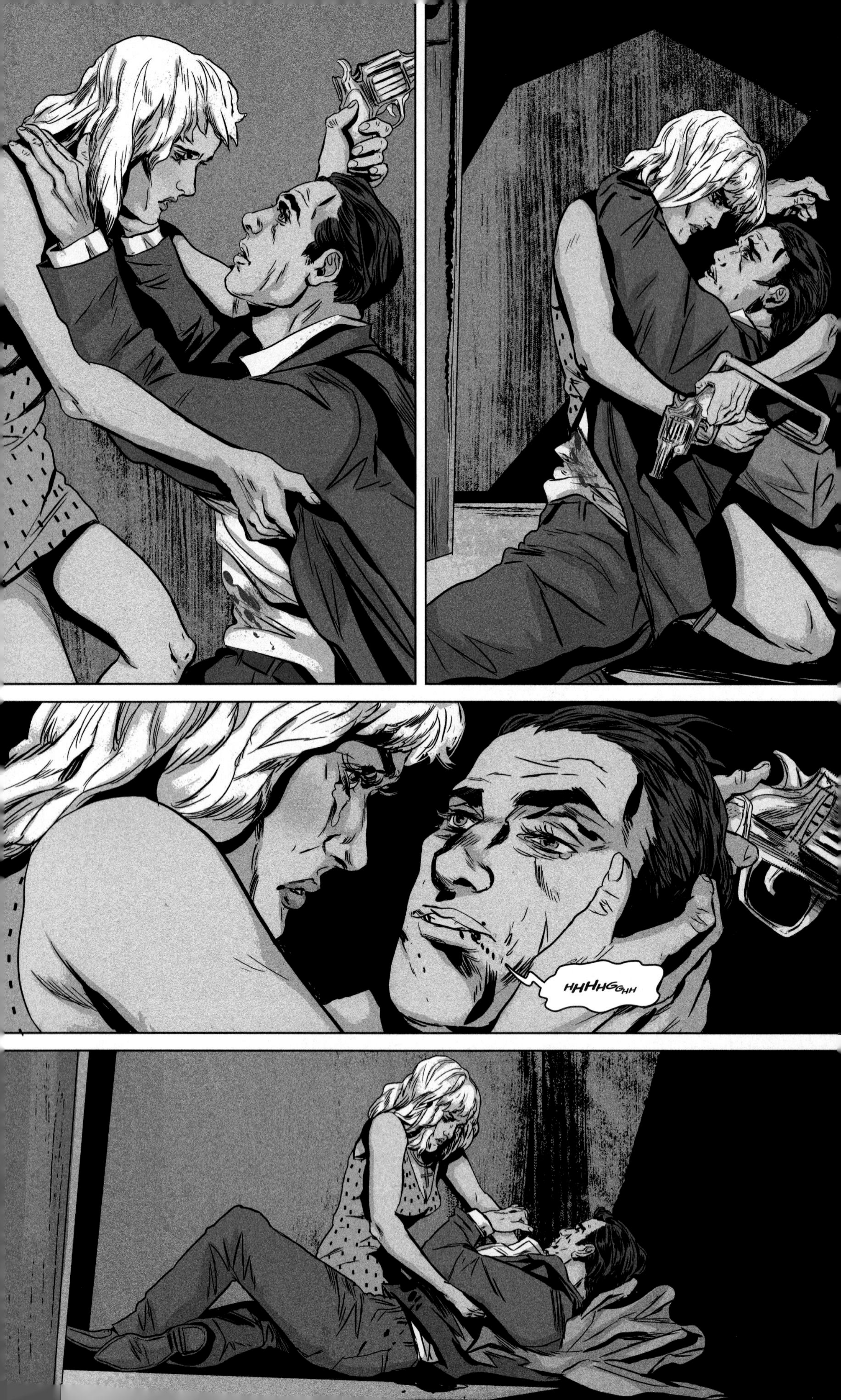
HHHHGGHH

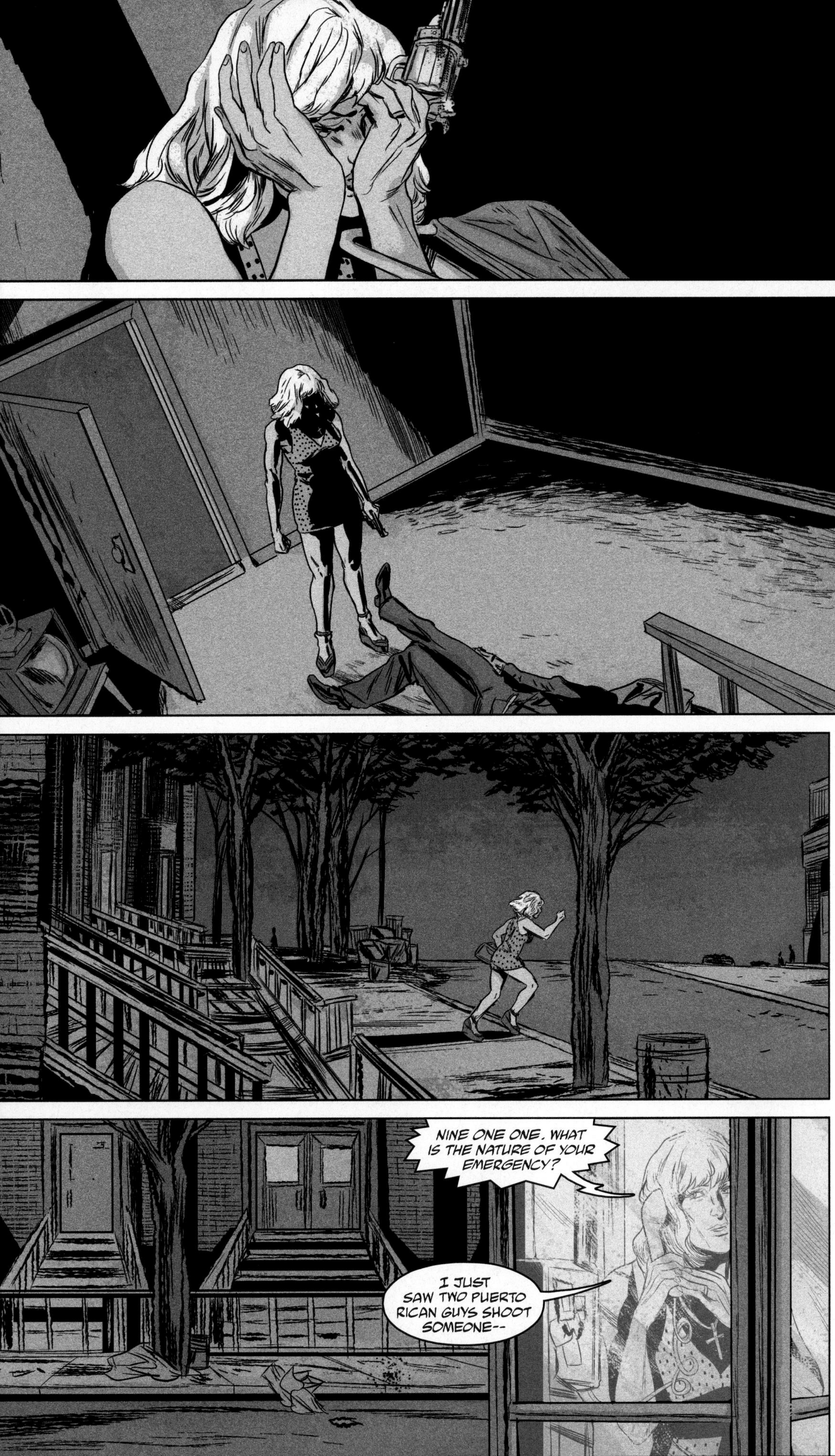
NINE ONE ONE. WHAT IS THE NATURE OF YOUR EMERGENCY?
I JUST SAW TWO PUERTO RICAN GUYS SHOOT SOMEONE--

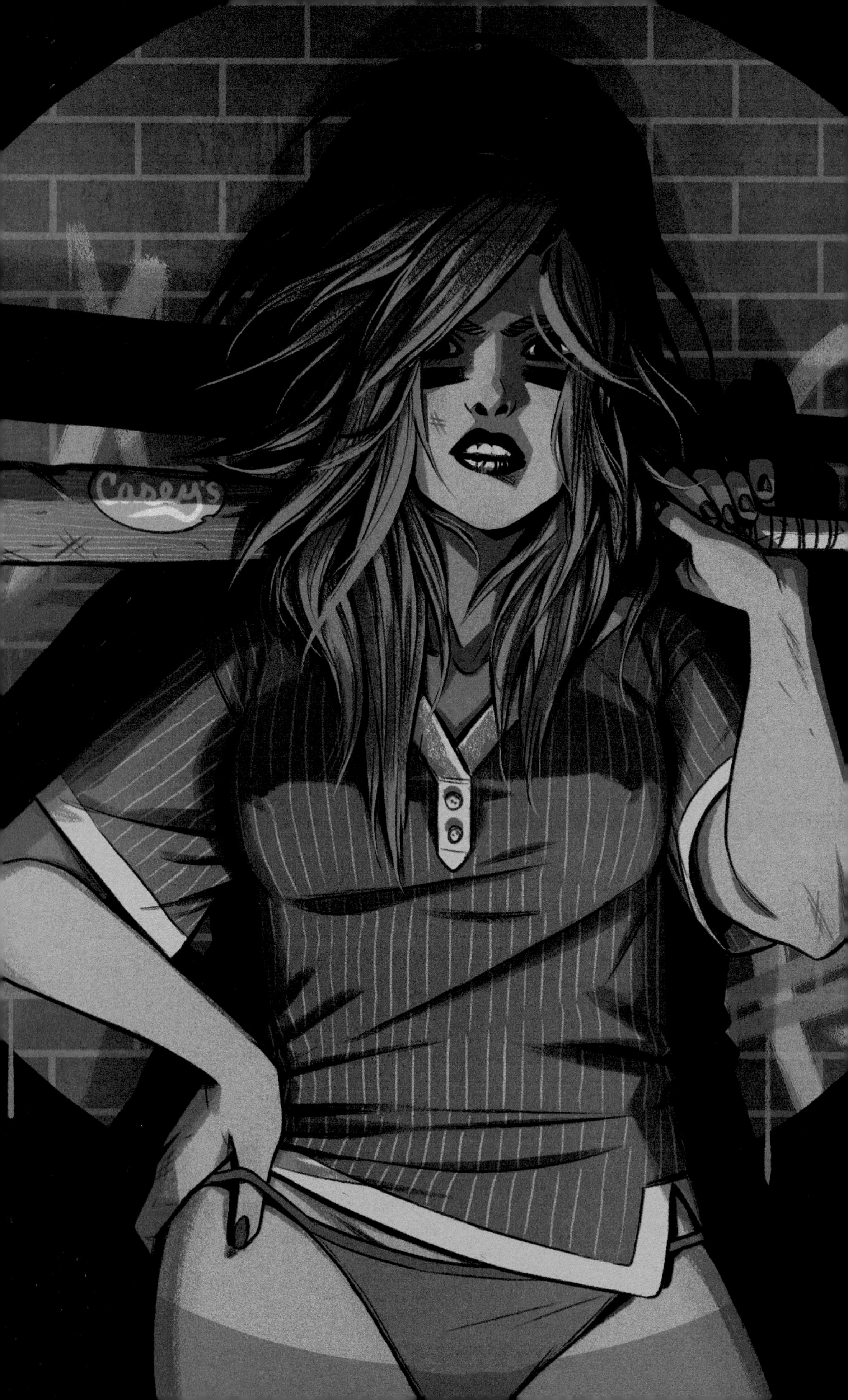
Casey's

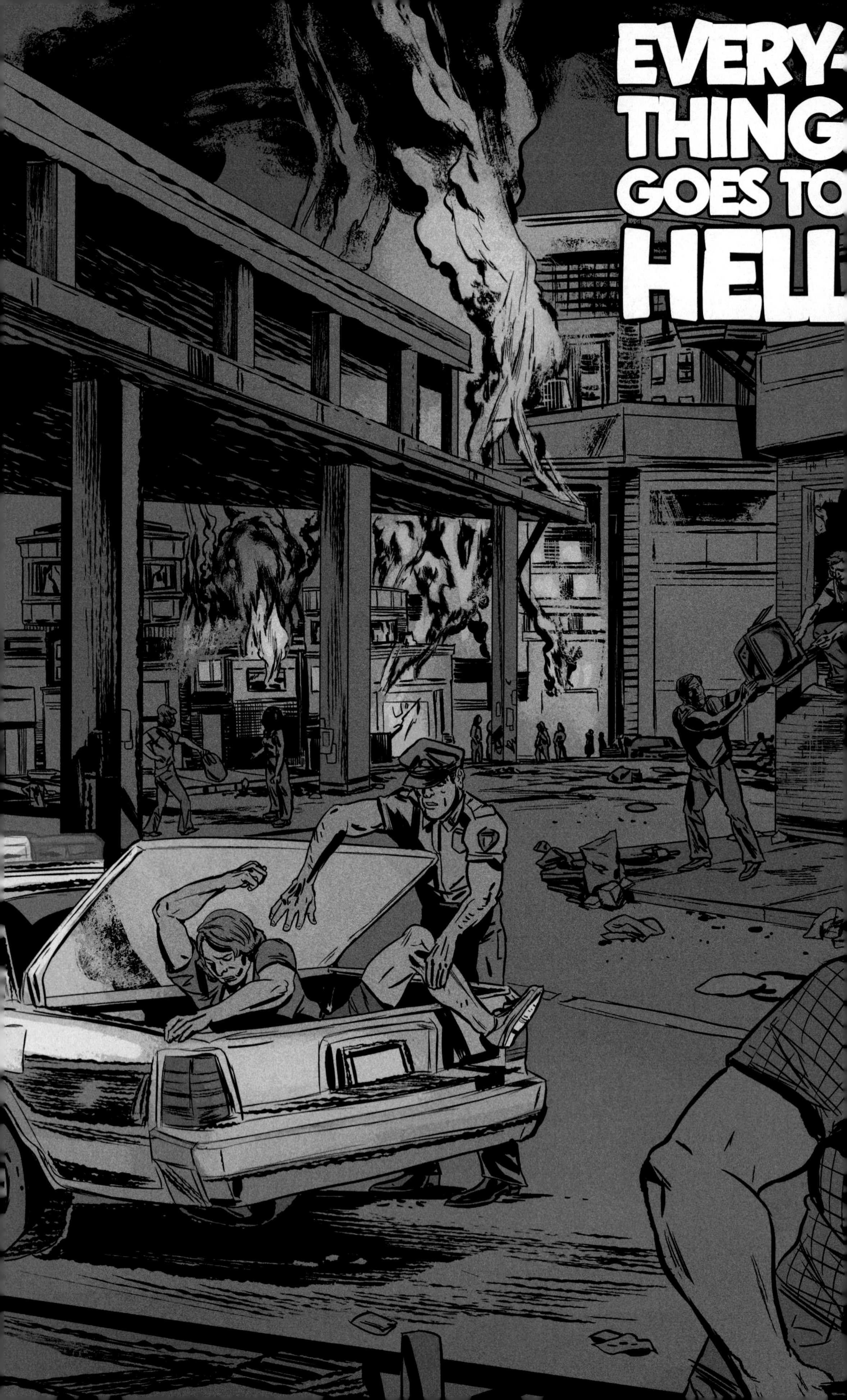
EVERY-
THING
GOES TO
HELL

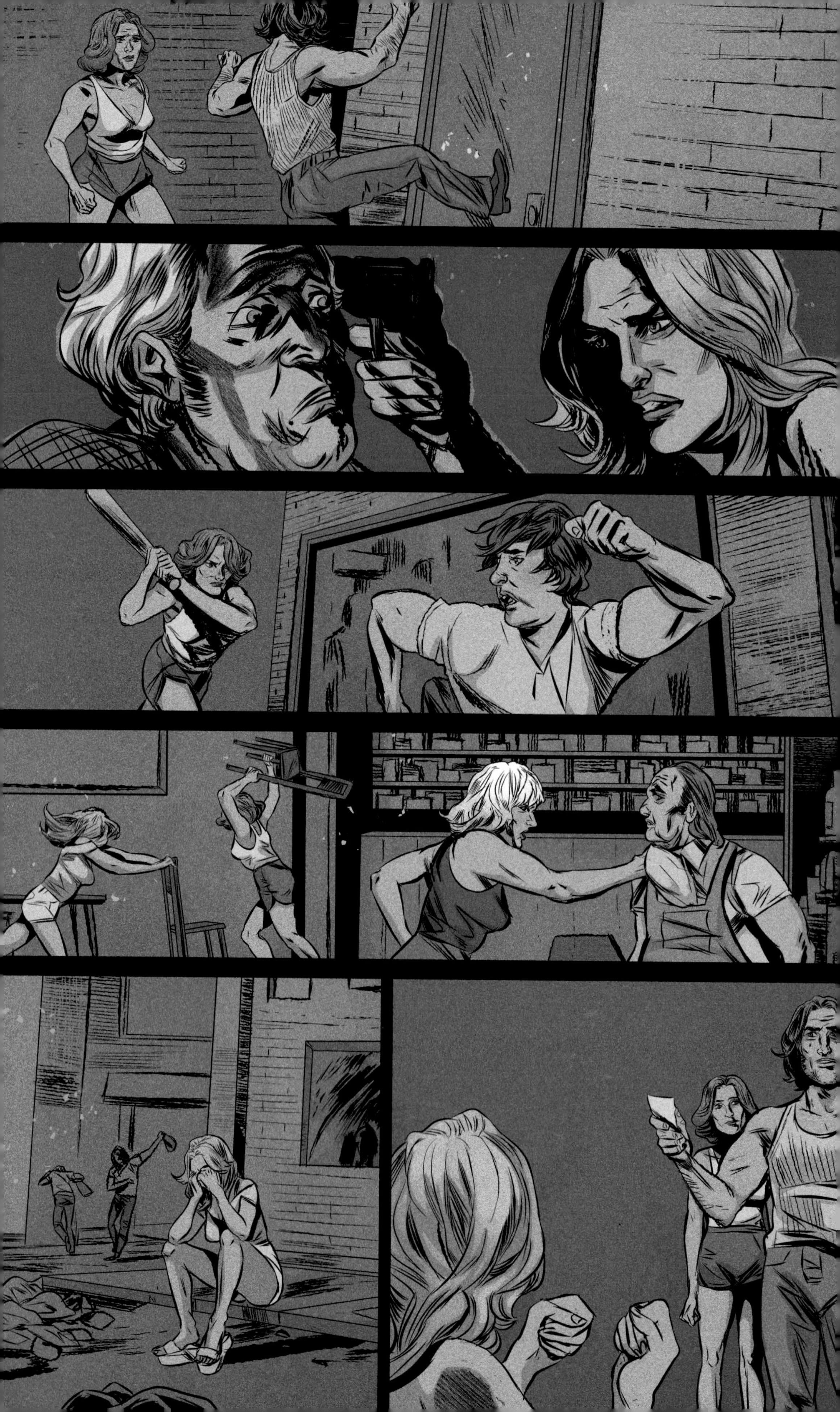

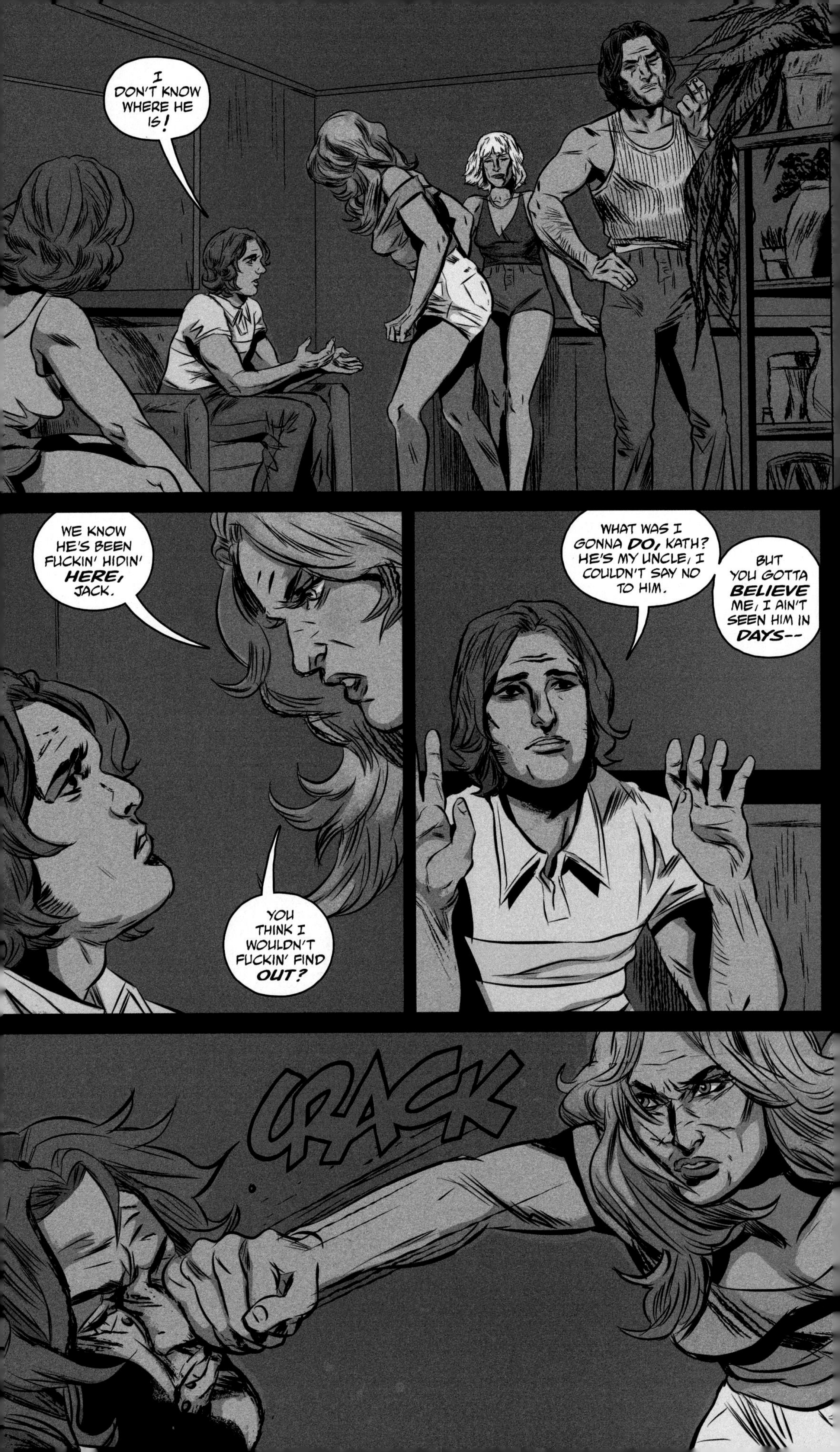
I DON'T KNOW WHERE HE IS!
WE KNOW HE'S BEEN FUCKIN' HIDIN' HERE, JACK.
YOU THINK I WOULDN'T FUCKIN' FIND OUT?
WHAT WAS I GONNA DO, KATH? HE'S MY UNCLE, I COULDN'T SAY NO TO HIM.
BUT YOU GOTTA BELIEVE ME, I AIN'T SEEN HIM IN DAYS--
CRACK

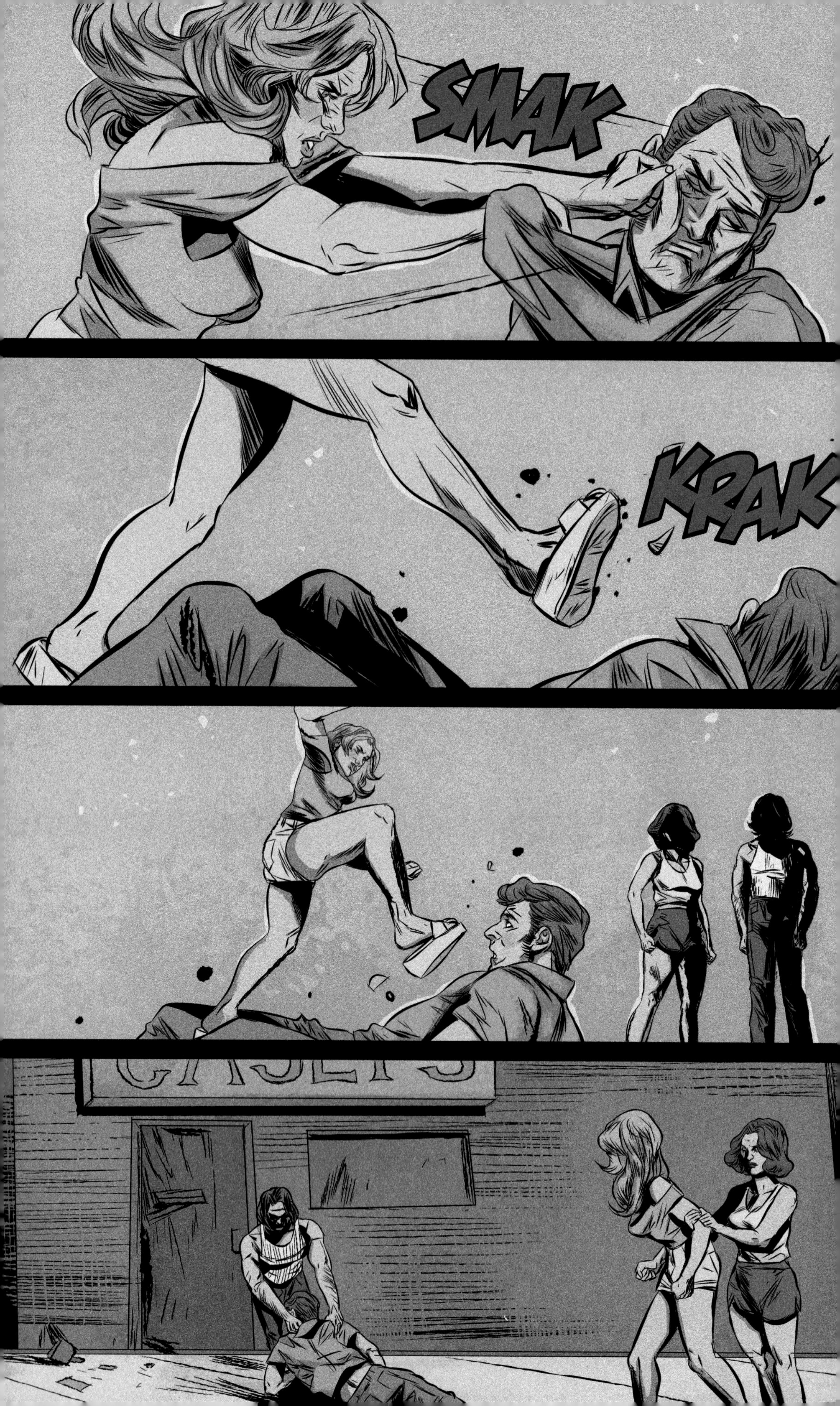
SMAK
KRAK

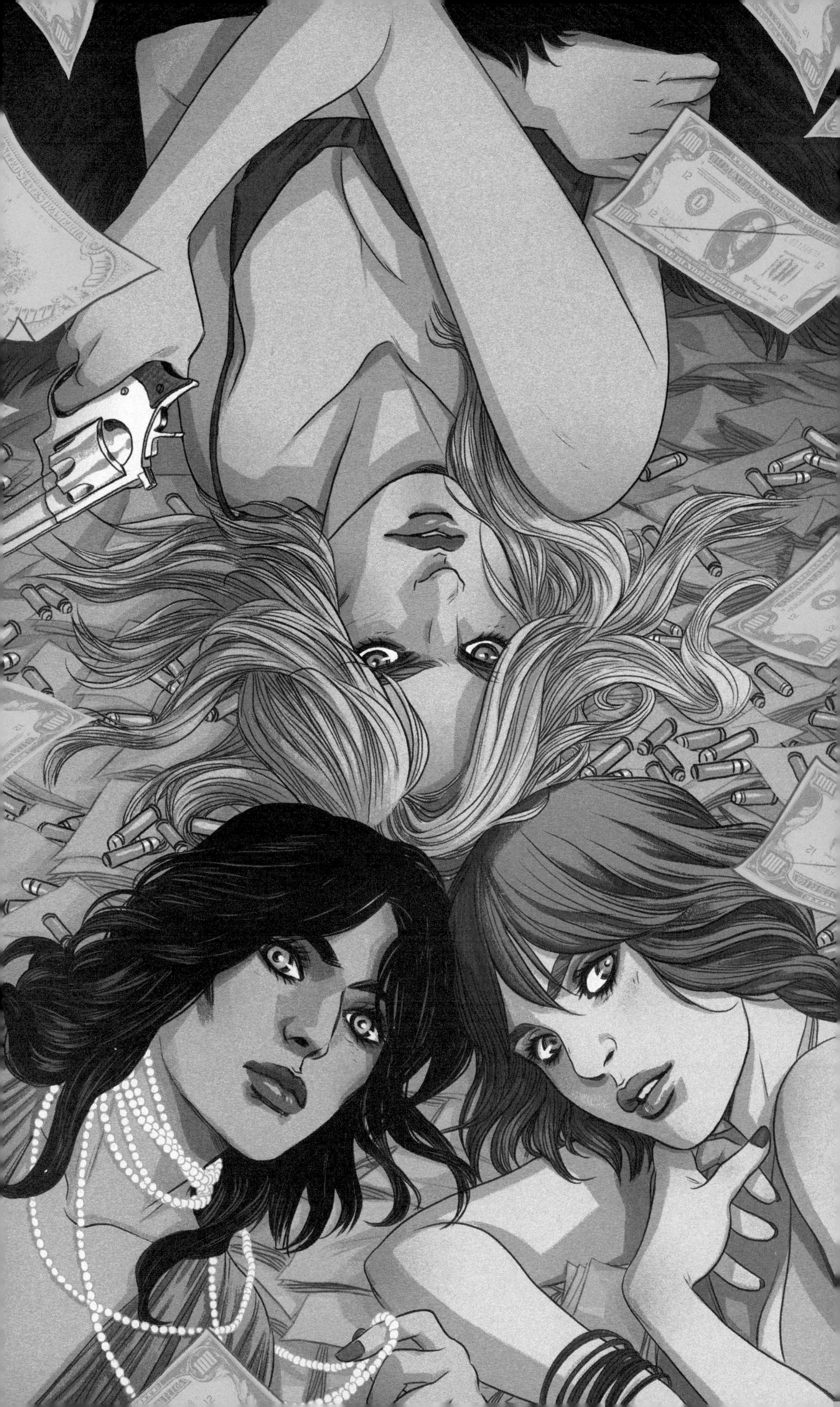

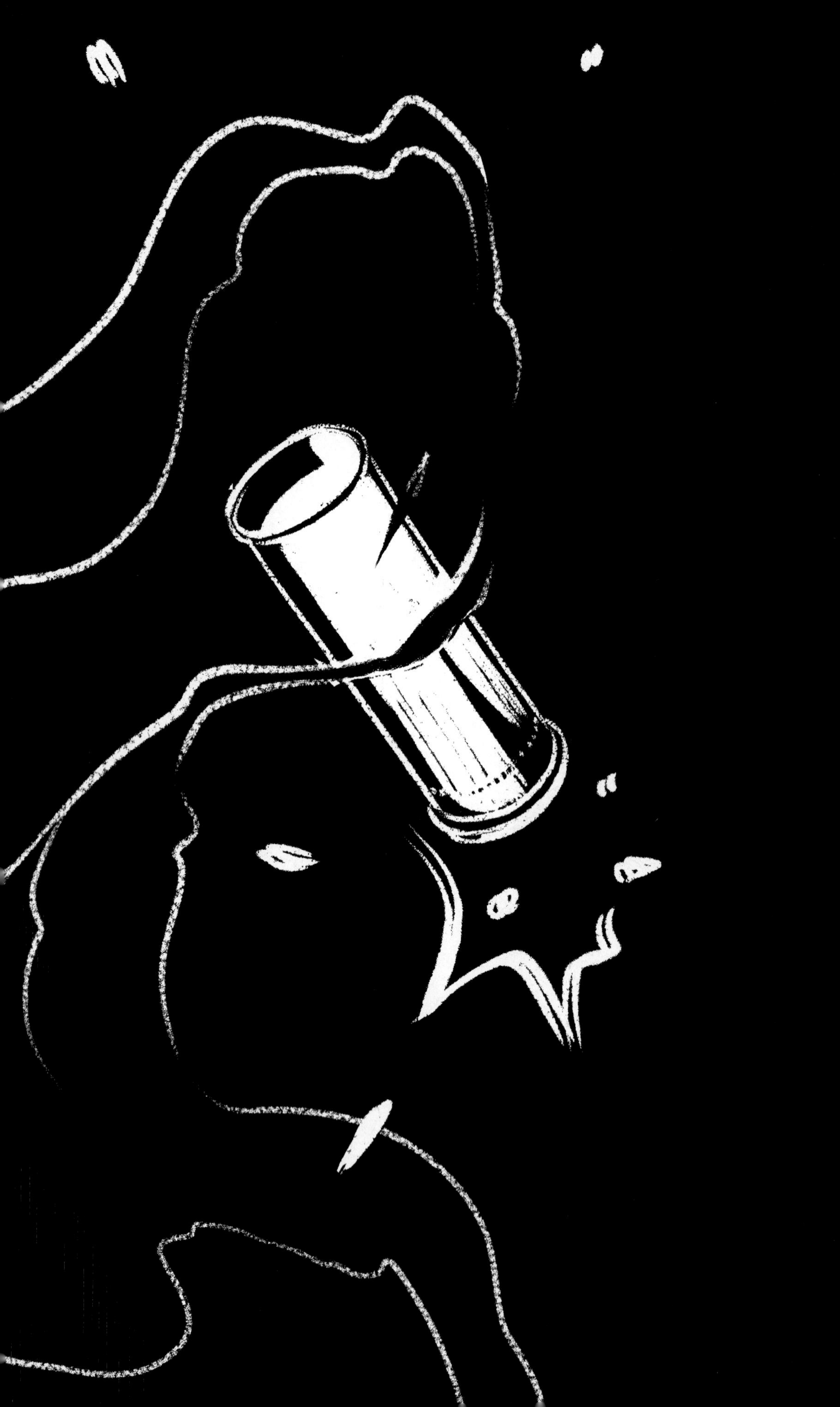

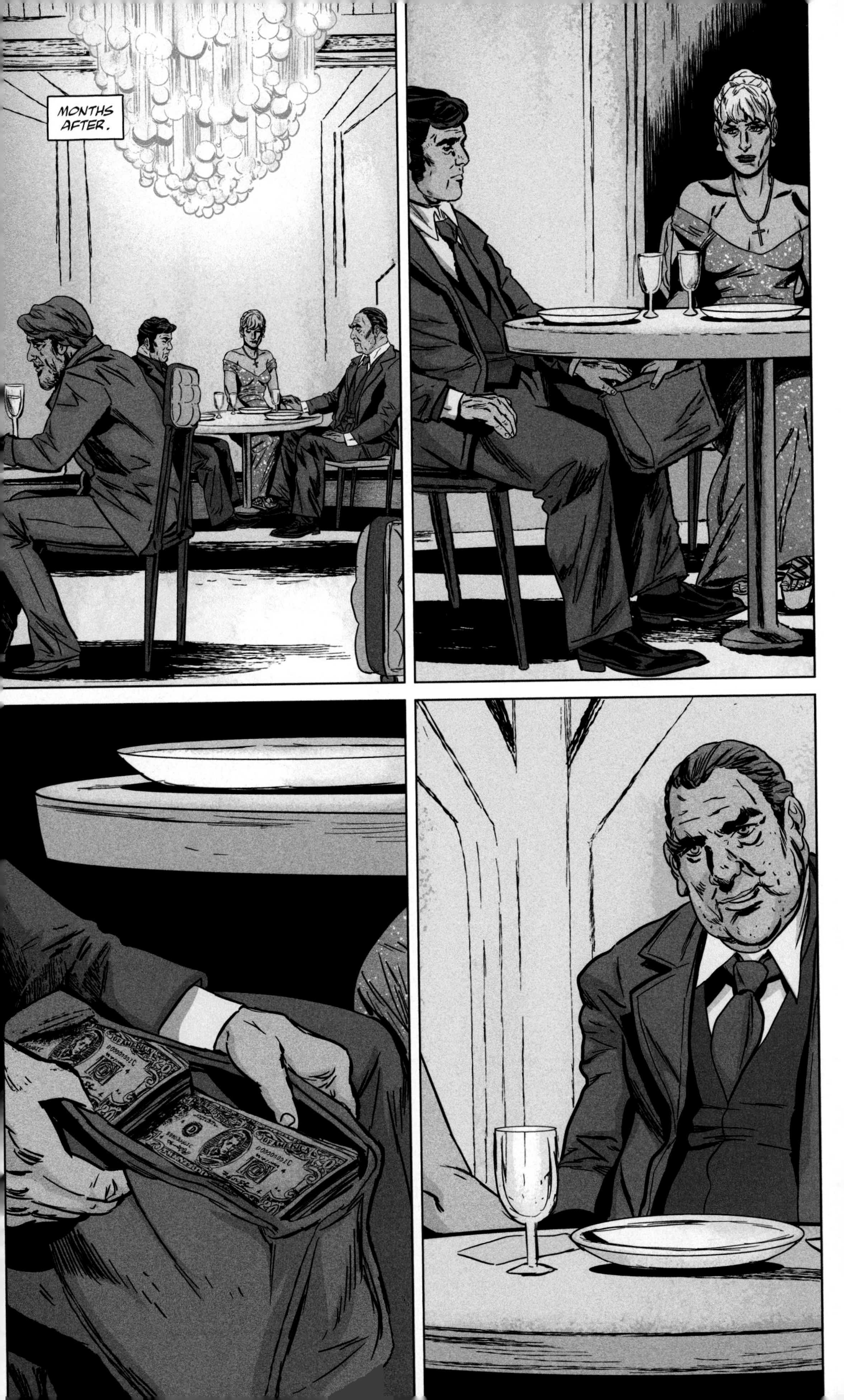
MONTHS AFTER.

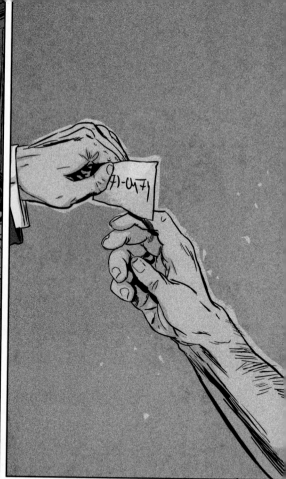

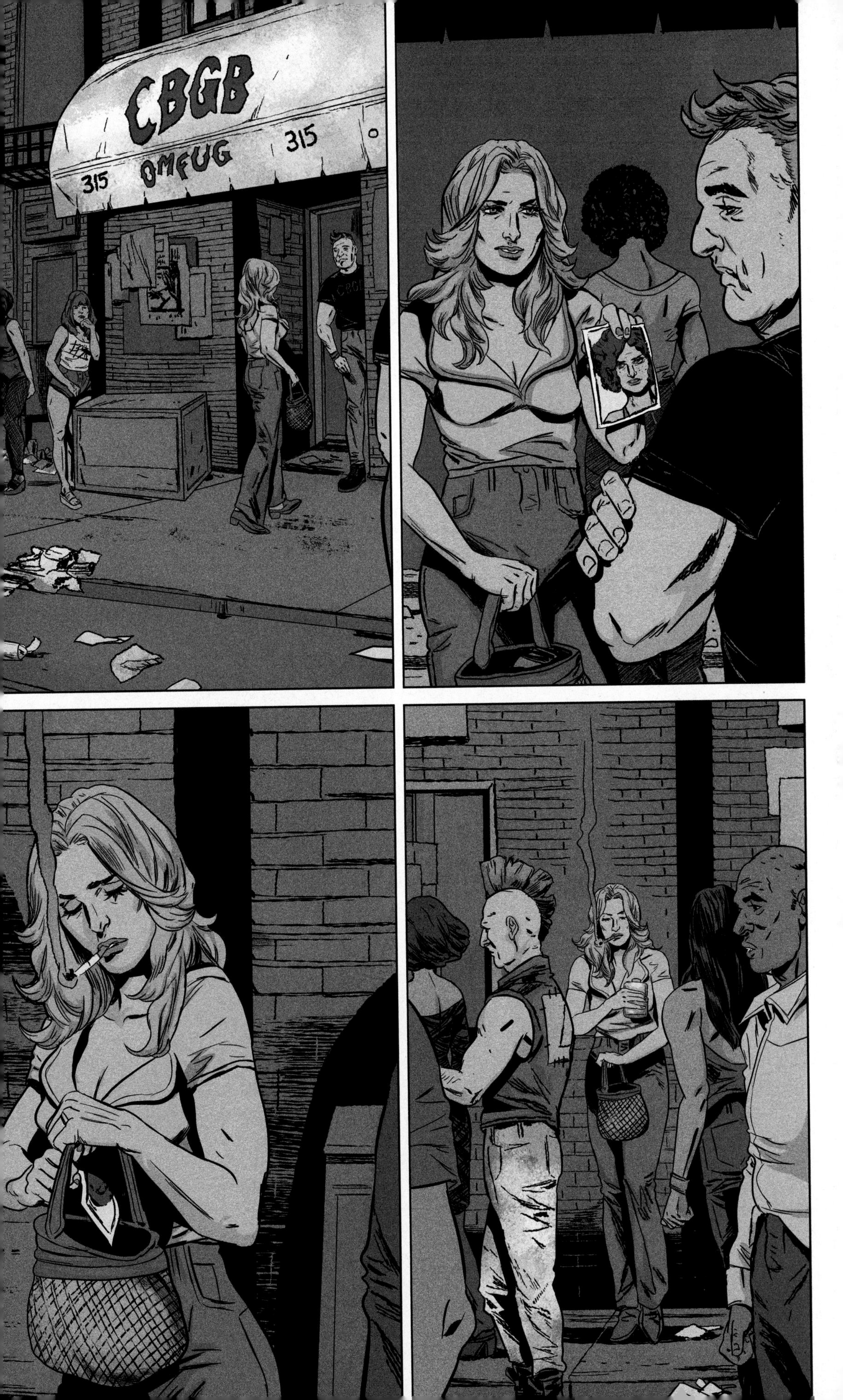
CBGB
315
OMFUG
315
CBGB

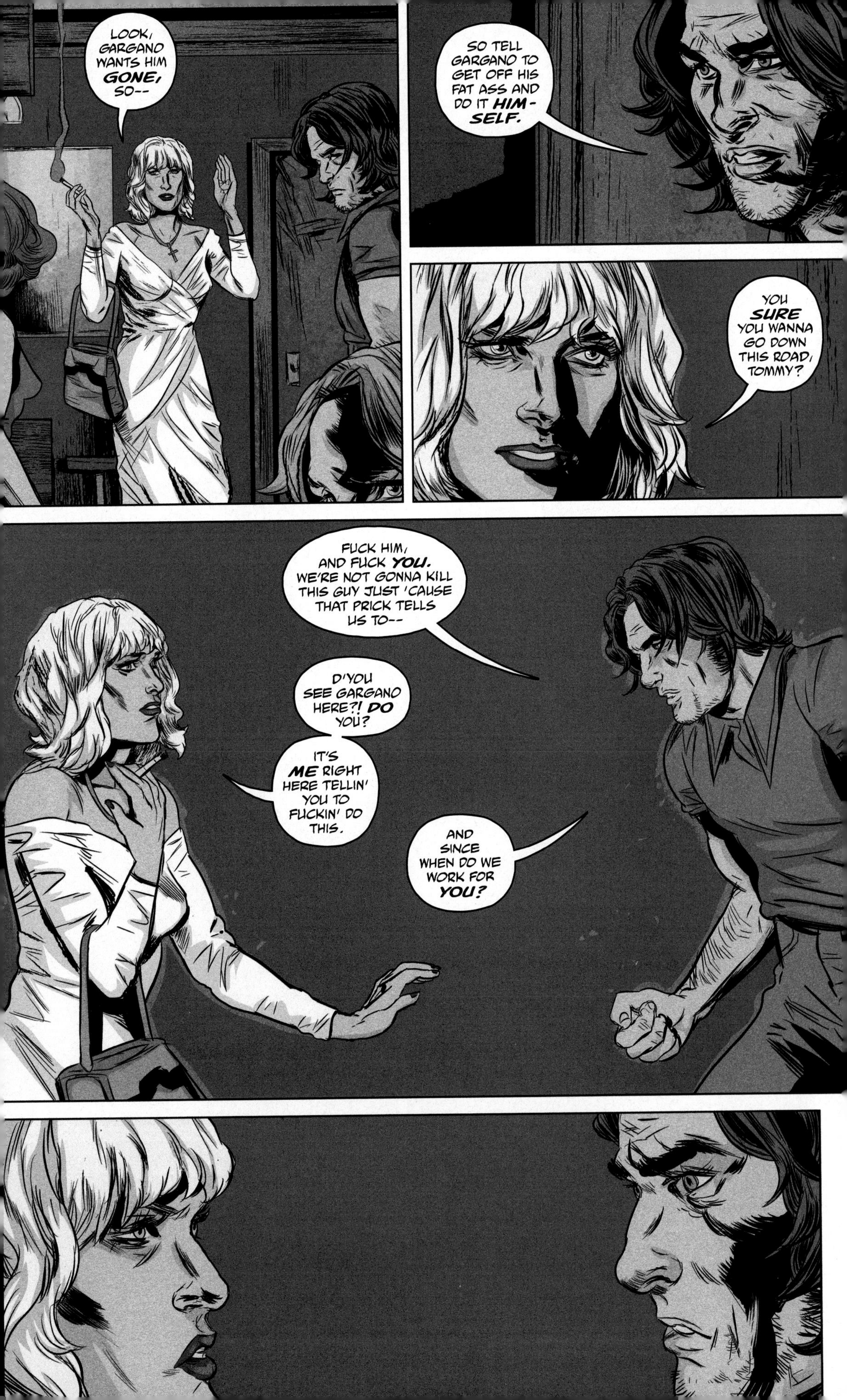
LOOK, GARGANO WANTS HIM GONE, SO--
SO TELL GARGANO TO GET OFF HIS FAT ASS AND DO IT HIM-SELF.
YOU SURE YOU WANNA GO DOWN THIS ROAD, TOMMY?
FUCK HIM, AND FUCK YOU. WE'RE NOT GONNA KILL THIS GUY JUST 'CAUSE THAT PRICK TELLS US TO--
D'YOU SEE GARGANO HERE?! DO YOU?
IT'S ME RIGHT HERE TELLIN' YOU TO FUCKIN' DO THIS.
AND SINCE WHEN DO WE WORK FOR YOU?

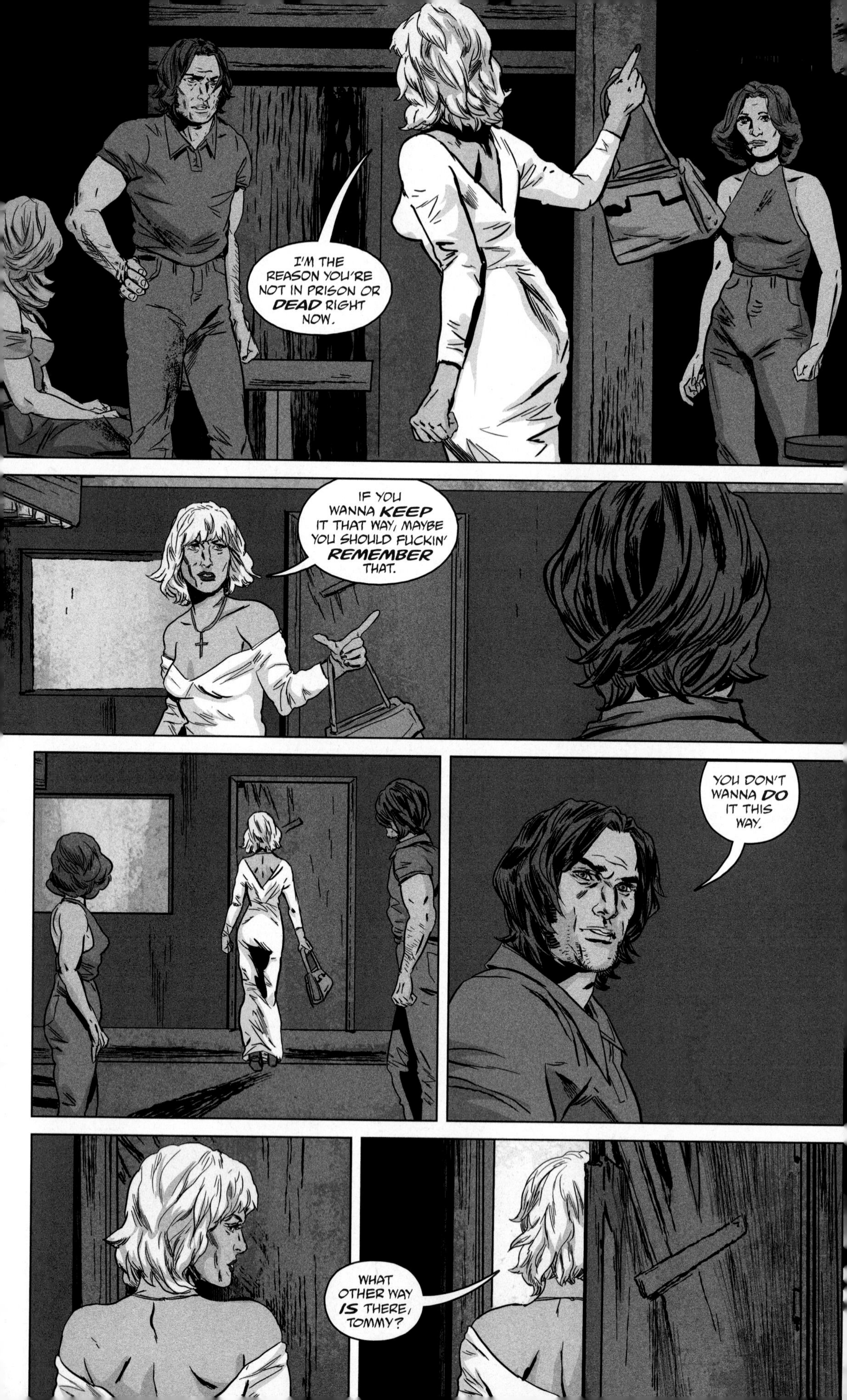
I'M THE REASON YOU'RE NOT IN PRISON OR DEAD RIGHT NOW.
IF YOU WANNA KEEP IT THAT WAY, MAYBE YOU SHOULD FUCKIN' REMEMBER THAT.
YOU DON'T WANNA DO IT THIS WAY.
WHAT OTHER WAY IS THERE, TOMMY?

FOR CHRIST'S SAKE, CAN'T YOU *SAY* SOMETHIN' TO HER?

WE DON'T TALK MUCH THESE DAYS.

THERE'S SOMETHIN' YOU'VE GOTTA *KNOW*, KATH.

ME AND TOMMY, WE'VE BEEN TALKIN' AND...WE'RE LEAVIN' *TOWN* TOMORROW.

WHAT'RE YOU *TALKIN'* ABOUT?

WE CAN'T PUT *UP* WITH THIS CRAP NO MORE.

I KNOW SHE'S BEEN A *PRICK* LATELY, BUT SHE'S STILL--

YOU'VE BEEN SO WRAPPED UP WITH THIS SHIT WITH HEATHER GOIN' MISSIN' THAT YOU AIN'T BEEN PAYIN' ATTENTION.

DON'T YOU THINK SOMETHIN' STINKS ABOUT *EVERYTHIN'* THAT'S BEEN GOIN' ON?

TONY GETTIN' *WHACKED* THE SAME NIGHT SHE KILLED *JOHNNY?* FRANKY MYSTERIOUSLY DYIN' JUST BEFORE HE COULD TALK TO THE *COPS?*

WHAT YOU SAYIN'? *RAVEN* KILLED TONY AND FRANKY?

WE'RE SAYIN' THAT SHE AIN'T TELLIN' US *EVERYTHIN'* ABOUT HOW SHE SUDDENLY BECAME OUR FUCKIN' *BOSS.*

SHE DIDN'T KILL *FRANKY*. SHE DIDN'T HAVE THE *REACH* BACK THEN.

BUT THE NIGHT'VE THE BLACKOUT. SHE SAID SOMETHIN' TO ME, AND I DIDN'T THINK NOTHIN' OF IT THEN, BUT...YEAH, I THINK SHE KILLED *TONY*.

BUT FRANKY... WHO DO WE KNOW WHO *DOES* HAVE THAT KINDA REACH?

GARGANO...

MAYBE...MAYBE WE'RE JUST BEIN' PARANOID. BUT SOMETHIN'S FUCKIN' GOIN' ON HERE.

AND WE DON'T WANT *NO* PART IN ALL THIS BACKSTABBIN' BULLSHIT.

GEORGE AND JAMES JUNIOR ARE STILL STAYIN' WITH *FAMILY*, RIGHT?

YEAH...

YOU SHOULD COME WITH US, KATH. YOU DON'T NEED TO BE SUCKED INTO THIS MESS.

FUCK. EVEN IF IT'S ALL *TRUE*, I CAN'T GO 'TIL I'VE FOUND *HEATHER*.

C'MON, KATH, SHE PROBABLY SKIPPED TOWN 'CAUSE OF ALL THE SHIT WITH *JIMMY*.

SHE WOULDN'T'VE LEFT WITHOUT TELLIN' *ME*...

OKAY, IF YOU THINK YOU CAN, *YOU* GO FIND HER.

BUT LOOK AFTER YOURSELF, KATH--

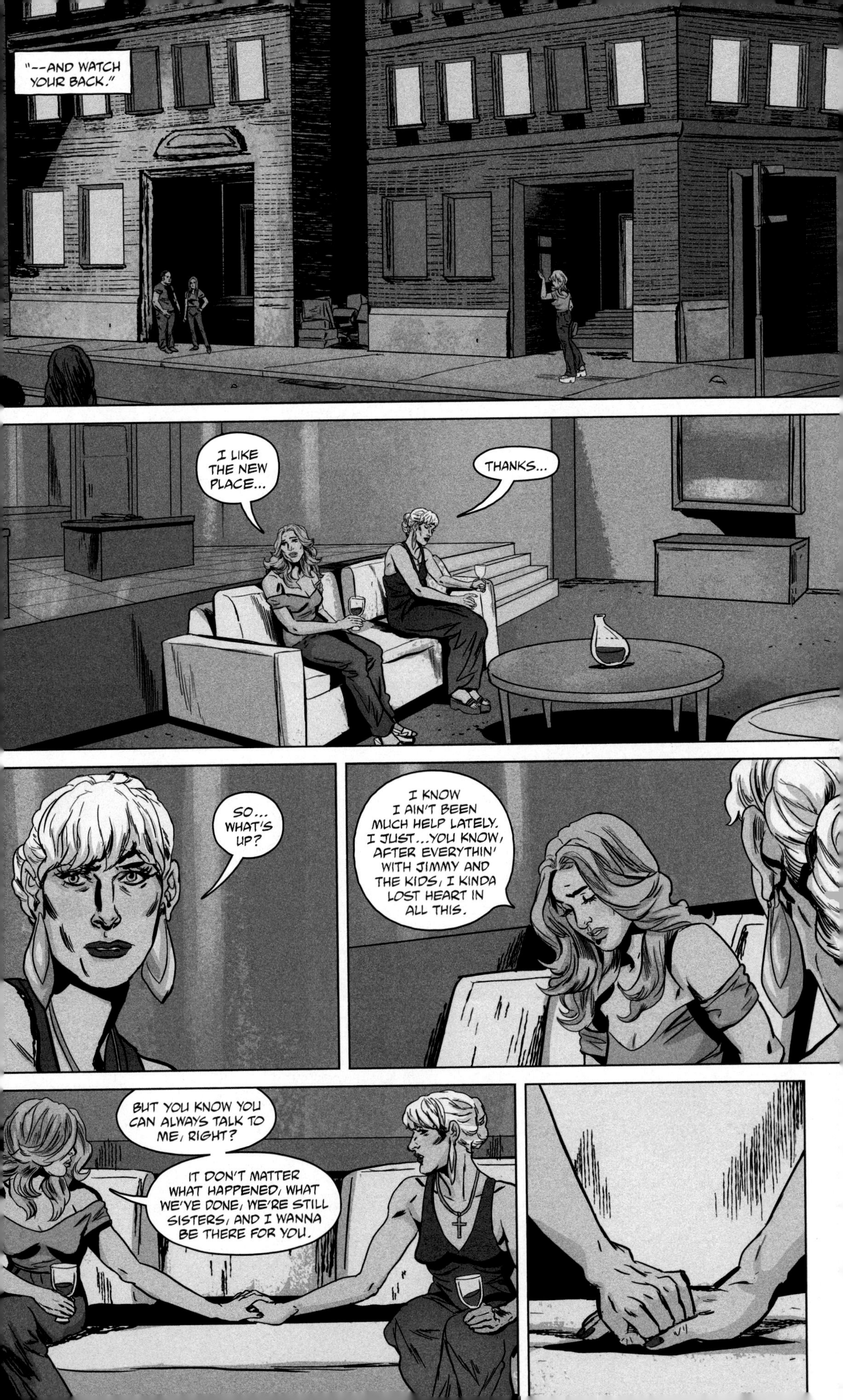
"--AND WATCH YOUR BACK."
I LIKE THE NEW PLACE...
THANKS...
SO... WHAT'S UP?
I KNOW I AIN'T BEEN MUCH HELP LATELY. I JUST...YOU KNOW, AFTER EVERYTHIN' WITH JIMMY AND THE KIDS, I KINDA LOST HEART IN ALL THIS.
BUT YOU KNOW YOU CAN ALWAYS TALK TO ME, RIGHT?
IT DON'T MATTER WHAT HAPPENED, WHAT WE'VE DONE, WE'RE STILL SISTERS, AND I WANNA BE THERE FOR YOU.

YOU KILLED TONY, DIDN'T YOU...?

FUCK...

HOW D'YOU KNOW?

JESUS, RAVEN. WHY'D YOU *DO* IT?

IT'S LIKE TOMMY SAID BACK BEFORE OUR MEET WITH GARGANO, THESE ITALIANS...

THEY ALL TALK ABOUT HONOR AND THEIR CODE, BUT THEY'RE ALWAYS FUCKIN' EACH OTHER *OVER.*

FUCK...I DID IT TO PROTECT THE CREW, KATH. TO PROTECT *US.*

WHY THE FUCK DIDN'T YOU *TELL* ME?!

YOU EVER *KILLED* ANYONE? SOMEONE YOU REALLY *CARED* ABOUT?

IT AIN'T SOMETHIN' YOU EVER WANNA *TALK* ABOUT.

WHY DIDN'T YOU KILL *FRANKY?*

WHAT?

YOU SAID YOU WANTED TO TALK, SO LET'S TALK.

BACK IN THAT ALLEYWAY, WHEN WE FOUND OUT WHO HE *WAS.* WHY DIDN'T YOU *KILL* HIM?

JUST FUCKIN' GET HIM OUTTA THE *WAY,* THERE AND THEN.

I DUNNO. WE WEREN'T REALLY *THINKIN'*, WERE WE? IT ALL JUST *HAPPENED.*

FUCK... MAYBE I JUST COULDN'T BRING MYSELF TO *DO* IT.

I COULDN'T EVEN FINISH OFF *JIMMY* WHEN IT CAME TO IT... *ANGIE* HAD TO FUCKIN' DO IT.

AND THERE WAS *ME,* THINKIN' I WAS SOME BIG-SHOT *GANGSTER.*

YOU KNOW WHAT GARGANO SAID TO ME? HE SAID YOU DIDN'T HAVE THE *HEART* FOR THIS.

REALLY? I GUESS THAT GUINEA FUCK'S SMARTER THAN HE *LOOKS.*

HOW DID WE END UP *HERE?*

WHO THE FUCK KNOWS...

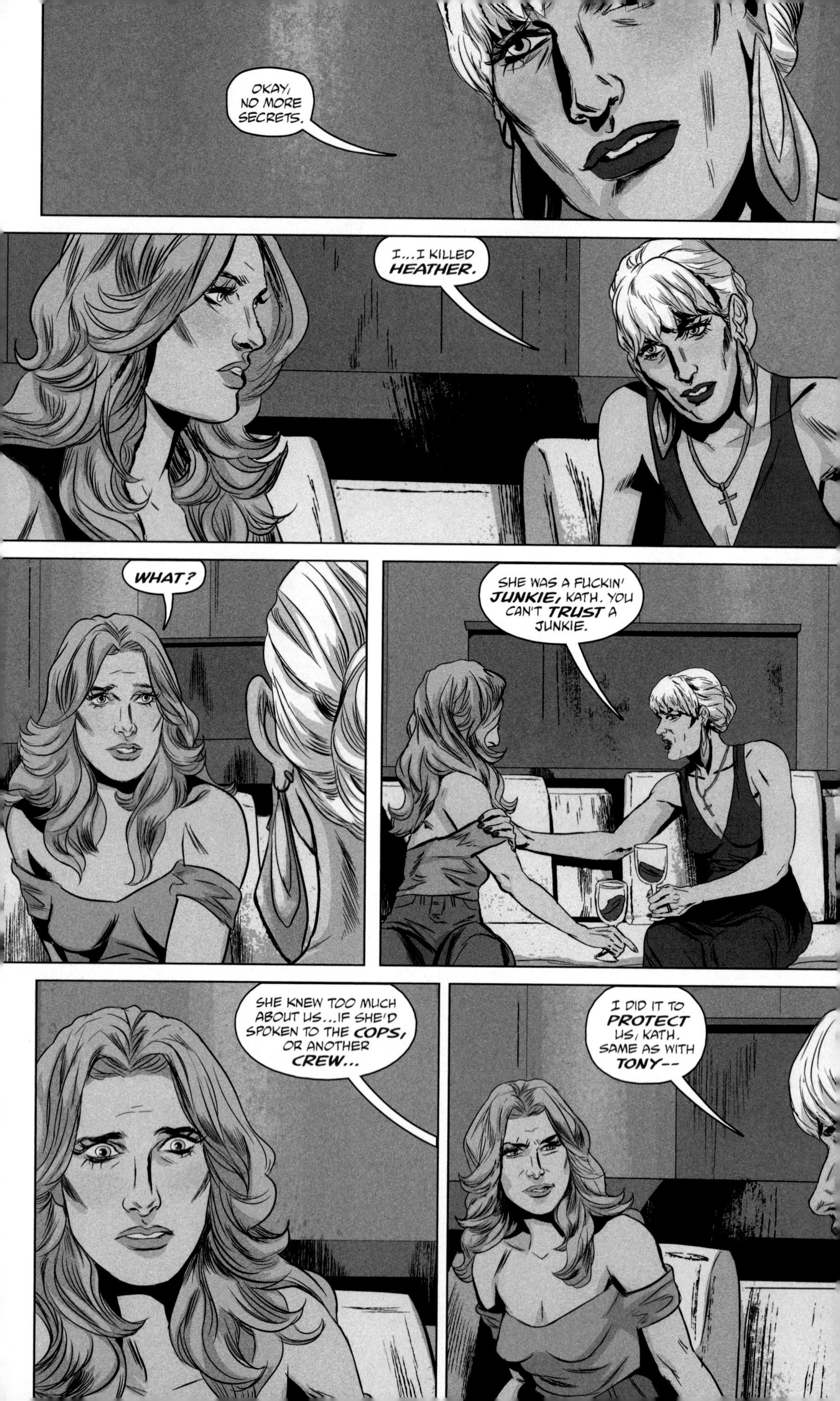
OKAY, NO MORE SECRETS.
I...I KILLED **HEATHER.**
WHAT?
SHE WAS A FUCKIN' **JUNKIE,** KATH. YOU CAN'T **TRUST** A JUNKIE.
SHE KNEW TOO MUCH ABOUT US...IF SHE'D SPOKEN TO THE **COPS,** OR ANOTHER **CREW...**
I DID IT TO **PROTECT** US, KATH. SAME AS WITH **TONY--**

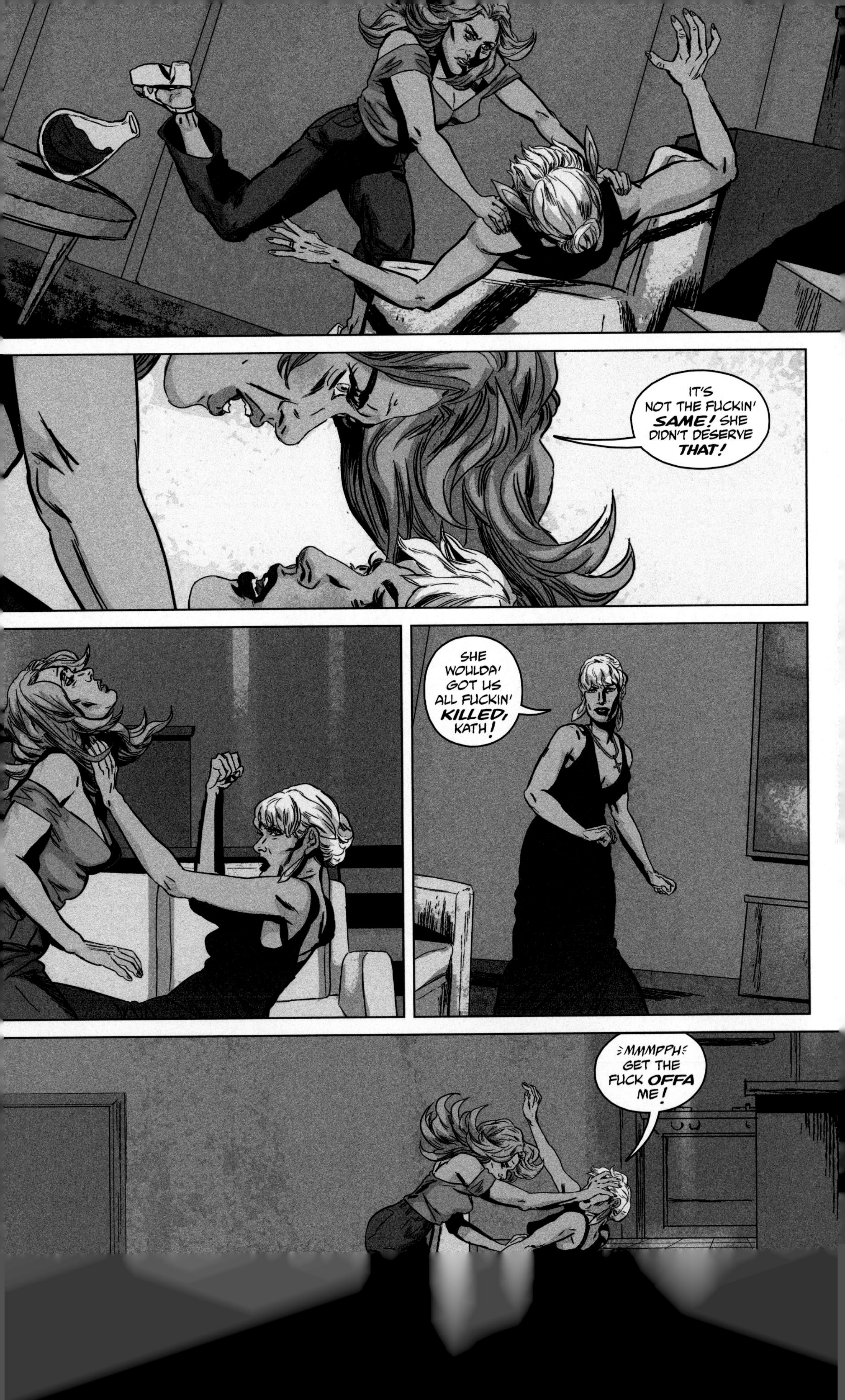
IT'S NOT THE FUCKIN' SAME! SHE DIDN'T DESERVE THAT!
SHE WOULDA' GOT US ALL FUCKIN' KILLED, KATH!
MMMPPH GET THE FUCK OFFA ME!

SMAK

YOU HEARTLESS FUCKIN' *BITCH!*

SOK

IF ONLY DAD WAS ALIVE TODAY, HE WOULDA' BEEN FUCKIN' PROUD TO SEE THE *SCUMBAG* YOU TURNED INTO!

LIKE FATHER, LIKE FUCKIN' *DAUGHTER--*

KLOK

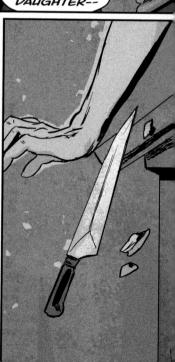

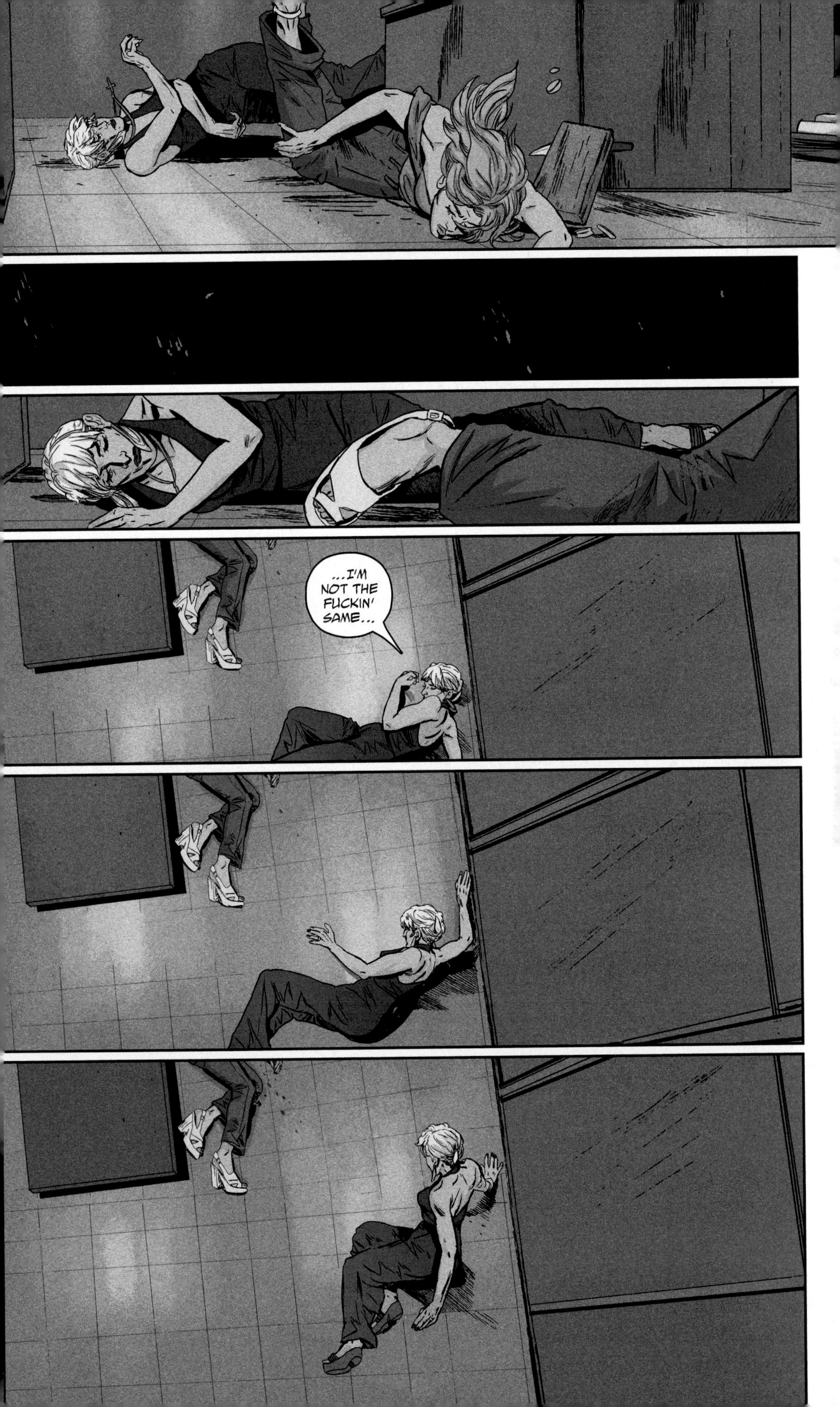
...I'M NOT THE FUCKIN' SAME...

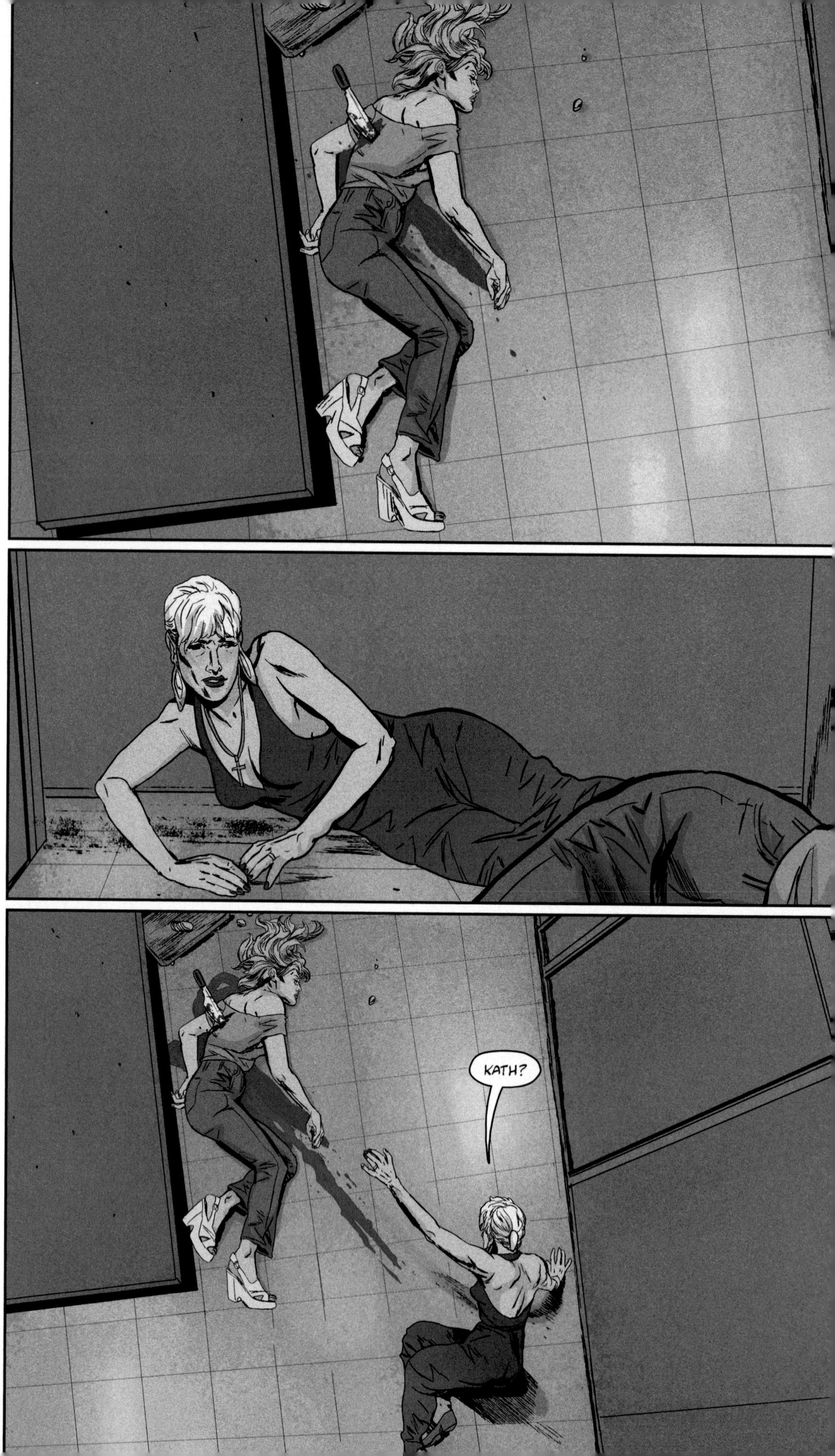
KATH?

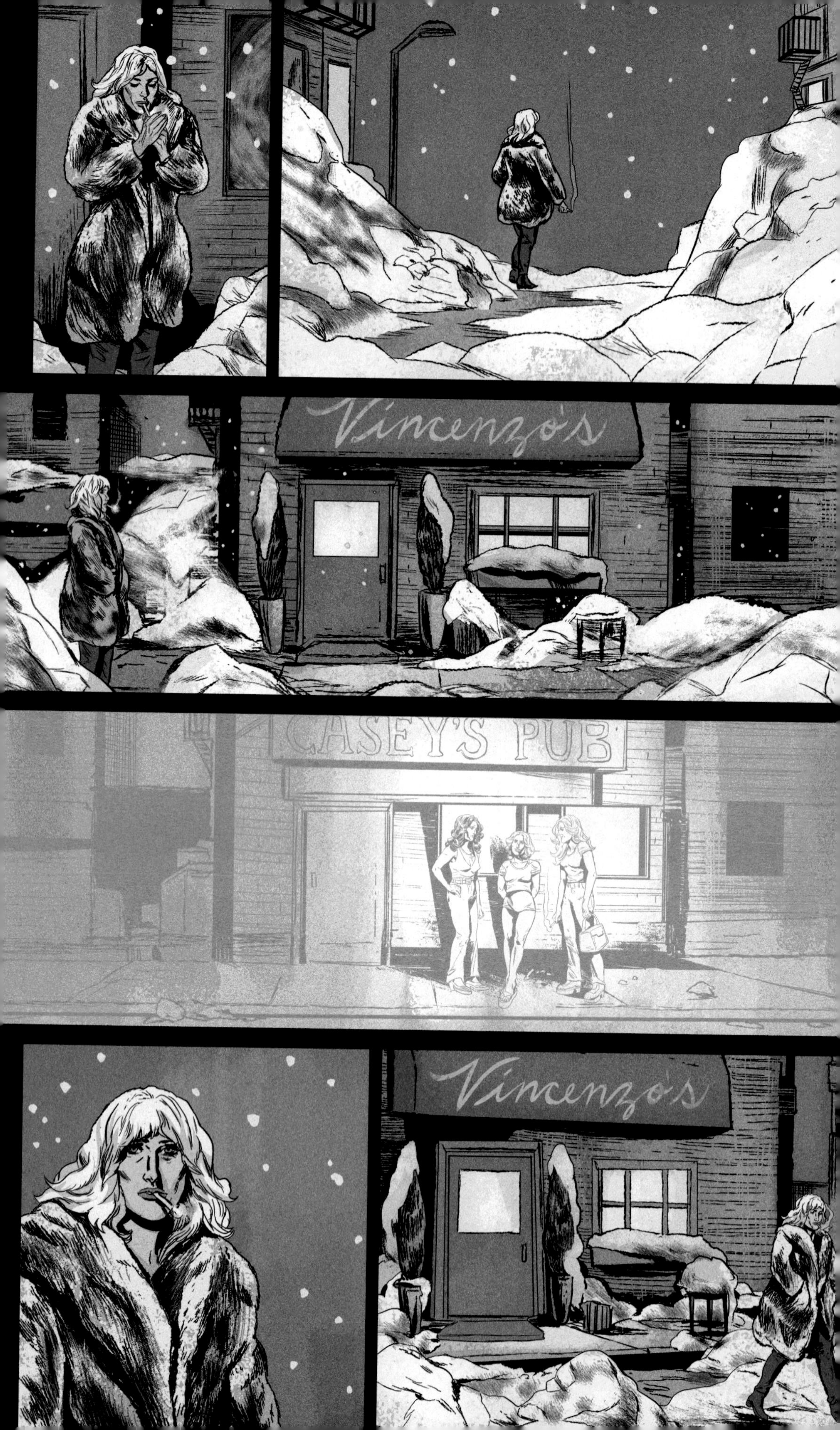
Vincenzo's
CASEY'S PUB
Vincenzo's

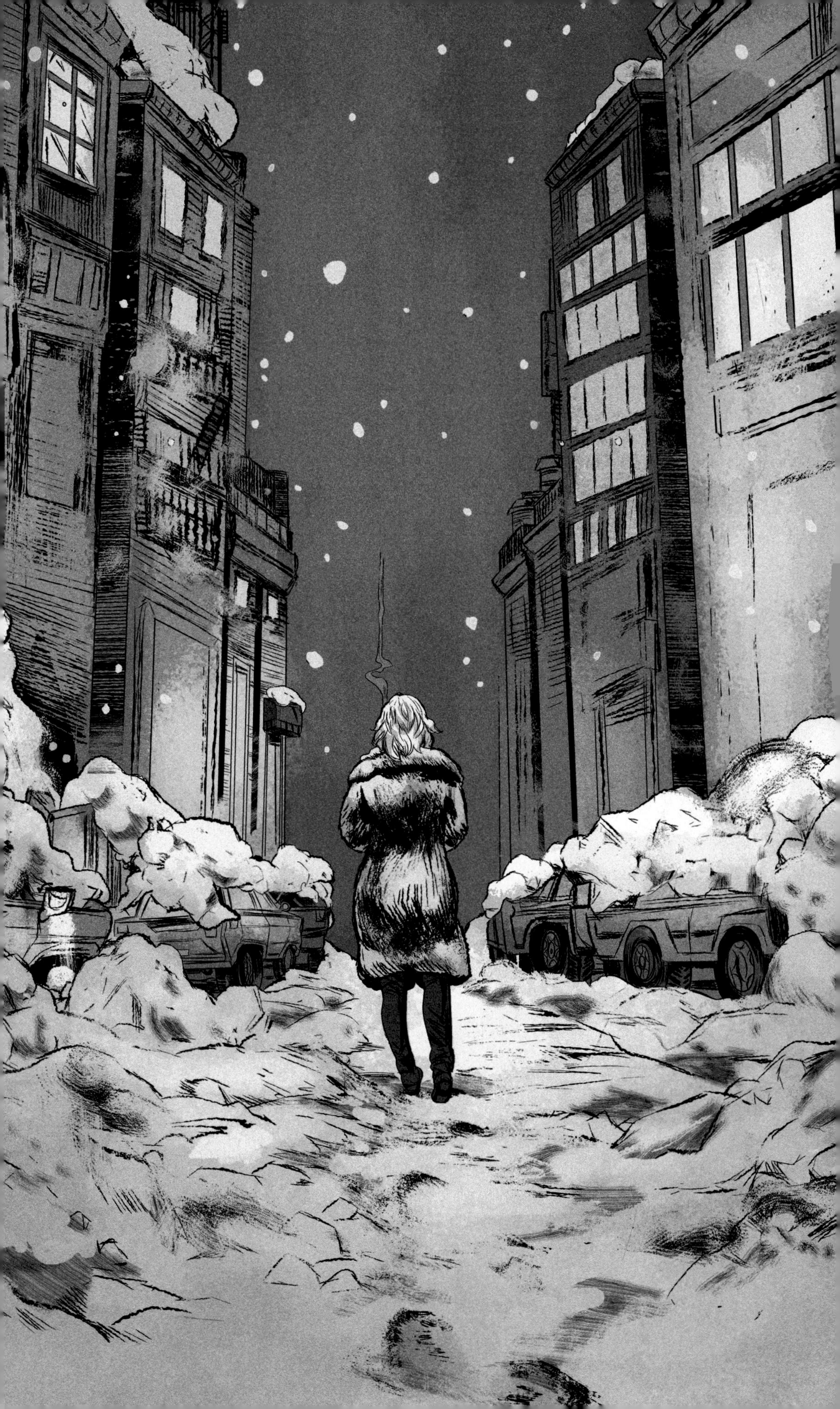

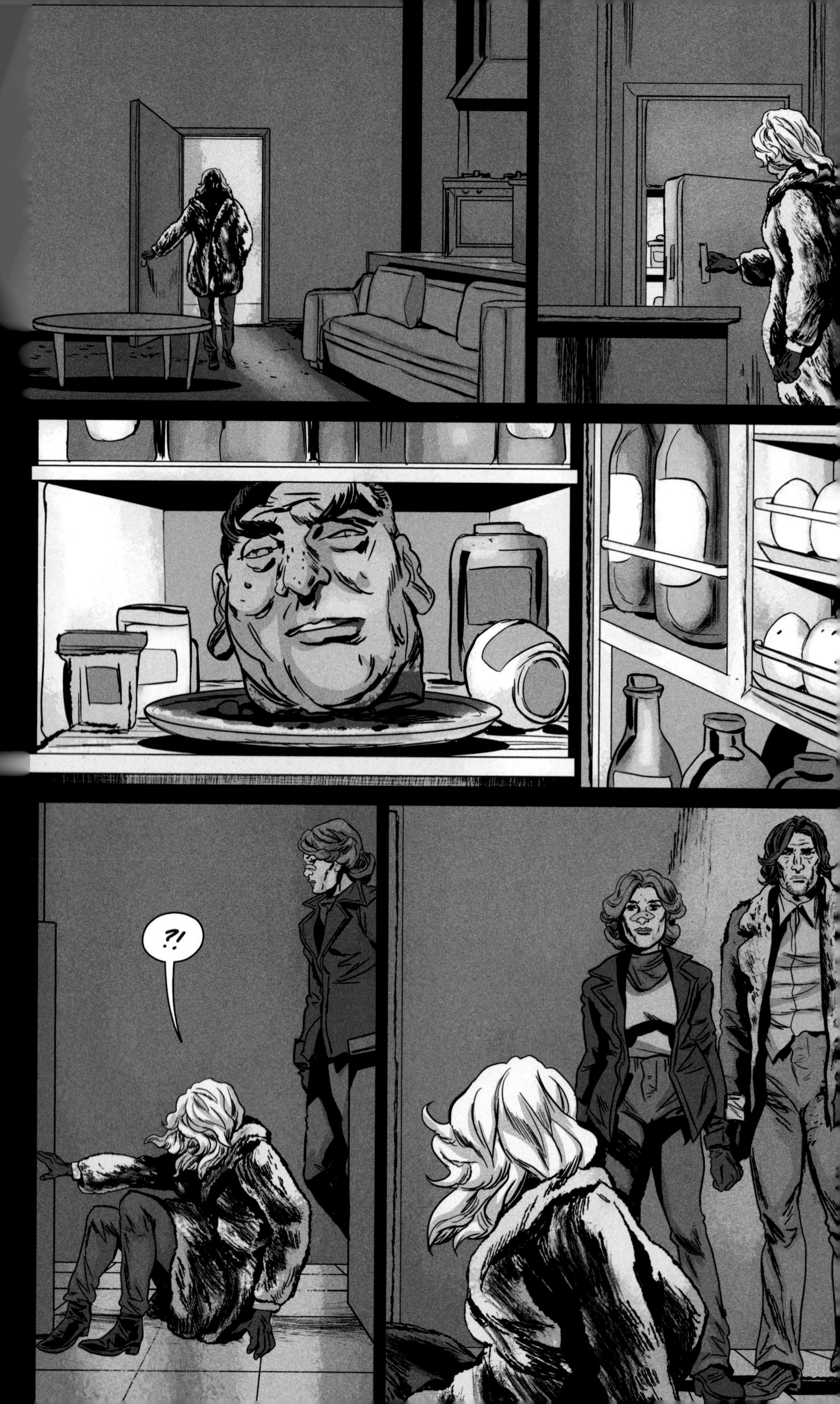
?!

ANGIE, LISTEN, WE CAN FUCKIN' *TALK* ABOUT THIS. YOU DON'T KNOW WHAT HAPPENED. I...

YOU KNOW WHAT? *FUCK* YOU! I DID WHAT *NEEDED* TO BE DONE.

THEY'RE GONNA REMEMBER *MY* NAME AFTER I DIE. NOT MY *DAD'S*, NOT *JOHNNY'S* OR *JIMMY'S*. *MINE*.

I *MADE* MY MARK ON THE FUCKIN' WORLD. I--

OKAY. JUST FUCKIN'--

BAM

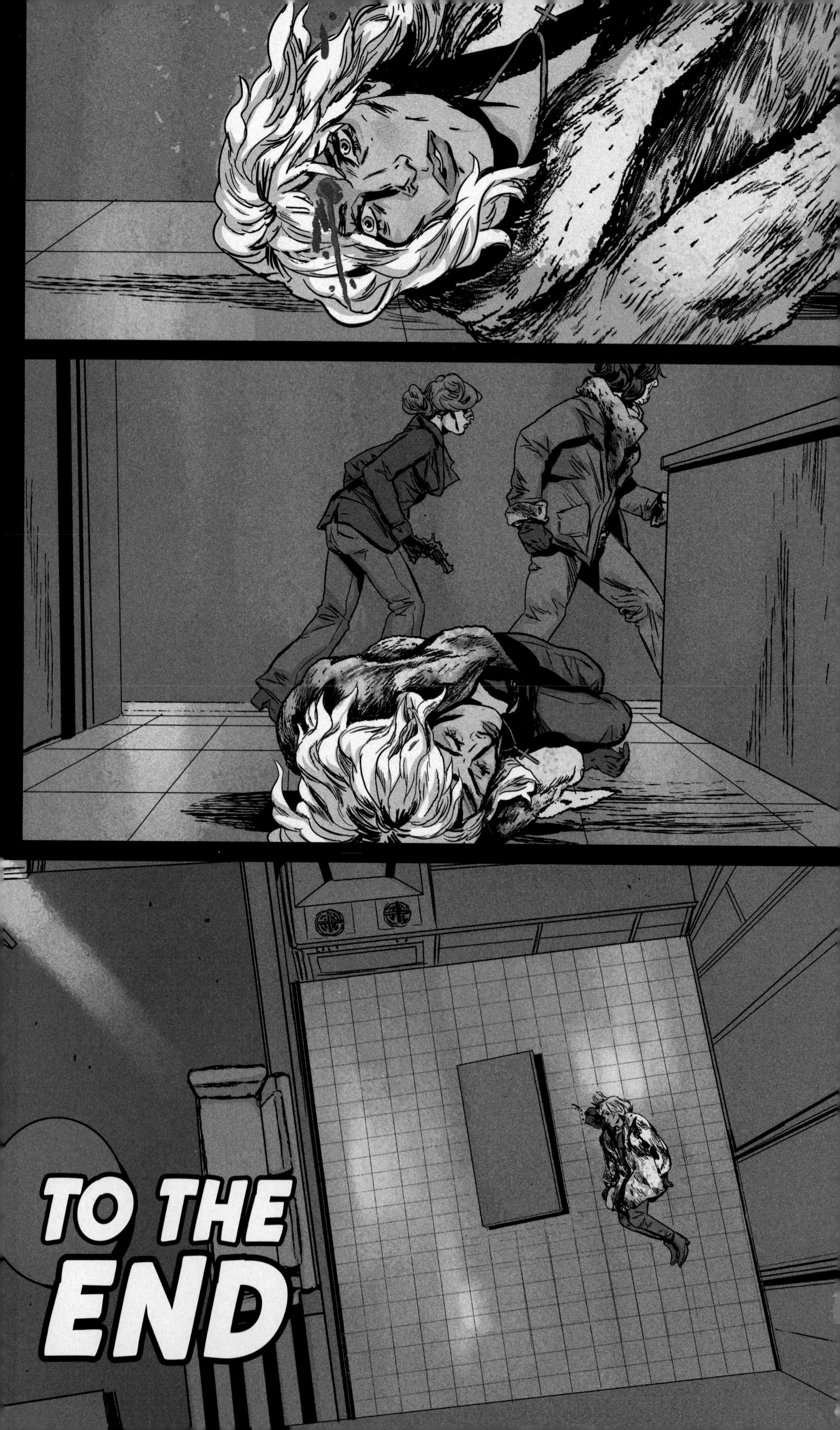
TO THE
END